ELIZABETH GASKELL: THE ARTIST IN CONFLICT

ELIZABETH GASKELL: THE ARTIST IN CONFLICT

by

MARGARET GANZ

TWAYNE PUBLISHERS, INC. • NEW YORK

Library of Congress Catalog Card Number: 68-24279

MANUFACTURED IN THE UNITED STATES OF AMERICA

For ARTHUR

Preface

IT IS an understandable if perhaps not very meaningful tribute to Elizabeth Cleghorn Gaskell that a revival of interest in her work should have coincided with the approaching centennial of her death. Since November 1965 an edition of her collected letters has appeared and two critical studies (a third is in preparation) have been published, one of them offering a "basis for reassessment" of the writer in the light of her steady, consistent development as a "social observer" and a craftsman.

This present study (concluded before the appearance of these recent works) was not intended either to commemorate Mrs. Gaskell or particularly to challenge her present reputation among Victorian novelists, but to do justice as fully and fairly as possible to her achievements. In this attempt her writings have been approached in some ways not fully explored by previous critics. All her works are included in a detailed critical analysis (some earlier studies omit the biography of Charlotte Brontë and many do not discuss the essays and short stories); moreover the writings are dealt with in *thematic* rather than *chronological* terms. To sacrifice chronology in order to clarify artistic intention and execution seemed appropriate as long as a certain progressive growth and maturity (perhaps not quite as consistent as others have deemed it) could still be suggested. Thus in Chapter 2 ("The Social Conscience"), because of the similarity in subject matter, the discussion of *North and South* directly follows that of *Mary Barton* even though *Ruth* is Mrs. Gaskell's second social novel. The significant contrasts and comparisons in her handling of conflicts between masters and workmen could thus be more easily pinpointed, yet the technical sophistication of *North and South* as her fourth exercise in fiction (the humorous *Cranford* also precedes it) has not been overlooked.

Perhaps the most unorthodox alteration of chronology is the inclusion of Mrs. Gaskell's last novel *Wives and Daughters* in Chapter 3 ("The Humorist's Vision"). Yet only by considering that work in conjunction with *Cranford* could Mrs. Gaskell's most meaningful achievement—her humor—be fully encompassed. Though its appeal has generally been acknowledged, earlier and present critics have not been impelled closely to analyze its particular quality and impact on the reader. It is the richness and subtlety of the often praised but rarely probed humorist's vision which this study has especially tried to illuminate. If there is indeed to be some meaningful "reassessment," Mrs. Gaskell's humor must significantly contribute to it. For her particular comic vision, transcending the conventions which so often trammeled her, was responsible for her finest, most sophisticated, most universal artistic expression.

While fear of oversimplifying made it impossible to assign a specific rank and status in Victorian fiction to Mrs. Gaskell or neatly to resume her general flaws and virtues in a few final pages, her merits and deficiencies have consistently been suggested, not only through full critical analyses and references to those aspects of her correspondence which highlight her mind and art but through appropriate comparisons with contemporary novelists. These are particularly instructive since she was in the rather awkward position of having to contend with formidable rivals like Dickens, Thackeray, Charlotte Brontë, and George Eliot.

Above all, this study has attempted to suggest some of the less apparent but fascinating elements in Mrs. Gaskell's failure to reach a level of achievement on a par with that of such contemporaries. It has thus often focused on those flaws in her work the result not of deficient craftsmanship, not of imperfect intellect, not of excessive sentimentality, but of a basic temperamental ambivalence whose repercussions often prevented her from achieving the universality of the great artist. The conflict between her instinctive impulses and the demands of both social conventions and spiritual commitments was the central personal dilemma which on both a conscious and unconscious level contributed to the imperfect development or marring of many of her works (*Ruth* and *Sylvia's Lovers* show striking instances of such weaknesses). Her failure to resolve that conflict so characteristic of her age essentially spelled her failure to achieve artistic wholeness. It is a tribute to her intelligence, sensitivity, and a certain innate shrewdness that she so early adumbrated her problem and at least managed to transcend it through the sublimation of humor. For it is the very struggle of instincts with conventions which, projected in humorous terms, guaranteed the greatness of *Cranford*. As she enshrined the struggle in its pages, the alchemy of art forged out of her central failing the substance of her one masterpiece, her major and lasting achievement as a novelist.

M. G.

Acknowledgments

SINCE the collected letters had not appeared when I was writing this study, I relied heavily on correspondence in manuscript. For permission to quote from the letters and other documents I wish to thank the following: the Trustees of the British Museum; the Brotherton Collection at the University of Leeds; the Gaskell Collection, Manchester Public Libraries, Manchester (England), by kind permission of the Libraries Committee; the Victoria and Albert Museum; the Henry W. and Albert Berg Collection of the New York Public Library, Astor, Lenox, and Tilden Foundations; the Morris L. Parrish Collection of the Princeton University Library; the Yale University Library.

My special thanks go to all the English libraries for their courtesy, their helpfulness beyond the call of duty, and their generosity in making material easily available to the researcher.

I owe my deepest gratitude to my husband who listened, advised, criticized, supported, sustained, even typed.

Contents

Chronology

1810 Elizabeth Cleghorn Stevenson born on September 29 in London (Chelsea) at 12 Lindsay Row (now 93 Cheyne Walk), the second child of William Stevenson, a former Unitarian minister, classical tutor, magazine editor and contributor, and, after 1806, Keeper of the Treasury Records.

1811 At fifteen months, after the death of her mother (Elizabeth Holland), went to reside with her mother's sister (Mrs. Hannah Lumb) in Knutsford, the small Cheshire town in which she would spend her youth. Her father remarried in 1814.

1822– 1827 Attended Avonbank school in Stratford-on-Avon. Was inspired to write her first essay by a visit made at that time to a neighboring mansion (Clopton House).

1827– 1829 Resettled in London after the mysterious disappearance during a sea voyage of her brother, John Stevenson, a naval lieutenant. Under the very uncongenial family circumstances of living with a stepmother and her children, helped nurse her father through the protracted illness which preceded his death in 1829.

1829– 1831 Finished her education at Newcastle-on-Tyne in the home of a distant relative, the prominent Unitarian minister William Turner. In the last year of her stay went to Edinburgh with the Reverend Turner's daughter Ann. Through Ann's sister, whom she then visited, she met her future husband.

1832 Married at Knutsford (August 30) to the Reverend William Gaskell, assistant pastor of the Cross Street Unitarian Chapel in Manchester. After honeymoon in Wales, removed to Manchester as a permanent residence.

1836– Wrote diary recording growth of oldest daughter Marianne
1837 (b. 1834) and later of second daughter Margaret Emily [Meta] (b. 1837). Sole poem of projected series—*Sketches Among the Poor*—(written with her husband) published by *Blackwood's Magazine.*

1840 Sketch of Clopton House (sent to William Howitt in 1838) published in *Visits to Remarkable Places.*

1845 Encouraged by her husband to write in order to counteract the depression induced by the death of her little boy Willie (b. 1844).

1847– Three stories published in *Howitt's Journal*: "Libbie Marsh's
1848 Three Eras" and "The Sexton's Hero" in the first year, "Christmas Storms and Sunshine" in the next.

1848 *Mary Barton* published anonymously, with great popular success and many critical accolades.

1849 Entered literary world, making the acquaintance of Samuel Rogers, Dickens, John Forster, Monckton Milnes, Guizot, F. D. Maurice, Carlyle, Wordsworth.

1850 Moved with her family (two more children Florence Elizabeth and Julia Bradford born in 1842 and 1846) to a permanent home in Manchester: 42 (later 84) Plymouth Grove. At Dickens' request became a contributor to *Household Words* which soon published some of her short stories ("Lizzie Leigh" appearing in the first number of the magazine). Began friendship with Charlotte Brontë while both were visitors at the home of Sir James Kay-Shuttleworth in the Lake District (Windermere). Published *The Moorland Cottage* as a *Christmas Book.*

1851 Published "Mr. Harrison's Confessions" in *The Ladies' Companion* (Feb.–April). Publication of *Cranford* began in *Household Words* (Dec. 1851–May 1853).

1852 Published "The Old Nurse's Story" in *Household Words.*

1853 Published *Ruth,* which aroused severe public reaction against liberal treatment of the "fallen woman" but also won praise from discriminating critics, writers, religious figures.

1854 On fall voyage to France probably met for the first time Madame Mohl, a clever Englishwoman through whose Paris salon she came to know many French intellectuals and whom she regularly visited on her continental trips.

1855 Acceded to the request of the Reverend Brontë that she undertake the biography of the recently deceased Charlotte (spending the next two years on research including visits to all pertinent places). Published *North and South* in book form (after much conflict with Dickens during the work's serialization in *Household Words*—Sept. 1854–Jan. 1855). Published in *Household Words* "An Accursed Race" and "Half a Lifetime Ago" and the next year "The Poor Clare."

1857 Published *The Life of Charlotte Brontë*. On a trip to Rome immediately after completing the work met and began what was to be a close friendship with Charles Eliot Norton with whom she corresponded to the end of her life. Returned to find herself threatened by libel suits growing out of statements in the *Life* and also assailed by complaints from minor figures in the biography. Resolved the difficulties by emendations and deletions incorporated in the third edition.

1858 "My Lady Ludlow" published in *Household Words*. Visits to Germany and France.

1859 Traveled to Whitby in preparation for *Sylvia's Lovers*. Published in Dickens' *All the Year Round* "The Crooked Branch" as "The Ghost in the Garden Room" and "Lois the Witch."

1862 Traveled through northern France. Published "Six Weeks at Heppenheim" in *The Cornhill Magazine*. Was active in attempts to alleviate the deprivation in Manchester during the "cotton famine" resulting from the American Civil War.

1863 Published "A Dark Night's Work" in *All the Year Round* and "Cousin Phillis" in the *Cornhill* (Nov.–Feb. 1864). Published *Sylvia's Lovers*.

1864 Published "French Life" in *Fraser's Magazine*. Used stay in Pontresina for working at *Wives and Daughters*. Began publishing this last novel in August in the *Cornhill* where it was serialized until after her death (to January 1866).

1865 Died suddenly in Holybourne (Hampshire) where she was making final preparations to surprise her husband with a house purchased for him and for her daughters. Was buried at Knutsford.

CHAPTER 1

A Portrait of the Novelist

THE GENERAL picture of Mrs. Gaskell as woman and writer which emerges from most contemporary and later appraisals is hardly unjust yet it does not fully encompass the nature of her temperament or the quality of her art. The limitations of that picture may partly result from her secondary position among the novelists of her age, since few critics are tempted to probe beyond the most salient characteristics of a minor writer. Certain assumptions about her personality which affect the evaluation of her work can also be traced to the protracted absence of detailed information about her life, the result of her own reluctance to be the subject of a biography.[1] Yet, though that difficulty has now been surmounted, the suggestions of an intriguing versatility of temperament furnished by Annette Hopkins' exhaustive biography have not yet been fully explored. Indeed Margaret Lane, in reviewing that very biography, exemplifies a pervasive attitude as she attempts to account for the previous absence of full-length studies of the novelist:

> . . . Mrs. Gaskell is a peculiarly difficult subject. She is like a gentle landscape of orchards and fields, charming, reassuring, undramatic; soothing rather than exciting, she offers the psycho-analyst the mini-

> mum of scope. She is like, indeed, one of those good and charming friends whom one sincerely loves and rarely discusses, simply because they *are* so admirable and good.[2]

The term "charming" is familiar from many previous tributes (Dickens indeed speaks to her of her "charming writing"[3]), while "soothing" is an indirect reminder that critics have generally not found Mrs. Gaskell intellectually challenging. That limitation is, however, made to seem negligible precisely because of her charm in George Eliot's reference to her "charming mind,"[4] and in Henry James's suave circumlocution about the "charming facts" of her "genius":

> For Mrs. Gaskell's genius . . . was so obviously the offspring of her affections, her feelings, her associations, and . . . was so little of an intellectual matter, that it seems almost like slighting these charming facts to talk of them under that collective name, especially when that name is a term so coarsely and disrespectfully synthetic as the word genius has grown to be. But genius is of many kinds, and we are almost tempted to say that that of Mrs. Gaskell strikes us as being little else than a peculiar play of her personal character. In saying this we wish to be understood as valuing not her intellect the less, but her character the more.[5]

The evaluations quoted above are unquestionably pertinent. One need only, as critics have so often been impelled to do, compare Mrs. Gaskell with two prominent women novelists of her time to realize that she lacks Charlotte Brontë's passionate apprehension or the intellectual and psychological penetration of George Eliot. Doing full justice to her, however, requires a modification of that portrait of a sweet, sensible, kind-hearted, and above all, even-tempered woman so often presented to us, and perhaps most dramatically by David Cecil as he contrasts her with Charlotte Brontë and George Eliot:

> In the placid dovecotes of Victorian womanhood, they were eagles.
>
> But we have only to look at a portrait of Mrs. Gaskell, soft-eyed, beneath her charming veil, to see that she was a dove.[6]

That she did not invariably possess what A. W. Ward calls

"her sweet serenity of soul"[7] should not be adduced from her indignation at social ills, since an amiable and cheerful disposition hardly precludes an active sympathy with the deprivations of others. The clue to the qualification of such judgments as those of Ward and Cecil lies rather in the remarks of the rare critic who, without pursuing his insight, sensed her temperamental inclination to a rather somber appraisal of earthly life. Thus, neither G. B. Smith nor David Masson denies her capacity for optimism, yet both imply contrasting aspects to her temperament. Smith suggests that "hers must have been a brooding nature; one which often reviewed the moral mysteries of the universe" and was capable from the beginning of "mirroring upon itself the sorrows of those with whom she came into contact"[8]; Masson notes that "in all her works, there is a certain subdued weariness, as though the world would be a very dreary one if we were not all to rest ere long."[9] Such comments, reinforcing one's sense of certain morbid tendencies in Mrs. Gaskell,[10] despite her overtly cheerful gospel of resignation to life, suggest that the familiar connotations she evokes are only partially valid. An accurate portrait must encompass complexities and paradoxes in her nature and her work not as yet sufficiently emphasized.

Aside from the possibility of "a brooding nature," her very capacity for humor implies a measure of conflict in appraising reality. As in Dickens, the comic vision undercuts the tendency to sentimentality—especially pathos—though the two impulses are of course not mutually exclusive in English humorists. The *bizarrerie* and gratuitous extravagance of Dickens' humor to some extent explain his predilection for melodrama and Gothic mystery. Given the more muted whimsy and sly irony of Mrs. Gaskell, however, her own delight in sensationalism, in the uncanny, in the supernatural, in the grotesque—so evident in many of her shorter stories—seems a more unexpected manifestation of her temperament, even after taking into account the general taste of the age to which Dickens' *Household Words* and *All The Year Round* (in which most of Mrs. Gaskell's stories appeared) undoubtedly catered. The paradoxes of her nature are aptly suggested when we find K. L. Montgomery saying of this "dove" that "possibly no one except Poe possesses an equal power of 'making one's flesh creep',"[11] and Elizabeth Haldane noting that her conventional life as a "wife of a Nonconformist minister of the best type" appears "quite inconsistent with her love of dreadful deeds and wicked men."[12]

Critics almost invariably praise Mrs. Gaskell's versatility in being not only an able social novelist whose depiction of industrial problems touched the public conscience but a skillful humorist who diverted readers with whimsical pictures of genteel small-town life. Yet to these two main achievements must be added another evidence of flexibility. She was an effective journalist who satisfied her own vivid imagination while successfully catering to the Victorian appetite for inspiring dramas, thrilling adventures, gory mysteries, and supernatural terrors.

That aspect of Mrs. Gaskell's art has not been ignored by critics, but since her penchant for sensational themes is less apparent in her finished novels, it has not been given consideration sufficient to suggest the versatility of both her nature and her art. Thus Ward's judgment, though partly accurate, falls short in evaluating the significance of this tendency in Mrs. Gaskell:

> Though reasonableness and a lucidity of mind which mirrored itself in a style of perfect clearness were among her most unfailing characteristics as a writer, yet her imagination was unmistakably attracted by whatever bordered on, or partook of, the supernatural. . . . Her reputation as a teller of ghost-stories extended beyond the immediate circle of her home life; and in her earlier as well as in her later writings . . . she subjects her readers to the same spell. But these were fancies only, to which she allowed no place in her conception of life, or in the expression which that conception found in her principal works.[13]

Such manifestations of imaginative sensibility should not be dismissed as "fancies only," since there is a qualitative similarity between her emotional susceptibility to possible supernatural phenomena and her comprehension of a different kind of haunting—the obsession with guilt and fear, "the working out of the subtle poisons of remorse and dread"[14] (as the critic of *The Westminster Review* called it), a subject hardly limited to her shorter works. In her ability to fathom some nightmarish mental states, she again shows a temperamental kinship to Dickens, and reveals a less equable temperament than one might have expected.

If the complexity of Mrs. Gaskell's nature and the variety of her literary productions must be stressed, so must her failure to realize her artistic potential. Critics acknowledge that the demands made on the wife of a Unitarian minister, who eventually headed a large household, brought up four daughters, and served as hostess to many celebrities visiting Manchester, were bound to interfere with the concentration essential to producing finished work. In many letters Mrs. Gaskell herself testifies to the distractions which prevented a full commitment to writing; indeed the desire for money to travel abroad or refurbish the household made the quick production of many a story a tempting solution. Yet what critics should have consistently stressed is the crucial restriction imposed by her acute sensitivity to the proprieties of her age and reinforced by her conventional upbringing. Her agonies over the reception of her novel *Ruth*, punctuated by the anxious feeling that she "must be an improper woman without knowing it"[15] (though from the vantage point of the present nothing more proper than her treatment of the "fallen woman" in this work could be conceived) are a case in point.

In the privacy of her correspondence, however, when she does not have to sustain that exalted propriety which would lead a critic to assert in 1874 that "there is no purer author in modern times,"[16] she emerges as a woman of no less basic goodness and piety, but of far greater sophistication, frankness, shrewdness, and witty common sense. At a trying period in her life, we discover her longing for "the delicious quiet and dolce far niente of Italy";[17] she confesses in another letter that a story she is writing is merely the reworking of "an old rubbishy one," that "if [she] were a servant, & suspected and things locked up . . . [she]

should . . . be . . . a very clever thief," and that she is a "sermon hater."[18] On another occasion she deplores "a want of the sense of humour" in "two of the most deeply religious young men I ever met with," reiterating emphatically "But it *is* a *want*."[19] She advises and questions her daughter Marianne with loving firmness: "About yr. bonnet get it *large*, and trimmed with (*-or*) white. ARE your shoulders lower?"[20] With Dickensian sprightliness, she notifies her sister-in-law of an impending departure by announcing that "We are 'here today, & gone tomorrow,' as the fat scullion maid said in some extract in Holland's Exercise book"; she exults in Marianne's improved health which she owes to the "Rivington air," by exclaiming "Good air for ever! Hurrah!" and goes on to complain: "Oh! who *must* we ask to meet the Bradfords—hang 'em."[21] After an exalted paean of praise to Florence Nightingale, she ruefully comments to a friend: "I dare say all this sounds rather like 'bosh'—but indeed if you had heard all about her that I have you would feel as I do."[22] She depicts for her children her impatience at a "slow reader" in the train over whose shoulder she was trying to get as fast ahead as possible on *Little Dorrit*: "*We* only read the first two chapters, so I never found who 'little Dorrit' is."[23] She maintains that she objects to "biographies of *living* people," and slyly comments "I always let people *invent* mine, & have often learnt some curious particulars about myself from what they choose to say."[24]

Liveliness, humor, and informality are indeed the distinguishing characteristics of her correspondence. Her very first letter to George Eliot whimsically suggests her inclination to usurp the fame of the as yet unidentified writer, now that she herself is thought to have written *Adam Bede*: "I have hitherto denied it; but I really think, that as you want to keep your real name a secret, it would be very pleasant for me to blush acquiescence. Will you give me leave."[25] She closes one letter to Charles Eliot Norton in a gently teasing vein: "I don't believe from what I hear of your books, that a republic agrees with your health; do try a little aristocracy, and as a step to it try a visit to us, who are admirers of that 'effete institution.'"[26] With a flair for the grotesque she mischievously dramatizes for him Rossetti's penchant for Pre-Raphaelite ladies:

> It did not signify what we were talking about or how agreeable I was; if a particular kind of reddish brown, crepe wavy hair came in, he was away in a moment struggling for an introduction to the owner of said head of hair. He is not mad as a March hare, but hair-mad.[27]

She confesses to him: "I believe I *am* Mediaeval,—and *un* Manchester, and un American."[28]

The very deletions from her own letters used in her biography of Charlotte Brontë show her awareness of a necessary circumspection in presenting her subject before the public; that she nevertheless incurred condemnation for what were felt to be severe breaches of taste is but another instance of a spirited frankness given to asserting itself *malgré elle*. In appraising her we must then take into account not only the woman divided between the demands of her family life and her art but also the writer intensely affected by the attitudes of the reading public[29] and the strictures of the critics to whose conventional standards—it must always be remembered—she was herself partially committed.

It is precisely because she was more than a gentle, pious spokesman for social reform or a kindly humorist of small-town life that her intentions were often misunderstood and that two of her works—*Ruth* and *The Life of Charlotte Brontë*—met with an indignant reception they seem hardly to have warranted. But, since she did not possess an unsocial nature or that total intellectual commitment to one's art which makes the safeguarding of integrity essential, she often failed to carry through the ideas or the psychological insights which she undoubtedly had. Of the contemporary critics of *Ruth*, only W. R. Greg fully discerned the ambiguities in her attempt to show that a "fallen woman" could be redeemed and, better still, perceived that she had a far more sophisticated view than she allowed herself to express. After pointing out that the Pharisaical employer of

Ruth, Mr. Bradshaw, is by implication shown to be far more guilty in his righteousness than Ruth in her sin, Greg comments:

> But what we object to in her book is this; that the tone and language habitually adopted throughout, both by Ruth herself and by her friends when alluding to her fault, is at war with this impression and with the true tenor of the facts recorded. *Mrs. Gaskell scarcely seems at one with herself in this matter* [italics mine].[30]

V. S. Pritchett calls attention to her ambiguous handling of character in *North and South* as he questions the nature of Margaret Hale's anguish about "telling . . . one of those awful lies which wreck love affairs according to the Victorian convention," and wonders whether Margaret is "mortified by her wickedness, or . . . really afraid, in her pride, that she has shown a weakness to a lover she has so far kept at arm's length?"[31]

Conflicted between the artistic impulse to interpret Philip Hepburn's lie in *Sylvia's Lovers* in such psychological terms as make it less reprehensible and the moral need to condemn any deviation from the truth regardless of circumstances, Mrs. Gaskell denies the character its full dimension; few critics as a result even credit the measure of psychological sophistication her portrait of Philip does possess. Diffidence seems partly responsible for her failure to translate into meaningful actions the unpleasant implications of Mrs. Gibson's behavior in *Wives and Daughters*. It is hard to blame her when one perceives the limitations of her audience: one critic, for instance, proclaims the moral "relief" experienced in being able "to get away from" the unscrupulous Mrs. Gibson and her mercurial daughter Cynthia "into the company of Molly,"[32] the virtuous heroine. The net result of that diffidence, however, is that her most mature work is weakened by the static nature of the relationships it portrays.

The oscillation between artistic sophistication and conventional reticence is at the heart of Mrs. Gaskell's undeniable limitations as a writer; no true judgment of her nature and of her achievement can be reached without concentrating on the conflict between her artistic impulses and her commitments to conventional standards of moral and social behavior.

Since Mrs. Gaskell's work was deeply affected by her upbringing and the existence she led as a writer, the details of her life are particularly suggestive. Like many other creative artists, she relied heavily on her experiences, the places in which she had lived, and the people she had known as material for her art, but because she lacked the imaginative power which totally transfigures reality, it is easier to find the sources of her writing in the facts, circumstances, and relationships of her life than in those of a very complex creative artist.[33] Thus the city of Manchester in which she spent all of her married life provided the background and the source material for her social novels (*Mary Barton* and *North and South*) and some of her first short stories. The town of Knutsford in which she grew up and its immediate surroundings inspired her stories and novels of provincial life: "Mr. Harrison's Confessions," *Cranford*, "My Lady Ludlow," *Wives and Daughters*, "Cousin Phillis." Her stay in Newcastle-on-Tyne and Edinburgh, her honeymoon in Wales, her vacations in Silverdale (in the Lake District), her travels to Germany, France, and Italy yielded the settings for several stories.

Because she was a writer whose creativity very much depended on the facts of her experience, many of her works (but especially *Cranford* and *Wives and Daughters*) have fascinated what Ward dryly calls "that pensive portion of the public which is never satisfied till in a work of fiction every place, character, incident, and situation has been identified."[34] One might add that "the public" has hardly been the only culprit. After reading Mrs. Ellis H. Chadwick's *Mrs. Gaskell: Haunts, Homes and Stories*, an exhaustive exploration of conjunctions between the author's life and her art (in which indeed the facts of her life are so often deduced from her art), one fully sympathizes with William E. A. Axon's assertion in reviewing the book that "It is a degradation of literature to think of the poet or novelist as merely a mirror reflecting the images of persons met in social intercourse."[35] The *possible* sources for her inspiration in real life cannot be ignored; one must simply be wary of assuming too close a correspondence between actual and fictional settings, characters, and situations.

Another question which one approaches with reservations is that of family influence on her literary career. The hereditary impact of having a father of remarkable cultivation and high intellectual gifts and a paternal grandmother related to the poet James Thomson can of course hardly be ascertained. Yet the nature of her father's immediate influence on her artistic development also remains mere conjecture. For she was only a year old when she came to live at her aunt's house soon after her mother's death and made only periodic visits to the London of her birth until she spent two years helping to nurse her father through the lingering illness which preceded his death. We know that she was not happy in these visits to a home where a stepmother and other children may have proved difficult companions;[36] we do not clearly know whether William Stevenson, eminently capable of supervising his daughter's education, was responsible for first instilling in her a love for literature and the desire to be an artist.

But family traditions and vocations undoubtedly predisposed her to certain interests and preoccupations which eventually found literary expression. A playfully romantic predilection for the Viking spirit is apparent in Mrs. Gaskell's reaction to the tradition that the Stevensons had Norwegian ancestors (the name was spelt "Stevensen" in some family documents):

> Mrs. Gaskell liked to think of her Scandinavian forefathers, and when she went away now and again for little jaunts and expeditions, such as she always enjoyed, she used to laugh and say that the blood of the Vikings her ancestors was rising in her veins.[37]

The dramatic portrayal of the seafaring life in *Sylvia's Lovers* is but one manifestation of her involvement with a mode of existence to which both her paternal grandfather (a Royal Navy captain) and her brother were committed. The tragic career of that brother, John Stevenson, who, as a lieutenant in the merchant marine, disappeared and was never heard of again had a profound effect both on her father (whose final illness dated from that time) and on herself. The influence of personal feelings is unmistakable in Mrs. Gaskell's recurrence to the subject of the sailor who has been severed from family and friends, to their great sorrow and anguish. The fortuitous reappearance of Miss Matty Jenkyns' hapless brother as the picturesque "Aga Jenkyns" near the conclusion of *Cranford* is a classic case of wish-fulfillment in fiction.

The details of her father's own career are also richly suggestive of that indirect play of certain experiences on a creative artist. Perhaps the most significant aspects of that career to a reader familiar with *North and South* is William Stevenson's early renunciation of his Unitarian ministry because of conscientious scruples. Possibly through the influence of another minister, the Reverend George Wicke, who had given up his calling and published a pamphlet vindicating his scruples against the payment of preachers, Stevenson, then Minister of Dob Lane Unitarian Chapel (he was also a classical tutor at Manchester Academy), resigned his post. For a while he practiced scientific farming without much success in East Lothian (together with James Cleghorn whose last name he probably bestowed on his daughter in tribute to his friendship with the family),[38] and then combined the keeping of a boarding house with the tutoring of Edinburgh University students. A journalistic career which included editing *The Scots Magazine* and contributing to *The Edinburgh Review* and *The Westminster Review* commanded his considerable abilities until he received the position of Keeper of the Treasury Records, which he held to the end of his life.

The many facets of such a career, in themselves a testimony to the integrity, the versatility, the general cultivation, and the literary skill of the novelist's father, are particularly relevant in that they illumine the handling of certain situations and characters in Mrs. Gaskell's novels. She was in part inspired by her father's spiritual crisis when in *North and South* she had Mr. Hale resign his ministry and seek employment as a tutor, and probably paid special tribute to her father's diversity of interests in her portrait of the Reverend Ebenezer Holman in "Cousin Phillis," a man dedicated not only to the spiritual demands of his pastorate but to the scientific challenge of successfully operating his farm.

The impact of her mother's family and its mode of life on Elizabeth Stevenson was to be more simple and direct. Introduced to the Holland family by Philip Holland, the former teacher of a Manchester friend (Dr. Thomas Barnes), William Stevenson eventually married Elizabeth Holland in 1797. Not only were the Hollands, a Cheshire branch of a prominent Lancashire family, connected with the Wedgewoods and the Darwins, but the prosperous farm at Sandlebridge owned by Samuel Holland, Stevenson's father-in-law, was apparently the scene of childish pranks by none other than the future Lord Clive, who, at school in Knutsford, "spent some of his holidays at Sandle Bridge, where it was his joy to terrify the Hollands by jumping from the ball on the top of one of the two stone gateposts to its fellow on the other."[39]

Elizabeth Stevenson was to become very well-acquainted with her grandparents in Sandlebridge and with the rest of the family in nearby Knutsford; both places and persons were to provide material for her inspiration. For, as we have already indicated, though she was born in London (on September 29, 1810 in a house at what was then 12 Lindsey Row and is now 93 Cheyne Walk), she remained there for not much more than one year. After her mother's death, she was sent to live with her mother's sister, Mrs. Hannah Lumb, who, forced to separate from her mentally unstable husband, had settled in Knutsford with her little crippled daughter. That Mrs. Lumb's decision to bring up her niece was not entirely impulsive is demonstrated by a touching letter from Mary Ann Lumb to her mother, entreating her to allow her baby cousin to come and share their lives.[40] A warm, devoted relationship developed between Elizabeth and Mrs. Lumb, to whom she undoubtedly proved a great consolation after Mary Ann's early death; Mrs. Gaskell's later references to her aunt testify to her own lasting love, regard, and loyalty.[41] Though there were periodic visits to her father's household in London, Knutsford, a quaint Cheshire village, was her home. Her adoptive mother at Heathside House in Knutsford, her grandparents at Sandlebridge and her uncle, Peter Holland, the Knutsford surgeon who lived at Church House, formed the family circle. That quiet life in the country, to which, despite its intermittent childish disappointments, she would later refer with great fondness[42] only terminated when she was sent to school at Stratford-on-Avon. She never really returned to stay at Knutsford, for the tragic news of her brother's disappearance and her father's illness called her to London and, after his death, she completed her education at the home of the Reverend William Turner in Newcastle. Through one of his daughters she met the man who was soon to become her husband, the Reverend William Gaskell, Junior Minister at the Cross Street Unitarian Chapel in Manchester.

But the Manchester life that was to follow would never eradicate "the thoughts and feelings arising from the happy circumstances of rural life,"[43] and the elements out of which her youthful existence at Knutsford had been wrought would provide the matter of fiction quite soon after she had embarked on her writing career. Sandlebridge bears some resemblance to "Woodley" in *Cranford* and to "Heathbridge" in "Cousin Phillis" (in both stories the farms are reminiscent of her grandparents' home). Knutsford is first re-created in "Mr. Harrison's Confessions" as "Dunscombe," is immortalized as "Cranford," reappears in several short stories, and receives its final tribute as "Hollingford" in *Wives and Daughters.* If Dr. Peter Holland's daughters may have suggested the Misses Jenkyns in *Cranford,* Holland himself perhaps provided some of the traits of the older country doctor in "Mr. Harrison's Confessions," of Mr. Hoggins in *Cranford,* and of Dr. Gibson in *Wives and Daughters.*[44] Most important of all, a whole mode of experience and view of life were impressed upon her; she absorbed particular values and assumptions which contrasted sharply with the sophistication of the not-too-distant urban center of Manchester. Whereas the experience of her married life in that city forges *Mary Barton* and *North and South,* the memories of youth in her "dear *adopted native* town"[45] are fully relived in *Cranford* and in her last novel, *Wives and Daughters.* It seems psychologically appropriate that her greatest artistry should have been achieved while handling the material she had most unconsciously absorbed.

The Knutsford and Manchester experiences are thus the central sources of inspiration for the novelist and determine the twofold nature of her accomplishment as the humorous chronicler of small-town life and as the thoughtful and sympathetic appraiser of the urban conflicts between masters and workmen. Nor are these two aspects of her art completely separate impulses which never find expression in the same work. *North and South,* as its title suggests, does explore the respective claims of the rural and urban worlds, but, characteristically enough, it is not the Knutsford setting nor distinctly the Knutsford views which are contrasted with the Manchester spirit. The Southern village which is Margaret Hale's first home has the beauties of landscape and the absence of hectic excitement we associate with Knutsford, but lacks the Knutsford characters—eccentric, genteel spinsters and their maidservants, a rare country doctor, tradesman, or titled lady—and the whimsical pattern of eventfully uneventful lives mirrored for us in "Mr. Harrison's Confession," *Cranford,* "My Lady Ludlow," and *Wives and Daughters.* Like *Mary Barton, North and South* is, to use Louis Cazamian's term, a *roman à thèse* (a thesis novel) and consequently the rural world in the novel functions not to celebrate a memory but to propound an idea. It is used to heighten the dramatic impact of Milton-Northern (Manchester) on those who are strangers to its way of life and its strivings, and in the end to do justice to the drawbacks and attractions of both town and country. Indeed it had also functioned in *Mary Barton* for purposes of contrast, though in a much simpler way; that country of her childhood for which Alice Wilson yearns exemplifies the peace, serenity, and beauty which one longs to recapture amidst the hopeless, blighted life which is the destiny of the Manchester poor.

A lesser but no less genuine source of inspiration is to be found in the experiences that bridged the gap between the author's childhood years at Knutsford and her married life in Manchester. The schooling at Avonbank (1822–1827) was undoubtedly a good preparation for a future writer.[46] There is evidence that the Misses Byerley who directed the school were extremely well-educated (indeed Catherine Byerley herself became a writer) and that the curriculum was an unusually sophisticated one as compared with that of standard girls' schools at the time. It is certain that the inspiration for her first published work dates from her stay in that region, for an excursion to nearby Clopton House (a mansion which tradition claimed to have been briefly visited by Shakespeare) led to a sketch of this visit which was later sent to William Howitt and anonymously published by him in his *Visits to Remarkable Places;* indeed on the strength of it Howitt encouraged her to continue to write and was later influential in the creation of her first novel, *Mary Barton.* The sketch itself, interestingly enough, foreshadows not the future talents of the social novelist or of the humorist but those of the writer of Gothic tales which exploit the quaintness of the past, as it is exemplified in old mansions, their traditions, and the strange histories of their former inhabitants.[47]

The two years which Elizabeth spent with her father, nursing him through that long illness which in 1829 culminated in his death have been described as "probably the most trying years of [her] . . . life." One cannot assume, however, that in depicting Margaret Hale's anguish in *North and South* while nursing her ailing mother, "the recollection of that dark time in her father's sick room at Chelsea was evidently with her."[48] Yet that early contact with protracted illness and death in someone close to her, along with the later loss of two children—her first child was stillborn and an eleven-month-old boy died of scarlet fever in Wales—no doubt lent a special authenticity in her novels not only to the portrayal of the dying but of their desperately anguished and helpless relatives.

Why Elizabeth Stevenson did not, after her father's death, return to her adoptive mother at Knutsford or even take up residence at the home of London relatives, has never been clearly established. Earlier biographers suggest that financial need led to a decision that she prepare herself for teaching by a thorough course of study at the Newcastle-on-Tyne home of the Reverend William Turner (a relative of her mother's through marriage and a prominent Unitarian minister). Yet her own daughter, Meta Gaskell, later maintained that "her stay in Newcastle was just the ordinary visit of a girl to her connections."[49] Since there is general agreement that the Reverend Turner inspired the portrait of the worthy dissenting minister Thurston Benson in *Ruth,* it is likely that both her spiritual and intellectual development were greatly furthered by the two years (1829–31) spent in his home.

Apparently the threat of a cholera epidemic in Newcastle (the reality of such a siege figures significantly in the closing chapters of *Ruth*) led Elizabeth to move to Edinburgh with Ann Turner, the minister's daughter. The Edinburgh setting of the opening chapters of *Round the Sofa*[50] describing the kind of boredom and loneliness of a girl and companion which make any occasion for diversion attractive has led early critics to deduce that such tedium faced Elizabeth in that town. But her chief biographer finds no foundation for such an assumption and indeed suggests that "she must have seen a good deal of the social life of the city, for it was during this visit that the earliest extant likenesses of her are usually said to have been made—the marble bust by David Dunbar and the lovely miniature by W. John Thompson."[51]

The many changes of scene which encompassed Knutsford, Stratford-on-Avon, London, Newcastle, and Edinburgh had already produced, as we have seen, significant impressions. To have been brought in contact with so many different environments before the age of twenty-one might seem to bode a lengthy career of new adjustments. But the encounter with the Reverend William Gaskell, on a visit to Ann's sister in Manchester, was to determine a permanent settlement in that industrial center.

Though Mrs. Lumb lovingly teased the engaged girl by wondering what the sedate and mature William Gaskell could see in "such a little giddy thoughtless thing as you,"[52] his choice was quite understandable in almost those very terms: a natural desire to complement his own temperament. Beyond her beauty and good breeding, and the uniformity of their social and religious backgrounds, her vivacious and sociable nature must have had a singular appeal for a man who at least in later years amply demonstrated that he was essentially withdrawn and remote, loath to express his feelings, reluctant to meet the demands of social activities, happiest in his study,[53] and in teaching and working for his parish and the city of Manchester. That her own eminently social tendencies, her love of fun and gossip, her yearning for travel, her delight in entertaining friends and celebrities did not convert him to a more open and versatile way of life again seems inevitable. Only very fortuitous circumstances can alter basic inclinations; the very fact of having a wife who had become a literary celebrity and was much sought after must have been rather trying for a Victorian husband, however much sophistication, grace, and charm he possessed. The temptation to maintain his identity by entrenching himself in his leanings toward sedentary study and personal remoteness must have been irresistible.

On the same principle of the appeal of opposites, Elizabeth Stevenson might well initially be drawn to the solidity of William Gaskell's nature. As in his choice, other influences were also at work. She was undoubtedly won over by that great personal attractiveness and those intellectual accomplishments which Ward has so aptly suggested in a personal reminiscence:

He acted as lecturer on English literature in the evening classes' department of the Owens College, Manchester; and, as it so happened that (I think in 1866) I took over those classes on my appointment to a professorship in that vigorous young institution, I can testify to his popularity with the students, and to the enthusiasm which he inspired in them. He was a remarkably handsome man even in his later years, and the refinement and charm of his manner were well set off by a dignified reserve. A trained English scholar and accomplished writer, he also possessed a marked poetical gift which he chiefly exercised in the composition, and translation from the German, of hymns and other sacred verse.[54]

Many words have been expended on the question of their mutual compatibility and happiness. One suspects that the doubts cast on the perfection of their *entente* by later critics (who found evidence in the correspondence of conflicting interests, of William Gaskell's general reluctance to share his wife's travels or her worries, and even of his failure to sympathize with her during an illness)[55] are an inevitable reaction to the unreal panegyrics lavished by earlier writers on their relationship. Whatever difference in taste and temperament may have led them eventually to lead rather separate lives, the affection and loyalty which Mrs. Gaskell demonstrates in her correspondence —in her concern for her husband's health, in her secret plottings to secure vacations for him, in her pride at his achievements, in the unresentful if hopeless wishes that he would not confine himself to his study but keep his family company on their travels—in her final purchase of a country house as a surprise for him—sufficiently assert the reality of a sound relationship.[56] The idyllic picture of private lives so characteristic of many Victorian and turn-of-the-century biographical and critical studies too often substitutes fantasy for reality (one need only read the first few volumes of *The Dickensian* to surmise the devastating effect of eventual revelations about Dickens' private life on the idealistic gentlemen critics who had reveled in the perfections of his moral nature). But if that portrait of marital bliss so characteristic of early Gaskell criticism and biography is invalid, so is any suggestion of a profound, jarring incompatibility. Theirs was no doubt a relationship in which mutual fondness and regard survived the inevitable strains of life and the contrasts and contradictions of dissimilar natures.

It is a significant if almost self-explanatory attribute of Mrs. Gaskell's literary career that it began somewhat late in life. Indeed many years were to elapse between her marriage in 1832 and the publication of her first novel, *Mary Barton,* in 1848. The duties of managing what was at first a financially modest household, taking care of her children (her oldest daughter, Marianne, was born in 1834, Margaret Emily [Meta] in 1837, Florence Elizabeth in 1842, William in 1844, and Julia Bradford in 1846), and assisting her husband in his parish duties must have required most of her attention. Yet the general picture of her basic "interests" which David Cecil presents surely does not do full justice to her concerns even if applied only to those early years of her married life:

> . . . when she had finished with her prayers and her personal tour of the parish, she was perfectly content to sit down and gossip to a neighbour about marriage and clothes and servants and children. As Trollope was the typical Victorian man, so Mrs. Gaskell was the typical Victorian woman.[57]

Undoubtedly she was fascinated with the pedestrian details of daily life, the cut of clothes and the fashion of bonnets (both of which she sometimes illustrates in her letters), the price and quality of food, the challenge of new recipes. Indeed those persistent interests so frequently displayed in her correspondence with her daughters, her female friends, and even when writing to men she knew intimately, are part of her charm. For they suggest one of her most winning qualities, often stressed by critics, the total absence of pretentiousness. But just as her letters show that she could move with whimsical abruptness from the description of household matters to the expression of deep emotions or the display of intellectual curiosity, so her attitudes and activities even in the early years demonstrate that different propensities in her nature asserted themselves. A concern to maintain her individuality underlies the decision that parish work (to which she truly devoted much effort) be performed solely on her own initiative, not made an absolute condition of her status as a minister's wife. Grief and joy were to find outlet in literary expression: in 1836 a small poem paid tribute to her stillborn child, and she chronicled the growth of her eldest and later of her second daughter in the "Diary of my daughter Marianne." The conditions of the poor, so deep a concern of both husband and wife, inspired them with the idea, as Mrs. Gaskell later explained, "of *trying* to write sketches among the poor, *rather* in the manner of Crabbe . . . but in a more seeing-beauty spirit."[58] One poem (indeed the only one they produced) was published in *Blackwood's Magazine* in 1837. The next year she was impelled to send the sketch of Clopton House (perhaps a reworking of a school composition) to William Howitt who, as we have previously mentioned, included it in his *Visits to Remarkable Places* (1840).

Such instances of early literary efforts show that her life was not solely that of the "district visitor" and gossiping housewife. Indeed the philanthropic work to which she devoted so much time and interest because she was naturally kind-hearted was also challenging her artistic imagination: in *Mary Barton*, a fund of accumulated experience of social conditions was eventually transmuted into literature. Moreover, as Yvonne ffrench aptly points out, while Manchester was often "the discouraging parochial scene," giving one a sense "of the remorseless nature of the thousand looms that demanded groans for bread and tears for water," it also offered opportunities for intercourse with "a prosperous, intellectual and progressive society . . . actively philanthropic and of a high cultural standard."[59] Mrs. Gaskell's lifelong friendship with the intellectual Winkworth sisters—some of her most interesting letters are written to Catherine and Emily—is an instance of the possibility of sharing more than mere gossip with neighbors. Susanna Winkworth has testified to that vitality in her which made the sisters "say to each other that we were sure she could write books, or do anything else in the world that she liked."[60]

The question of the immediate impulse for producing her first novel has often been debated. William Howitt (whom she had finally met in 1841 on a tour of the Rhine with her husband) and who, as we have noted, had encouraged her to continue writing, claimed much of the responsibility for the inception of *Mary Barton.* But, according to the testimony of her daughter, the direct suggestion apparently came from the Reverend Gaskell who felt that writing would alleviate the deep and lasting sorrow of his wife after the death of her little boy in 1845.[61] This personal feeling of grief would seem to have predisposed her to the choice of her theme, for she put aside an earlier story with a rural setting to grapple with a subject which would readily awaken the sympathy of one who had endured a tragic deprivation. That the suffering of Manchester workmen had for her a very personal connection with her own mournful experience is evident in her revelation to Travers Madge, the Manchester philanthropist, of the immediate circumstances which impelled her to write a novel like *Mary Barton.* While on a visit to a very poor workman's family, her efforts to counteract their rancor were dramatically cut short as the workman fiercely seized her arm and exclaimed: "Ay, ma'am; but have you ever seen a child clemmed [starved] to death?"[62]

Yet neither this moving incident, nor the memory of a great loss, could necessarily account for the total commitment to her theme and the obviously profound comprehension which she brought to bear upon the question of the rift between "the two nations" of rich and poor. Her own Preface to *Mary Barton* suggests an extended absorption of social realities;[63] it was to find appropriate expression in fiction during a long period of physical recovery (barely alluded to in the Preface) probably under the impetus of personal encouragement from both William Howitt and her husband. The unconscious growth of this specific creative impulse is suggested in an unfinished draft of a letter to a relative of W. R. Greg:

> The whole tale grew up in my mind as imperceptibly as a seed germinates in the earth, so I cannot trace back now why or how such

a thing was written, or such a character or circumstance introduced. (There is one exception to this which I will name afterwards [the character of John Barton].) I can remember now that the prevailing thought in my mind at the time when the tale was silently forming itself and impressing me with the force of a reality, was the seeming injustice of the inequalities of fortune.[64]

The details of the inception of *Mary Barton,* an intriguing example of the complex circumstances that can foster a latent creativity, are particularly pertinent in clarifying one aspect of her achievements. When her confrontation with the social problems of Manchester was made even more meaningful by personal sorrow, it was no doubt psychologically impossible for her to pursue the leanings to romance which the sketch of Clopton House exemplifies or the flair for humor which her correspondence already reveals at that time. She could be nothing if not *engagée.* And though her greatest achievement as a humorist, *Cranford* (1851–53), soon fully displayed the most significant of her talents, that aspect of her nature which came to terms with social problems by preaching Christian charity and sweet reasonableness asserted itself again not long after in *North and South* (1854–55). That novel continues the work begun in *Mary Barton* but in a less one-sided manner; having dedicated herself in her first work largely to vindicating the attitudes of the workers, she went on to redress the balance by also doing justice to the point of view of the manufacturers. The breadth of her commitment to social issues had been demonstrated two years earlier in *Ruth* (1853) as she challenged unfeeling and hypocritical attitudes toward the "fallen woman."

That the reforming impulse was not to be a permanent incitement to creativity is not only suggested by the writing of *Cranford* so early in her career but demonstrated by such later novels as *Sylvia's Lovers* (1863) and *Wives and Daughters* (1864–66). One could hardly supply for these works the evidence of didactic intentions given in Mrs. Gaskell's own words (whether in a preface or in her correspondence) for *Mary Barton* and *Ruth,* and implicit in the text of *North and South.* Aside from the many short stories which reflect her predilection for Gothic romance, suspense, and mystery, her major works exemplify conflicting impulses which must have asserted themselves from the beginning of her Manchester life. Her allegiance was no doubt divided between the *Weltanschauung* of Knutsford and of Manchester, between the appeal of a simple rural existence and the challenge of urban complexity. But, unlike the heroine of *North and South,* Margaret Hale, she could not leave behind her the world of her youth; the universe of Knutsford with its archaic charm wins out at last in the final celebration of country life which is *Wives and Daughters.* Because didacticism was for her more a moral obligation than an instinctive impulse, she did not, as her social novels testify, really succeed in transmuting a specific exhortation into a universally meaningful artistic statement. The transcription of rural innocence and eccentricity, on the other hand, naturally lent itself to a gratuitous exercise of the imagination. Assisted by her genuine talent for observation and for a certain kind of generalization, she was able rather effortlessly to endow seemingly limited experiences with universal significance, in a manner reminiscent of Jane Austen. Though she rightly sensed that she was "Mediaeval—and *un* Manchester"—she could not indulge her tendencies persistently but tried earnestly to do justice to those aspects of life which commanded another sort of allegiance than a spontaneous temperamental affinity. Yvonne ffrench perceptively suggests this conflict inherent in her nature and her art:

> Two dominant traits in her nature control in effect her literary work: a constant attempt at reconciliation between her natural escapism and the sense of moral obligation forced upon her by period, circumstances and upbringing. . . . Largely her literary struggle appears to be an effort to reconcile the antiquarian with the social reformer. The result was a clash between her affection for past, and regard for present, conditions.[65]

Yet the first embodiment of that "sense of moral obligations" —*Mary Barton*—was indirectly to make possible the expression of "her natural escapism" to a large and sympathetic audience. For the immediate success of that novel (so peculiarly pertinent a document after the social agitation of "the hungry forties") made her at once a recognized author, earned her the praises of many literary men, and introduced her to the literary society of London. Meeting Carlyle, Dickens, John Forster (who, as a reader for Chapman and Hall, had recommended the publication of *Mary Barton*), and even Wordsworth in that first year of fame was undoubtedly gratifying,[66] but Dickens' suggestion in 1850 that she become a regular contributor to his new magazine *Household Words* spelled the true beginning of a regular literary career.[67] The impulse to write no longer had to come from external circumstances, and *Cranford*—the reflection of a humorous view of life—was produced *gratia artis.*

Her existence was not altered in a drastic way, however, for she was still housewife and district visitor and to a certain extent remained so to the end of her days. But the greater financial ease (secured both by her writing and by a family inheritance) in turn made possible a more gracious way of living, allowing her to develop the opportunities for social intercourse with literary figures to which her fame entitled her. The family had previously moved in 1842 from 14 Dover Street to 121 Upper Rumford Street, a change necessitated by the growth of the Gaskell children. In 1850, not without some qualms on Mrs. Gaskell's part about the rightness of purchasing an elegant house when many poor people lacked passable accommodations,[68] they settled in 42 (later 84) Plymouth Grove, a spacious house with a garden in which the children could play and a field in which a cow could be kept. It was to be their permanent residence. Entertaining such celebrities as Dickens, Carlyle, Ruskin, Charlotte Brontë, and Harriet Beecher Stowe[69] (as well as many family friends and acquaintances), supervising the education and recreation of her four daughters, managing and indeed training the many servants such a household required, planning trips abroad, tending to the produce of her garden, corresponding with many of those friends and relatives she could not frequently see—all these activities had to be reconciled with her literary ambitions. In what is perhaps an overstatement, not of her activities but of her attitude to them, Susanna Winkworth has suggested the secondary place authorship took in this life crowded with responsibilities:

> Her books, indeed, were only written when all possible domestic and social claims had been satisfied. Not only was she a devoted wife and mother, but her actual household cares were a positive delight to her. She was more proud of her cows and poultry, pigs and vegetables, than of her literary triumphs, and trained a succession of young women into first-rate cooks.[70]

That the perfect reconciliation of duties had not been achieved is, however, evident in her letters. She would not so carefully weigh the appropriateness of an artistic career for a woman were she not herself conflicted between the respective claims of household activities and literary strivings;[71] she waxes enthusiastic at the mere thought of a "library" like Charles Eliot Norton's where one might retire to write "undisturbed for hours," and yet with a whimsical enumeration of tasks already performed that morning she vindicates the scene of her labors—the dining room—as the most suitable place from which to supervise children and servants;[72] the delights of solitude at Lea Hurst (the home of Florence Nightingale's parents) where she has retired for a while to work on *North and South* are only too apparent;[73] she often complains of physical exhaustion. But her correspondence also shows that she could not have foregone social activities. She loves far too well the bustle of daily life, though it is exhausting and distracting. She enjoys the exercise of maternal authority, reproving and praising her daughters, and very frequently analyzing their respective qualities and failings. She delights in interesting gossip whether it concerns literary figures or Manchester friends and acquaintances.[74]

The pattern of her existence remained much the same till the end, though, as her health began to fade in the last years, she realized more and more the necessity of long trips abroad to counteract the unfortunate effect of the Manchester air and climate. Her last artistic production is an appropriate example of how closely the claims of art and home were interwoven for her; the income from *Wives and Daughters* was destined to the purchase of a country house to which her husband could retire and which her daughters might inherit.

That life so filled with activity was on the whole free from unusually eventful experiences but could hardly in so sociable a woman be devoid of meaningful relationships. The year 1850 marks not only the beginning of her friendship with Dickens and collaboration with him, first on *Household Words* and then on *All the Year Round*, but also her significant encounter with Charlotte Brontë at the home of Sir James Kay-Shuttleworth on Lake Windermere. Several letters to friends vividly illumine this meeting and the inception of a friendship which correspondence and mutual visits (Charlotte Brontë went to Manchester in 1851 and 1853, Mrs. Gaskell to Haworth in 1853) were to sustain. If Dickens' letter requesting her to work for his magazine provided opportunities for the novelist and short-story writer, the encounter with Charlotte Brontë paved the way for the accomplishments of the biographer. Though the friendship was never very intimate—no doubt the result of Charlotte's innate reticence—its genuine cordiality and Mrs. Gaskell's abilities as a writer made her the likely choice to reveal to the world the true nature of "the authoress of *Jane Eyre*" after the latter's early death in 1855. Having to cope with the negative reactions her *Life of Charlotte Brontë* (1857) provoked in certain circles marked the second painful experience in her authorship. But as in the case of *Ruth* two years earlier, there were many enthusiastic tributes from friends, literary figures, and even from Charlotte's father to console her for the agony of having offended against Victorian reticence.

Fortunately also, the impact of adverse criticism reached her only after her return from what she later considered to be the happiest experience of her life, a trip to Rome with her four daughters as a guest of the William Wetmore Storys.[75] Her romantic encounter with Charles Eliot Norton (in the picturesque setting of the Roman Carnival) laid the foundation for a lasting friendship sustained by an eight-year correspondence only her death ended. The liveliness, whimsy, intelligence, breadth of interest and warmth of feeling which these letters so consistently display make them perhaps the best clue to the attractiveness of her personality, while the talent for easy and informal expression they reveal demonstrates her instinctive gifts as a writer.[76] Another close if more formal friendship was to grow indirectly out of her experience as a biographer, for *The Life of Charlotte Brontë* was not printed by her own firm, Chapman and Hall, but by Smith, Elder & Co., Charlotte's publishers. George Smith, very favorably impressed by Mrs. Gaskell, eventually became not only the publisher of her last works but an intimate friend. The author's lengthy correspondence with him gives us another instance of her outgoing nature and her capacity to maintain lifelong friendships, while it offers us some fascinating insights into her attitude toward Thackeray, George Henry Lewes, and George Eliot.[77]

Though Mrs. Gaskell's relationship with George Eliot did not extend beyond a brief correspondence (as we have seen, one that began auspiciously), that correspondence testifies to their mutual respect and admiration. Perhaps the greatest tribute to Mrs. Gaskell's artistic stature is that which George Eliot paid to her in her letter of November 11, 1859 acknowledging her "sweet encouraging words" regarding *Scenes of Clerical Life* and *Adam Bede*:

I had indulged the idea that if my books turned out to be worth much, you would be among my willing readers; for I was conscious, while the question of my power was still undecided for me, that my feeling towards Life and Art had some affinity with the feeling which had inspired "Cranford" and the earlier Chapters of "Mary Barton." That idea was brought the nearer to me, because I had the pleasure of reading Cranford for the first time in 1857, when I was writing the "Scenes of Clerical Life," and going up the Rhine one dim wet day in the spring of the next year, when I was writing "Adam Bede,"

I satisfied myself for the lack of a prospect by reading over again those earlier chapters of "Mary Barton." I like to tell you these slight details because they will prove to you that your letter must have a peculiar value for me, and that I am not expressing vague gratitude toward a writer whom I only remember vaguely as one who charmed me in the past.[78]

A personal friendship gave impetus to Mrs. Gaskell's fascination with French history, traditions, literature, and manners. Her interest in France is demonstrated as early as 1853 in the essay "Traits and Stories of the Huguenots" which relates exciting stories of actual escapes from Catholic persecutions and in the little story "My French Master," a charming portrait of a kindly, courageous, and impeccably mannered *émigré* who supports himself by teaching his native language in a small English town (a piece based on reminiscences of a French teacher in Knutsford). It is discernible again in her sketch "Company Manners" (1854) inspired by the social arts of Mme de Sablé, in her essay "An Accursed Race" (1855) dealing with a proscribed group in France, in the lengthy tale of the French Revolution which forms part of "My Lady Ludlow" (1858), and in "French Life" (1864), a series of sprightly essays assessing Parisian family life and society and depicting excursions into northern and southern France (e. g., Chartres and Avignon). It is finally evident in the intention, unfortunately never executed, of writing a biography of Madame de Sévigné. That penchant for France was undoubtedly encouraged by her friendship with Madame Mohl, and the contact with French society which that relationship made possible.[79] For, though English by birth, Madame Mohl, the wife of the Orientalist Julius Mohl, had resided in Paris from a very early age; she had been a favorite of Madame Récamier's salon and had had the distinction of dispelling by her vivacity the gloom of the aging Chateaubriand. She now reigned over a salon (at 120, rue du Bac) where her great wit and originality provided the appropriate atmosphere for the gathering of many French intellectuals. That her friendship with Mrs. Gaskell (who may have been introduced to her by the William Wetmore Storys) was very meaningful to a woman who from early youth had been conversant with the most accomplished men of letters, science, and politics is perhaps the greatest tribute to the novelist's sophistication and charm. From 1855 on (they probably met for the first time in 1854) visits to her became a regular feature of Mrs. Gaskell's trips abroad; indeed, standing before the mantelpiece in Madame Mohl's salon, the author worked away at many chapters of *Wives and Daughters.*[80]

In view of the great physical and mental exertions which Mrs. Gaskell's personal life and literary activities imposed upon her, her progressively failing health in the last years and her untimely death are not surprising. Her physical weakness provides touching evidence of her abiding involvement with social problems. For it resulted in part from unusual personal exertions to allay suffering during the 1862 Manchester "cotton famine" which followed in the wake of the American Civil War.[81] The longer and more frequent trips abroad apparently could not counteract the expenditure of energy demanded not only by her social life and active correspondence but by her continuing authorship. For, despite a certain creative decline of two years after *The Life of Charlotte Brontë* (which most critics assign to her extreme sensitivity to critical strictures), the years 1859 to 1865 witnessed the production of such lengthy stories as "My Lady Ludlow" (1858), "Lois the Witch" (1859), "The Grey Woman" (1861), "A Dark Night's Work" (1863), "Cousin Phillis" (1863–64), and of two major novels, *Sylvia's Lovers* (1863) and *Wives and Daughters* (1864–66). Few of her travels could have been free from the demands of the creative process. Her journey to Heidelberg in 1858 in all likelihood provided suggestions for "The Grey Woman" and "Six Weeks at Heppenheim." Her trip to Whitby in 1859 was probably undertaken for the specific purpose of doing research for *Sylvia's Lovers.* The impressions gathered during her visits to Normandy, Brittany, Paris, and Provence in 1862 seem in part to have been recorded on the spot, for "French Life" is written in the form of a journal. Her stay in Pontresina in 1864 was definitely not designed for the carefree delight of tourism but to allow opportunities for working on her last novel. As we have seen, the living room of Madame Mohl functioned intermittently as the writer's study.

Nothing is more understandable than the overwhelming desire for a restful life that led her to purchase a home in Alton, Hampshire—which she unfortunately never lived to enjoy. Her sudden death from heart failure (on November 12, 1865), while spending a weekend there in final preparations for the disclosure of her thoughtful surprise gift to her husband, left her last novel unfinished. A photograph of her in the last years shows her to have aged remarkably, but most critics agree that her last work does not reveal signs of physical strain. Yet her reference to the house never includes plans for her enjoyment of it.[82] A courageous acceptance of death as long as her family would be assured of security and happiness is not unlikely in someone who long before had already demonstrated a stoic resignation to it. An early letter (undated) to her sister-in-law, while it cheerfully asserts that she is not morbidly concerned with the thought of death, yet touchingly enjoins her to take care of her daughters Marianne and Meta in that eventuality, particularly since, as she quietly says, "we all know the probability of widowers marrying again."[83]

Much care and worry must have tried that overtly even-tempered, cheerful, and lively disposition, and much fatigue drained that energy that stopped only when her heart ceased to function. Had she been conscious of the coming end, her feeling might perhaps have paralleled, as several critics have remarked, that sense of contented lassitude expressed by Mrs. Gibson as she lies down to rest and dream of a pleasing future in the last words ever written by the novelist.

CHAPTER 2

The Social Conscience

I *Mary Barton* (1848)

THE IMMEDIATE APPEAL of *Mary Barton* is easily demonstrable by the many enthusiastic critical reviews, the large audience of readers, and the accolades of such important literary figures as Dickens, Carlyle, and Walter Savage Landor,[1] but the precise reasons for that appeal are not so immediately evident. The work did appropriately appear at the end of a decade of social unrest and, although it rehearsed only the beginnings of that period (the years 1839–42 in particular) its basic appraisal of social problems had not lost its pertinence.[2] Sheer timeliness, however, was not fully responsible for its success.

Inevitably led to compare Mrs. Gaskell's work with previous studies of social conditions in fiction, critics generally agree that *Mary Barton*'s special significance, aside from its great authenticity, lay in its capacity not only to stimulate the imagination but to arouse the social conscience of its readers. Obviously Harriet Martineau's *Illustrations of Political Economy* (1834) could hardly have achieved the same result: such "pictures of what those principles [of Political Economy] are actually doing in communities"[3] as *The Hill and the Valley* and *A Manchester Strike* were specifically calculated to appeal not to man's moral but to his rational nature, not to his heart but to his common sense and enlightened self-interest. Though Mrs. Trollope's *Michael Armstrong, the Factory Boy* (1840) has been underrated by critics, both that work and Charlotte Elizabeth's *Helen Fleetwood* (1841), which seek to evoke pity and indignation regarding social problems and are indeed often moving in their depiction of human suffering, lack the power of *Mary Barton.* The authors are not only more limited in the scope of their social criticism (both focus on the problem of child labor in the cotton mills) but in artistic execution (Mrs. Trollope's powers of characterization are intermittent, while those of Charlotte Elizabeth are almost nonexistent) and in basic viewpoint (Mrs. Trollope's is belied by the work's artificial conclusion and Charlotte Elizabeth's is so parochial that it must alienate many readers).[4]

Critics are surely justified in acknowledging only Disraeli as a significant precursor in that attack on social conditions by novelists which would soon enlist not only Mrs. Gaskell's efforts but those of Charles Kingsley in *Alton Locke* (1850) and *Yeast* (1851). Yet they basically agree that, for several reasons, even Disraeli's impressive denunciation of the gulf between "the two nations"[5] in *Sybil* (1845) was not as effective as Mrs. Gaskell's treatment of the same focal problem in *Mary Barton.* Because Disraeli's commentary on social problems had a political *raison d'être,* its scope and effect were restricted while Mrs. Gaskell's broadly humanitarian appraisal invariably had a wider appeal. Whereas Disraeli's knowledge of social conditions was the result of planned research over a limited period of time, Mrs. Gaskell's grasp of the subject was the fruit of many years of personal experience with poverty in her husband's parish. While the mind of the one deftly exposed social ills with thoughtful indignation and a biting contempt for human exploitation, the heart and conscience of the other movingly dramatized the harrowing inequities of man's social condition.

The general humaneness of Mrs. Gaskell's approach indeed gives her, as Kathleen Tillotson points out, the advantage not only over her politically oriented predecessor but over the writer who would soon become the apostle of Christian Socialism in fiction:

> . . . Mrs. Gaskell differs from Disraeli and Kingsley in having no axe to grind. A wider impartiality, a tenderer humanity, and it may be a greater artistic integrity, raise this novel beyond the conditions and problems that give rise to it.[6]

Thus her greatest asset is that spontaneous, non-manipulative interest in humanity to which Arnold Kettle does justice in a suggestive comment:

> It would not be fair to compare Disraeli's presentation of scenes of poverty with the mode of exhibition—local color and feeding peculiarities included—employed in the reptile house in the London Zoo; but with Mrs. Gaskell such a comparison would never even enter one's head. She has a respect for her characters quite different from the social worker's interest or the responsible intellectual's effort of sympathy.[7]

Unencumbered then by a specific commitment—be it to a Young England or a Christian Socialist movement—Mrs. Gaskell exemplifies in her work the attempt to counteract Utilitarian rationalism with an appraisal of human needs and desires which makes sentiment the significant nexus of human relations. It is, as Louis Cazamian so aptly says, a "sentimental interventionism" which she preaches. We therefore associate her views with the gospel of Carlyle and, though not directly influenced by Dickens (nor indeed by any earlier writers on social questions), her appeal to the emotions is qualitatively similar to his. Cazamian points to that significant resemblance:

> While she was as unfitted as Dickens to erect a new system, to challenge orthodox political economy with new economic principles, she could, as effectively as he, suggest in the face of a pressing and painful reality, the *sentiments* which would give birth to actions in the present and to new theories in the future [italics mine].[8]

The impact of Dickens' denunciations regardless of their complete accuracy (e.g., his attack on the Poor Laws in *Oliver Twist*) suggests the force of an appeal to sentiment cast in fictional form. As Edmund Spenser well knew centuries before, humanity prefers to receive its lesson garbed in a story; it is much more disposed to have its emotions roused than its intellect challenged. When that appeal to readers had, as in Mrs. Gaskell's case, the quality of a religious injunction, its effect was further intensified: it challenged Christian consciences to re-evaluate standards of earthly conduct in the light of future salvation.

The authenticity of Mrs. Gaskell's descriptions of social conditions in Manchester was of course essential in retaining the interest and sympathy of readers who might justly demand a sufficient correlative for the feelings they were asked to experience. Yet not only did contemporary critics emphasize the accuracy of her portrayal[9] but even the formidable W. R. Greg, who severely criticized her for placing the responsibility for such conditions upon the masters, could not challenge the veracity of her descriptions. He was forced to admit that the author "has evidently lived much among the people she describes, made herself intimate at their firesides," and to grant that her dialogues "approach very nearly, both in tone and style, to the conversations actually carried on in the dingy cottages of Lancashire."[10]

In claiming that the vagaries of capitalistic production victimized masters as well as workmen, and that the latter's failure to lead disciplined and abstemious lives largely accounted for hardships in time of retrenchment, Greg revealed that very immunity to sentiment which Mrs. Gaskell was trying to counteract. The self-satisfaction with which he presented an instance (complete with chart) of the "actual progress upwards of a young mechanic" who developed saving habits and postponed marriage until he was solvent indicates that, like Harriet Martineau before him, Greg had brought his mind conscientiously to bear upon social problems while his imagination and heart had largely remained inoperative. (Considering that the average laborer was poorly housed, forced to work very long hours, wretchedly paid, and almost denied any leisure, he would have needed enormous self-control to renounce temporary enjoyments.) Like Mrs. Gaskell, Greg maintained that the basic want of the workers was, as he put it, "moral, not material." But the apostle of self-sufficiency was mainly criticizing the workmen's lack of moral fiber ("strength," "sense," "courage"), which accounted for the precariousness of their lives,[11] while Mrs. Gaskell, the "sentimental interventionist," repeatedly deplored the denial of moral support to the workers. For only the sympathy and the confidence of the masters could help to relieve the physical suffering and sense of alienation of the men.

This conflict of views is interesting not only as a classic illustration of two contrasting viewpoints concerning those social conditions fostered by the Industrial Revolution but as a dramatic instance of the gap between the assumptions, the standards, even the temperamental leanings of Utilitarianism and Social Interventionism. Many critics also suggest that Greg's reproaches were partly responsible for Mrs. Gaskell's far more sympathetic view of masters in *North and South.* Though she does do justice to their boldness, their inventiveness, and their self-reliance, she has not, however, altered her basic viewpoint in that novel. For the masters' sympathetic understanding of their workmen and their willingness to share business concerns with them are still the *sine qua non* of successful cooperation in capitalistic enterprise. After all it is in *North and South* that the master, Mr. Thornton, echoes Carlyle's condemnation of the "cash nexus."

While Cazamian views Mrs. Gaskell's particular insight into social questions as the logical product of her femininity for "it is feminine natures, more impulsive and tender, who have perceived the connection between the principles of Christian charity and the duties of social solidarity,"[12] David Cecil, interestingly enough, believes that very femininity to have been her greatest handicap in the handling of social questions:

It would have been impossible for her if she had tried, to have found a subject less suited to her talents. It was neither domestic nor pastoral. It gave scope neither to the humorous, the pathetic nor the charming. Further, it entailed an understanding of economics and history wholly outside the range of her Victorian feminine intellect. And the only emotions it could involve were masculine and violent ones.[13]

Yet the conscious purpose of Mrs. Gaskell was precisely not to grapple with "economics and history" but to bring to bear upon social conditions and those very "masculine and violent" emotions which she was well aware they aroused (as her portrayal of John Barton shows) the solution of womanly feelings of sympathy and solicitude which she hoped would, like an antidote, counteract their virulence. In that sense the subject was eminently "suited to her talents," and she could without qualms deny a knowledge of political economy (though she had read Adam Smith and perhaps other works on the subject[14]), as she pursued her aim of revealing the bitterness evoked by social conflicts and of suggesting ways to mitigate it. The scrupulosity of her modest intentions is amply demonstrated in her sensitive reaction to the criticism of her aims:

I do think that we must all acknowledge that there are duties connected with the manufacturing system not fully understood as yet, and evils existing in relation to it which may be remedied in some degree, although we as yet do not see how; but surely there is no harm in directing the attention to the existence of such evils. No one can feel more deeply than I how WICKED it is to do anything to excite class against class; and it has been most unconscious if I have done so . . . no praise could compensate me for the self-reproach I shall feel if I have written unjustly.[15]

That very absence of tendentiousness in *Mary Barton* has made it seem a purer work of art than the social novels of her predecessors (we have seen Kathleen Tillotson speak of its possibly "greater artistic integrity"). But it would be a mistake to assume that the breadth of her purpose and the selflessness of her impulse were wholly conducive to a controlled and harmonious artistic expression. For, to begin with, though she was under no compulsion to enjoin specific actions or to promote particular remedies, she was limited by profound moral and religious commitments which distinctly affected the handling of her subject. What Arthur Pollard calls "the moralizing intention of the work"[16] does indeed impair its artistic power, while the form which that intention takes is an even more immediate source of weakness. Instead of consistently suggesting her views through the interaction of characters and circumstances alone, she yields to the hortatory impulse; this preaching by doctrine rather than by example minimizes the impact of her dramatic presentation of human conflicts and their possible psychological implications. It is not surprising that Elizabeth Barrett Browning, though certainly committed to social reform, should find the effect rebuffing:

> There is power and truth—she can shake and she can pierce—but I wish half the book away, it is so tedious every now and then; and besides, I want more beauty, more air from the universal world—these class-books must always be defective as works of art.[17]

But it is not didacticism alone that mars the artistic coherence of the work. Her very diffidence and modesty, though in some ways so helpful a guarantee against one-sidedness, mitigate unfortunately, as we shall see, against the force of every deeply felt indictment inspired by her social sympathy.

Her basic theme, as she describes it in her Preface to the novel, seems undeniably promising from an artistic point of view, since it is concerned with the psychological rather than the economic implications of social conflict.[18] Her intention is not so much to chronicle a way of life as to convey a particular state of mind, *regardless of its justification*—that of those sympathetically observed "care-worn men, who looked as if doomed to struggle through their lives in strange alternations between work and want," and who feel (as she has personally discovered from "one or two of the more thoughtful among them") "sore and irritable against the rich, the even tenor of whose seemingly happy lives appeared to increase the anguish caused by the lottery-like nature of their own."[19]

Her apparent objectivity seems at first fortuitous; since she wants to reveal an ominous moral and psychological phenomenon, the justification for the workers' bitterness may not be as relevant a question as the threatening reality of a rancor which transforms "resignation" into "revenge," of "a state . . . in which the lips are compressed for curses, and the hands clenched and ready to smite." However, her statement that she wishes "to give some utterance to the agony which, from time to time, convulses this dumb people; *the agony of suffering without the sympathy of the happy, or of erroneously believing that such is the case* [italics mine]," reveals the weakness which underlies her objectivity. She intimates that the masters might be guilty yet immediately retracts the suggestion, seemingly temporizing with the truth. Yet her very refusal to identify herself with the viewpoint of the men indirectly supports her most significant conviction. The workers' possible misjudgment of their employers after all suggests that it is a failure in communication, what she later on in the novel itself calls a "feeling of alienation between the different classes of society," which is the focal problem in the social relations between masters and men.[20]

Thus her Preface already reveals the difficulties created by her basic intention not to establish the responsibility for social deprivation but to warn against the dangers of its moral and psychological repercussions. It foreshadows some of the problems actually faced by the author in the novel itself. She will be emotionally incapable of remaining an objective arbiter of disputes while exploring the state of mind of her "care-worn men," yet morally committed to oppose a rebellion against accepted standards and norms. She will persistently tend to qualify that allegiance with the downtrodden to which her sympathy impels her.

Discerning critics of *Mary Barton* have understandably singled out for praise the characterization of John Barton, Mary's father.

Only in the portrait of the Manchester weaver whose progressive disillusionment and embitterment lead him to commit murder at the behest of his union does Mrs. Gaskell achieve her stated intention of exemplifying the moral and psychological devastation that can be caused by alienation.[21] Indeed she carefully suggests the complex interaction of temperament, personal experience, and external circumstances which leads to the downfall of her hero. Early insights into Barton's nature and the quality of his bitterness clearly anticipate his future conflicts. The balance of his moral nature is shown as precarious because of his emotional intensity (his basic characteristic is that of "extreme earnestness; resolute either for good or evil"); moreover, severe mental suffering in one who possesses a "sort of latent enthusiasm" may already have distorted his moral values. At a time when his better impulses still prevail, John Barton can not only be so strongly aroused on the subject of "the gentlefolk" that his recriminations against them rush forth while "the latent fire" is "lighting up his eye," but his destructive feelings of rancor and hatred toward the rich are intimately related to the positive impulses of love and tenderness toward the child he has tragically lost:

"And what good have they ever done that I should like them? . . . If I am sick do they come and nurse me? If my child lies dying (as poor Tom lay, with his white wan lips quivering, for want of better food than I could give him), does the rich man bring the wine or broth that might save his life? If I am out of work for weeks in the bad times, and winter comes . . . and there is no coal for the grate, and no clothes for the bed, and the thin bones are seen through the ragged clothes, does the rich man share his plenty with me, as he ought to do, if his religion wasn't a humbug? . . . No, I tell you, it's the poor, and the poor only, as does such things for the poor. Don't think to come over me with th' old tale, that the rich know nothing of the trials of the poor; I say, if they don't know, they ought to know. We're their slaves as long as we can work; we pile up their fortunes with the sweat of our brows, and yet we are to live as separate as if we were in two worlds. . . ."[22]

The loss of his wife which soon follows this first scene in the novel is an appropriate psychological step in his alienation from "the gentle humanities of earth" for he now lacks a restraining influence on that emotionalism whose positive attributes almost imply negative ones. His very reaction to his wife's death exemplifies his potential for love and hatred and the inexorable connection between the two, for his overwhelming tenderness for the departed soon gives way to a strong vindictiveness against the person he believes responsible for his loss. The very man who is impelled by "a strange curiosity" to look again at "his first gift to her, a bead necklace," and breaks down in tears when his discovery of "piled-up tea-things" reminds him of "his wife's daily round of duties" unreasonably conjectures that the recent disappearance of his wife's flighty sister, Esther, may have caused that fatal "shock to the system" of Mrs. Barton:

> His feelings towards Esther almost amounted to curses. It was she who had brought on all this sorrow. Her giddiness, her lightness of conduct had wrought this woe. His previous thoughts about her had been tinged with wonder and pity, but now he hardened his heart against her for ever.[23]

Barton's inability to forgive is closely allied to the most dangerous tendency in his nature. Unlike Alice Wilson (the sister of Barton's good friend) who, when confronted with sorrow "would say it were sent, and fall to trying to find out what good it were to do,"[24] John Barton is incapable of resignation. His tragedy, like that of so many heroes, has its root in his rebellion against fate, in his obsession with challenging not only the existing realities of social conditions but the basic nature of justice.

His tendency to negate resignation is most dramatically exemplified at the bedside of Davenport, the dying workman whom John Barton and George Wilson have gone to assist. Nor does the author neglect to give Barton a psychological justification for his feeling. The horrifying picture of destitution both in the street piled with loathsome refuse and in the hovel where the dying man "lay on straw, so damp and mouldy, no dog would have chosen it in preference to flags," with "a piece of sacking, coming next to his worn skeleton of a body" in the fever of a delirium from which "every now and then he started up in his naked madness, looking like the prophet of woe in the fearful plague-picture," could hardly inspire abnegation. The difficulties of resignation are indeed only too apparent in the behavior of Davenport: that the saintly acceptance of hardships so characteristic of him before his illness must have been sustained at the cost of great mental effort is subtly suggested by the author's comment that in his delirium "he cursed and swore, which surprised Wilson, who knew his piety in health, and who did not know the unbridled tongue of delirium." It is not surprising that John Barton, confronted with mortal agony under such harrowing conditions, should find the gospel of resignation Davenport had preached in a letter to his wife wholly irrelevant and that he should meet Wilson's praise of this document with bitter cynicism. When Wilson comments that "it were as good as Bible-words; ne'er a word o' repining; a' about God being our Father, and that we mun bear patiently whate'er He sends," the following dialogue takes place:

"Don ye think He's the' masters' Father, too? I'd be loth to have 'em for brothers."

"Eh, John! donna talk so; sure there's many and many a master as good or better nor us."

"If you think so, tell me this. How comes it they're rich, and we're poor? I'd like to know that. Han they done as they'd be done by for us?"[25]

And Barton continues to denounce the inequities of the capitalistic system which denies to workers "interest" on their own capital—that "labour" which allows the building up of fortunes by the exploitation of the working man. In conclusion Barton clinches his argument by opposing to Wilson's suggestion that "th' masters suffer too" in difficult times the irrefutable argument which had haunted Mrs. Gaskell's mind when years earlier a workman had faced her with it: "Han they ever seen a child o' their'n die for want o' food?"[26]

In presenting the two final steps toward that ultimate alienation which makes the commission of murder possible, Mrs. Gaskell again strives to do justice to the complexities of Barton's nature—to the clash between possibilities of good and evil—and to the role played by unfortuitous circumstances in fostering his destructive tendencies. It is because he has such constructive feelings toward the Chartist petition, because he so lovingly feels "a really pure gladness of heart" in actively promoting "some grand relief" for the workingmen that he is so bitterly disappointed when he returns from London. What has again impressed him there is his sense of total alienation from the rich, his abiding apprehension of the great gap between two ways of existence and two concepts of what is deemed the significant "business" of life. He tells his friends that, as the procession of Chartists had moved past elegant carriages:

> "One o' th' police struck me. 'Whatten business have you to do that!' said I.
>
> " 'You're frightening them horses,' says he, in his mincing way . . . 'and it's our business to keep you from molesting the ladies and gentlemen going to her Majesty's drawing-room.'
>
> " 'And why are we to be molested?' asked I, 'going decently about our business, which is life and death to us, and many a little one clemming at home in Lancashire? Which business is of most consequence i' the sight o' God, think yo', our'n or them grand ladies and gentlemen as yo think so much on?'
>
> "But I might as well ha' held my peace, for he only laughed."[27]

By analyzing Barton's progressive despondency after his return from London, the author appropriately prepares us for his final indignation which will burst out during the strike (when mediation has failed) in the irrepressible "have at the masters!" Again external circumstances abet his tendencies, for the economic crisis which has now hit Manchester further inhibits Barton's better impulses. The physical weakness of hunger, the sense of unreality induced by the opium which staves off craving for food, and the desultoriness of unemployment enhance his tendency to brood and give to discontent the dimensions of an obsession. Mrs. Gaskell's ability to intuit a "state of feeling" to which the term "monomania" might be applied "so haunting, so incessant, were the thoughts that pressed upon him" is demonstrated in the following analogy:

> I have somewhere read a forcibly described punishment among the Italians, worthy of a Borgia. The supposed or real criminal was shut up in a room, supplied with every convenience and luxury; and at first mourned little over his imprisonment. But day by day he became aware that the space between the walls of his apartment was narrowing, and then he understood the end. Those painted walls would come into hideous nearness, and at last crush the life out of him.
>
> And so day by day, nearer and nearer, came the diseased thoughts of John Barton. They excluded the light of heaven, the cheering sounds of earth. They were preparing his death.[28]

There is genuine psychological insight in her realization that Barton's "overpowering thought," his perpetually reiterated questioning of "why" the "rich and poor" should be "so separate, so distinct, when God has made them all" and "it is not His will that their interests [be] so far apart," is especially destructive because it leads him away from the particulars of his own state to a questioning of the universal condition of man, to a probing of "the problems and mysteries of life." In his bafflement at these "mysteries," he clings to the one abiding reality, a characteristically dual emotion: "the only feeling that remained clear and undisturbed in the tumult of his heart, was hatred to one class, and keen sympathy with the other."[29]

The close relationship between "hatred" and "keen sympathy" is again evident in his final commitment to violence after the hopeless outcome of the meeting of masters and workmen during the strike. It is his very tenderness "for the childer, whose little voices are getting too faint and weak to cry aloud wi' hunger," his realization that the workers' demands for more money are made "not for our own lives . . . but for the lives of them little ones, who don't yet know what life is, and are afeard of death," which provokes his anger at the masters' obduracy and his violent indignation at the satiric cartoon of the bedraggled men made by young Harry Carson (the son of Wilson's master). While his solidarity with all workingmen leads him to reprove any violence against the "knobsticks" (scabs) who in their destitution "mun choose between vitriol and starvation," his alienation from the masters triumphs in the reckless assertion of his personal desire for revenge: "Set me to serve out the masters, and see if there's aught I'll stick at."[30] After the general decision to kill Harry Carson, Barton's act of *hybris* is requited by *nemesis* in the drawing of lots. In destroying Carson, he destroys himself, for a man capable of strong feelings of love and loyalty to some of his fellow men is not one to throw off lightly the denial of love even to those from whom he has become fully estranged. Only death can be the appropriate deliverance from that muddle of life which has led Barton to reject the moral principles that could sustain his own humanity.

For in the pathetic speeches that precede Barton's death, the author carefully reminds us that though he has committed a crime, his initial intentions were good, and had become corrupted by his bewilderment at the contradictions between moral injunctions and human behavior. In his youth, he says, he had studied the teachings of the Bible, "but you'd never believe black was black, or night was night, when you saw all about you acting as if black was white, and night was day." Even the way of resignation had once seemed eminently attractive, "liker heaven than any other bit of earth has been," until the harsh realities of existence made a commitment to it seem impossible. He could have resisted the arguments of those who urged him, "Stand up for thy rights," had not a far more personal and direct plea negated his attempt "to live Gospel-wise": "wife and children never spoke, but their helplessness cried aloud, and I was driven to do as others did,—and then Tom died." The psychological conflict growing out of the desire to adhere to the gospel of love for his fellow men is dramatically suggested in his confession that "I was tore in two oftentimes, between my sorrow for the poor suffering folk, and my trying to love them as caused their sufferings (to my mind)." To the last we are reminded that for Barton the ways of love and hatred were closely conjoined and that, given the social rift he constantly witnessed, constructive emotions toward some of his fellow men almost inexorably implied destructive ones toward others. When the positive power of the Christian ethos was for him made inoperative by the perpetual spectacle of its negation in human conduct, the natural impulse could only be one of rejection: "And I thought I'd no longer labour at following th' Bible myself."[31]

The general lines of John Barton's downfall are thus presented with a certain insight which gives it tragic dimensions and a larger significance, making us feel indeed that his "is the timeless history of how a man full of human kindness is hardened into (and by) hatred and violence,"[32] and that "apart from Heathcliff, he is the nearest approach to a tragic hero which the early Victorian novel permitted itself."[33]

But that he is only "the nearest approach"—if we may borrow Kettle's terms—is to be accounted for by Mrs. Gaskell's failure to commit herself boldly to her vision of the causes for his agony. Her basic diffidence about challenging the conventions of the status quo, her genuine desire not be "WICKED" in arousing contentious feelings, but rather to function as a "peacemaker" (a term critics so often use in connection with her), her pious commitment to the gospel of resignation—all conspire against the dramatic fulfillment of her conception of Barton's dilemma.

Just as she had done in her Preface, she feels obliged to insist in the novel that there may be no true correlative for the workers' feeling of rancor, even if the reality of this feeling must be coped with. Yet she sympathizes so deeply with John Barton that she often cannot help convincing us of the justice of his feelings. The scene with the policeman in London is a case in point as is also the spectacle of the Carsons' gracious life in which the longing for a hothouse rose contrasts painfully with the craving for bread among the poor. Probably the best example of her identification with Barton's view is that she assigns to him the irrefutable argument that a master never loses a child through starvation which we know to have been so personally meaningful to her. Her sympathy with that view accounts for the reiteration of this very argument in more moderate terms by the sensible friend of John Barton, Job Legh, in his final discussion with Mr. Carson. Yet at other times her desire to remain a moderator in the conflict between masters and men leads to a marked ambiguity in her evaluation, not only of Barton's position, but of his nature. One of the best examples of this ambiguity is the passage which follows the discussion of Barton's painful broodings and of the reaffirmation, growing out of his confusion, of his "hatred" for the rich "and keen sympathy" for the poor:

> But what availed his sympathy? No education had given him wisdom; and without wisdom, even love, with all its effects, too often works but harm. He acted to the best of his judgment, but it was a widely-erring judgment.
>
> The actions of the uneducated seem to be typified in those of Frankenstein, that monster of many human qualities, ungifted with a soul, a knowledge of the difference between good and evil.
>
> The people rise up to life; they irritate us, they terrify us, and we become their enemies. Then, in the sorrowful moment of our triumphant power, their eyes gaze on us with mute reproach. Why have we made them what they are; a powerful monster, yet without the inner means for peace and happiness?
>
> John Barton became a Chartist, a Communist, all that is commonly called wild and visionary. Ay! but being visionary is something. It shows a soul, a being not altogether sensual; a creature who looks forward for others, if not for himself.[34]

The beginning of this passage suggests a flaw in John Barton which W. R. Greg would undoubtedly have accepted as the source of all his conflicts: his love is almost as unconstructive as his hatred because he lacks the education which will enable him to express it wisely. The "widely-erring judgment" born of ignorance will lead him, like Frankenstein's monster, to immoral actions exemplifying the inability to distinguish between good and evil, the absence of a "soul." This reduction of Barton's psychological state to attributes befitting a robot rather than a man clashes strongly with the previous analysis of his moral and mental turmoil. Yet even this simplified and rather severe judgment of his failures is not allowed to stand as such for in the next paragraph there is a strong suggestion that the responsibility for Barton's shortcomings rests entirely with those who have caused him to be "a powerful monster, yet without the inner means for peace and happiness." And the last paragraph, to compound the confusion, endows him with the "soul" that has just been denied to him, for it suggests that a commitment to "wild and visionary" action is not only evidence of supra-"sensual" tendencies but allows for a positive expression of his capacity to love.

In such a passage as this her ambiguous feelings not only weaken what has seemed a convincing psychological portrait, but leave us at a loss as to her real convictions about social responsibility and the appropriateness of political action on the workmen's part. At other times, the oscillation is more simply between the presentation of social conditions that would seem amply to justify Barton's view, and the suggestion that they may be misinterpreted by such as he. Intermittently, there is even a swing of the pendulum back again to a near justification of the workmen's outlook, as in the following description of the bewildering contrast seen by a "poor weaver" during an economic depression:

> . . . when he would bear and endure much without complaining, could he also see that his employers were bearing their share; he is . . . bewildered and (to use his own word) "aggravated" to see that all goes on just as usual with the mill-owners. Large houses are still occupied, while spinners' and weavers' cottages stand empty, because the families that once filled them are obliged to live in rooms or cellars. Carriages still roll along the streets, concerts are still crowded by subscribers, the shops for expensive luxuries still find daily customers, while the workman loiters away his unemployed time in watching these things, and thinking of the pale, uncomplaining wife at home, and the wailing children asking in vain for enough food,—of the sinking health, of the dying life, of those near and dear to him. The contrast is too great. Why should he alone suffer from bad times?[35]

Such a statement transcends mere objectivity by its emotional force; not the worker alone, but Mrs. Gaskell herself seems to be posing the last question. Determined, however, to do justice both to the masters' plight and to the workers' weaknesses (an impulse not credited by W. R. Greg) she soon tones down the impact of her statements:

> I know that this is not really the case; and I know what is the

truth in such matters: but what I wish to impress is what the workman feels and thinks. True, that with child-like improvidence good times will often dissipate his grumbling, and make him forget all prudence and foresight.

What immediately follows is an attempt to restore to the workers some of the dignity of which she has divested them (not without a few additional contradictions indicated by my italics):

> But there are earnest men among these people, men who have *endured wrongs* without complaining, but without ever forgetting or forgiving those whom (*they believe*) have caused all their woe.
>
> Among these was John Barton.[36]

And though she has emotionally convinced us in the deathbed scene that the masters have set a poor example by their unchristian behavior, she does not even then allow Barton to express his desperation at "trying to love them as caused their [the poor's] sufferings" without immediately adding the saving parenthetical phrase "(to my mind)" to suggest that he may be in error.

What also attenuates her sympathy with Barton's attitude is her abiding sense that an embittered refusal to accept one's suffering is almost equivalent to a religious transgression insofar as it implies a questioning of divine will. Though, as we have seen, she realizes that it is the indifference of rich to poor which makes religion seem "a humbug," nevertheless the fact that social resentment so often provokes the poor to negate the possibility of divine justice impels her to compare that resentment unfavorably with resignation—which assumes that trouble in the world "is sent for good" and must be accepted.[37]

John Barton and Alice Wilson function almost symbolically in the novel in charting the two significant ways of coping with "the mysterious problems of life" and if Mrs. Gaskell's spontaneous sympathy goes out to the rebel, all the tendencies of her devout upbringing lead her to exalt the saint. The significance of this particular allegiance to the principles of self-abnegation, self-sacrifice, and resignation can never be overrated. Her commitment to these values is evident in much of her work and had indeed already found expression not only in the one poem of

Sketches of the Poor (the selfless woman whose devotion to others prevented her from ever achieving her dream of returning to the country home of her youth anticipates Alice Wilson) but in two of three stories published before *Mary Barton* ("Libbie Marsh's Three Eras" and "The Sexton's Hero").[38] That this commitment sometimes conflicts with other inclinations should also be firmly kept in mind, for the tensions between its dictates and those of her instinctive feelings deeply affect the texture and coherence of many of her writings.

Though loving care has been expended in characterizing Alice Wilson, the absence of any true conflict in this character denies it dramatic power. Alice's extraordinary virtue, exemplified in her fear of giving the wrong impression that she is repining about her hard life, dehumanizes her. Her principles may be admirable, but we are alienated from the character who practices them. Our interest and sympathy remain with Barton, who exhibits those imperfections and submits to that vulnerability which George Orwell in his "Reflections on Gandhi" calls "the essence of being human," who, in Orwell's terms "is prepared in the end to be defeated and broken up by life, which is the inevitable price of fastening one's love upon other human individuals."[39]

If resignation is made to contrast sharply with rebellion through the character of Alice Wilson (and that of Margaret Legh, Mary's patient blind friend),[40] a sensible acceptance of existing conditions is demonstrated by Margaret's grandfather, the scientifically minded workman, Job Legh. His emotional stability, common sense, and shrewdness enable him to avoid the pitfalls of probing the mystery of inequities in the human condition. The justice of introducing such a character into the novel is unquestionable, for it would be a negation of human variety to suggest that most Manchester men were John Bartons; it is indeed appropriate that these two men represent "different responses to life's hardships."[41] And yet the phenomenon of such self-controlled involvement with social issues as Job Legh exemplifies minimizes the author's original thesis of widespread hostility and alienation, in the absence of other important characters who share Barton's bewilderment and rancor.

When we recall that W. R. Greg attacked the author for seeming to imply that all workmen felt as John Barton did, it seems almost unfair to suggest that one weakness of the book lies in her failure to demonstrate in other characters than John Barton what she had in her Preface called "the state of feeling among too many of the factory-people in Manchester."[42] Diffidence was probably responsible for that failure—an understandable feeling in the light of critical reactions. If one such character was open to misrepresentation, one can imagine the effect of having an explosive point of view represented by other major characters (all we get are glimpses of the anger and sullenness of the Trade Union men). Yet the fact remains that her thesis is greatly weakened by such an omission. For, even though she herself says of John Barton that "such men were not uncommon,"[43] she leads us to feel in the novel that Barton may well be an exception—a man as alienated from his friends as from his enemies—and that his tragedy is a very private one.

Indeed more than mere timidity in challenging her public may be responsible for our feeling that Barton cannot represent a consensus among the Manchester poor. The violence of his ultimate downfall suggests the same reluctance to condone rebellious tendencies which affects her earlier treatment of her hero. Such an attitude would have made it very difficult for her to explore other significant instances of behavior morally reprehensible to her without violating probability by again positing a destructive outcome (death or a severe punishment) for the rebels.

For she cannot really conceive of redemptive possibilities in the anger and doubts of her hero. Much as she authenticates that anger, makes those doubts meaningful, means his sufferings to arouse the conscience of those who have refused him sympathy and confidence—the masters—his rebelliousness implies for her an inevitable retribution which must cast him out from his fellow men. Surely a violence born of bitterness need not have eventuated in murder. Yet the author's ambiguous feelings about the right to protest find resolution solely in a judgment against Barton's questionings of the "mysteries of life." Such questionings, she indirectly suggests, can only lead to the totally destructive action which destines Barton to the fate of most great sinners in fiction.

If an ambiguous treatment of the most significant character in

Mary Barton gravely limits its artistic power, the novel is also weakened by the prominent position eventually accorded to what would, from the title, have seemed to be the major character—Mary Barton. Critics have rightly judged that sufficient material for two novels is to be found in this work. For besides the psychological study of the harrowing effects of social alienation, there is the more conventional romantic story of the pretty and flighty daughter of John Barton who eventually overcomes her frivolity. Some effort is made to interweave the fates of father and daughter, for the two young men who court her, Harry Carson and Jem Wilson, are each victimized by Barton: Carson is killed and Wilson nearly meets the same fate since he is accused of the murder. Because Mary has guessed her father's guilt, she has the anguishing task of reconciling conflicting duties and loyalties, for she cannot denounce her father and yet must try to save Jem Wilson (to make matters worse, she has recently realized that she loves him and not the frivolous Harry Carson for whom she had earlier rejected Jem).

But if this aspect of the plot seems to preserve and even enhance the continuity of the theme—since Barton's tragic destructiveness is here shown to harm those he most wants to protect—the handling of character and situations lacks the psychological insight which often illumines Barton's problems. The failure resides mainly in the characterization of Mary Barton who does transcend the conventions of fiction by being a workman's daughter but lacks the depth and complexity to be a moving counterpart of her tragic father.[44] Even the dangerous frivolity which makes her accept the secret attentions of Harry Carson is not a complex psychological flaw offering a dramatic contrast to her father's dangerous earnestness. The author suggests that instability and rebelliousness may well abet Mary in her infatuation, for if she shares the vanity of her reckless aunt Esther in yearning for wealth and status, she feels thus "perhaps all the more, for her father's aversion to the rich and gentle." We are even told that Mary's love for the elegant young gentleman is "a bubble, blown out of vanity" which nevertheless "looked very real and very bright." Yet neither her instability nor her deluded love—which could lead to a disastrous seduction—are ever authenticated. The only clear motivation which Mary has is her hardly complex desire for ease and prosperity. Even the frivolity of her plans to enjoy life when married to Carson (owning a carriage, purchasing elegant gowns) is attenuated by a very worthy impulse; like little Emily in *David Copperfield,* she very much wishes to be "a lady" in order to improve the lot of others, to supply her father "with every comfort she could devise."[45] Such aspirations, even in the conditions of destitution in which she lives, are hardly very imaginative "Alnaschar visions" (as Mrs. Gaskell terms them); they do not imply that deluded romanticism which Dickens suggests so early in his novel in little Emily's childish dreams of the "sky-blue coat with diamond buttons" in which Mr. Peggotty would undoubtedly astonish the population of Yarmouth.

The unrealistic yearnings, the inner struggles, the ambiguous strivings (as romantic impulses contend with the dictates of duty and loyalty) which Dickens does manage to suggest in Emily before she abandons the humble Ham Peggotty for the dashing Steerforth are absent from Mary's initial conflict between two similarly contrasting suitors. Indeed her lack of insight into her feelings about Jem seems not a potentially tragic delusion but a rather self-satisfied insensitivity to her inclinations:

"I don't care for him, and yet, unless I'm always watching myself, I'm speaking to him in a loving voice. I think I cannot go right, for I either check myself till I'm downright cross to him, or else I speak just natural, and that's too kind and tender by half. And I'm as good as engaged to be married to another; and another far more handsomer than Jem; only I think I like Jem's face best for all that; liking's liking, and there's no help for it."[46]

Though meant to anticipate future actions, such a passage lays no meaningful groundwork for the dramatic turning point of Mary's life—the realization of her love for Jem which removes the unsuspected danger of seduction by Carson—because it does not reveal the psychological roots of her contradictory feelings. Accordingly, her decision to reject the erratic Carson for the faithful Jem seems merely a convenient turn in the plot, the more unconvincing because it follows an awkward and unreal scene in which Jem, after his proposal has been rejected, expresses his desperation in terms more appropriate to stage melodrama than to a serious novel (His threats that her "cruelty" may lead him to become "a drunkard, and maybe . . . a thief, and maybe . . . a murderer" also appear to be less a revelation of character than a plot device to prepare for suspense when Jem is accused of Carson's murder). Though Mrs. Gaskell tries to justify Mary's swift turnabout after the rejection by saying that "a few moments may change our character for life, by giving a totally different direction to our aims and energies," Mary's decision is conveyed through a sentimental, artificial rhetoric which negates any psychological authenticity. Now that the rejection "had unveiled her heart to her . . . had convinced her that she loved Jem above all persons or things," she finds that the once desired "circumstances of ease and luxury" have become meaningless:

> What were these hollow vanities to her, now she had discovered the passionate secret of her soul? She felt as if she almost hated Mr. Carson, who had decoyed her with his baubles. She now saw how vain, how nothing to her, would be all gaieties and pomps, all joys and pleasures, unless she might share them with Jem. . . . If he were poor, she loved him all the better. . . . She had hitherto been walking in gropelight towards a precipice; but in the clear revelation of that past hour, she saw her danger, and turned away resolutely, and for ever.[47]

Even the later realization of the other kind of "precipice" she was nearing has no emotional power; Mary's discovery that Carson had no intention of marrying her comes when she is already invulnerable to his appeal. (The author's eagerness to vindicate her heroine's good judgment and virtue undoubtedly leads her to give Mary that advantage over her base lover.)

Unfortunately, then, Mrs. Gaskell's treatment of Mary's problems is largely made subservient either to the needs of suspense (will Mary be seduced, and can she later save Jem and protect her father from discovery?) or the demands of convention (the heroine remains personally unscathed and triumphs over her dilemma) with little attention to psychological considerations, while the reverse is largely true of her depiction of John Barton's conflicts. In Mary's case the instincts of the storyteller definitely triumph over those of the analyst of character.

That tendency is perhaps even more evident in her handling of Mary's conflict regarding her father's crime than in the treatment of her sentimental difficulties. That a dilemma involving not only divided allegiances but moral transgression had a profound psychological interest for her is evident in later works (*Ruth, North and South, Sylvia's Lovers,* "A Dark Night's Work"). Again and again she will attempt to analyze the state of mind of those caught in such dilemmas. Here, however, she focuses not on *inward* conflicts but on *external* difficulties. Since Mary need not implicate her father if she can obtain an alibi for Jem, the focal question becomes whether Mary, left to her own resources in Liverpool, can reach Jem's cousin whose ship has already left port and who alone can testify to Jem's whereabouts on the fatal day.

Mrs. Gaskell's narrative talents, already suggested by the exciting portrayal of the fire at Carson's mill and by Margaret Legh's lively story of the scorpion, are fully demonstrated in the scene in which Mary, in a small boat chasing Will Wilson's departing ship, is progressively "sickening" under the "nervous fear" of not arriving on time:

> Both wind and tide were against the two men, and labour as they would they made but little way. Once Mary in her impatience had risen up to obtain a better view of the progress they had made; but the men had roughly told her to sit down immediately, and she had dropped on her seat like a chidden child, although the impatience was still at her heart.
>
> But now she grew sure they were turning off from the straight course which they had hitherto kept . . . and after a short time she could not help naming her conviction, as a kind of nightmare dread and belief came over her, that everything animate and inanimate was in league against her one sole aim and object of overtaking Will.
>
> They answered gruffly. . . . They knew what they were about.[48]

As the passage suggests, the dramatic power of this incident (and later of Jem's trial) depends not only on the successful generation of suspense but on a subtler aspect of the storyteller's ability: the capacity to suggest with great imaginative power the state of "nightmare dread" that overcomes a mind bent on one purpose and yet overwrought by accumulated anxiety, doubt, grief, and conflict. Mrs. Gaskell intuits and projects states of obsession and of near madness with a dramatic effectiveness which approaches that of Dickens. We have seen one example in her treatment of John Barton's brooding—though she handles that with far greater artistic restraint and psychological subtlety. Mary Barton's eerie sensations at the trial (when, her testimony over, she no longer needs to fight for self-control) suggest a mental and emotional upheaval which many of the characters in her short stories experience, for it is in these works, as we have said, that her fascination with unusual states of mind and feeling is particularly expressed. Here Mary's former anxious experiences at sea and the image of the guilty father absent from the proceedings blend in nightmarish fashion with the reality of the court's proceedings:

> Mary never let go her clutched hold on the rails. She wanted them to steady her, in that heaving, whirling court. She thought the feeling of something hard compressed within her hand would help her to listen, for it was such pain, such weary pain in her head, to strive to attend to what was being said. They were all at sea, sailing away on billowy waves, and every one speaking at once, and no one heeding her father, who was calling on them to be silent, and listen to him.[49]

Even though Mrs. Gaskell undermines the impact of her central theme by her undue emphasis on suspenseful action in the latter part of the novel, her ability to weave an exciting story seems in itself remarkable in such an early work, particularly since two of her earliest stories, "Libbie Marsh's Three Eras" and "Christmas Storms and Sunshine," show very few signs of such inventiveness. It is also in *Mary Barton* that she first truly displays that flair for humor soon to find its full scope in *Cranford*. The whimsical story of the predicament of Job Legh and his father-in-law who years ago, while bringing the orphaned Margaret Legh back to Manchester, exhausted their ingenuity to soothe the fretful "babby" during the long journey shows a playful, tender, and imaginative appreciation of incongruity. But the effectiveness of her humor in counteracting sentimentality is even more evident when it deals with the novel's central concerns, suggesting the at once comic and touching naïveté arising from the workers' ignorance of and alienation from the world of the rich—and specifically of the London aristocracy. In the meeting preceding the departure of the Chartist delegation for London, as John Barton's visitors name the particular grievances they want redressed, their bewilderment regarding their plight is suggested not only by pathetic self-defeating wishes for the destruction of machinery and the removal of restrictions on child labor but also by the comically naïve suggestion of one workman for stimulating the economy. Members of Parliament are to be asked to emulate the practice of Sir Francis Dashwood to whose family the workman's mother was an "under-laundry maid":

". . . when we were little ones, she'd tell us stories of their grandeur: and one thing she named were, that Sir Francis wore two shirts a day. Now he were all as one as a Parliament man; and many on 'em, I han no doubt, are like extravagant. Just tell 'em, John, do, that they'd be doing the Lancashire weavers a great kindness, if they'd ha' their shirts a' made o' calico; 't would make trade brisk, that would, wi' the power o' shirts they wear."[50]

In a similar vein, John Barton's description of fashionable life in London is an at once amusing and pathetic illustration of the limitations of his own insularity while it also serves the author as a deft satirical denunciation of the idle rich:

"Well, them undertaker folk are driving a pretty trade in London. Well nigh every lady we saw in a carriage had hired one o' them plumes for the day, and had it niddle noddling on her head. It were th' Queen's drawing-room, they said, and th' carriages went bowling along toward her house, some wi' dressed-up gentlemen like circus folk in 'em, and rucks o' ladies in others. Carriages themselves were great shakes too. Some o' th' gentlemen as couldn't get inside hung on behind, wi' nosegays to smell at, and sticks to keep off folk as might splash their silk stockings. I wonder why they didn't hire a cab rather than hang on like a whip-behind boy; but I suppose they wished to keep wi' their wives, Darby and Joan like."[51]

Even the author's objections to factory work for married women are voiced in part through Mrs. Wilson's touching yet absurd conviction that the problem could be easily resolved by those in power if only it were brought close to home—the royal home:

"I say it's Prince Albert as ought to be asked how he'd like his missis to be from home when he comes in, tired and worn, and wanting some one to cheer him; and maybe, her to come in by-and-by, just as tired and down in th' mouth; and how he'd like for her never to be at home to see to th' cleaning of his house, or to keep a bright fire in his grate. Let alone his meals being all hugger-mugger and comfortless."[52]

Thus her humor sometimes functions to sustain her vision of the estrangement of the poor and humble from the values and mode of life of the rich and great; the former's defenselessness and proneness to embitterment are but enhanced by their incongruous innocence of the complexity of social issues, of political life, of wealth and power.

Predictably, the weakest section of the novel is that in which Mrs. Gaskell offers a possible solution for the alienation so dramatically exemplified in John Barton's struggles. The concluding sections of the novel project her conviction, already suggested in earlier chapters, that a basic humanity is the only standard for successful relations between masters and men. Unfortunately the desire to dramatize the beauty and effectiveness of a feeling of brotherhood leads her to oversimplify the difficulties of a complete change of values in the deathbed reconciliation of Mr. Carson and John Barton. Each has been shown to nurture hatred; indeed Mr. Carson's initial eagerness to revenge his son has provoked Mrs. Gaskell to exclaim "Oh, Orestes! you would have made a very tolerable Christian of the nineteenth century!" Admittedly it is an apt illustration of her theme of alienation that both should begin to repent of their feelings when actual contact reveals to them human considerations which distance had obliterated. As John Barton witnesses Mr. Carson's sorrow for his son, a sorrow reminiscent of his own loss, he perceives him for the first time in human terms:

The mourner before him was no longer the employer, a being of another race, eternally placed in antagonistic attitude; going through the world glittering like gold, with a stony heart within, which knew no sorrow but through the accidents of Trade; no longer the enemy, the oppressor, but a very poor and desolate old man.[53]

By the same token, his employer's personal encounter with the reality of John Barton's sufferings breaks the barrier of alienation; as Carson, after refusing to forgive Barton, muses sadly over his own bereavement, his humanity asserts itself above all other claims:

In spite of his desire to retain the revengeful feeling he considered as a duty to his dead son, something of pity would steal in for the poor, wasted skeleton of a man, the smitten creature, who has told him of his sin, and implored his pardon that night.[54]

A thoughtful reading of the Gospel enables his better feelings to triumph over his destructive ones, and the words he speaks before Barton expires are characteristic: "Forgive us our trespasses as we forgive them that trespass against us."

Yet touching as the spirit of this reconciliation is, it seems to suggest what the author was far too perceptive really to believe, that the substitution of the Christian ideal of charitable interdependence for that principle of energetic self-reliance so dear to the Political Economists could be easily achieved if men but recognized that (in those words of the poet Samuel Bamford which she frequently quoted) "we have all of us one human heart."

She does attempt in a later scene to suggest the difficulties such a change of values entails, but the didactic means she chooses do not aptly convey the humaneness of her approach to social conflicts. Thus Mr. Carson is more fully enlightened on his moral duties, yet not through the drama of additional experiences as an employer or further psychological conflicts about his personal loss but through a didactic discussion. Job Legh, the enlightened, commonsensical representative of the workman's viewpoint, has the task of explaining to an employer not only the reasons for John Barton's former grievances but the general causes of that alienation which victimizes all workers. In this discussion the author not only rehearses some points previously made more tellingly by analyzing Barton's feelings, but also manages to suggest that, despite Mr. Carson's charitable forgiveness of the dying John Barton, he still clings to many of his former views. The values of the political economist confront those of the Christian interventionist as Carson answers Job's assertion that the divinely enjoined "duty of the happy is to help the suffering to bear their woe," with the seemingly indefensible argument that "facts have proved, and are daily proving, how much better it is for every man to be independent of help, and self-reliant." Job's counterrefutation, though emotionally appealing, does not really come to grips with the problem Mr. Carson has earnestly posed:

> "You can never work facts as you would fixed quantities, and say, given two facts, and the product is so and so. God has given men feelings and passions which cannot be worked into the problem, because they are for ever changing and uncertain. God has also made some weak; not in any one way, but in all. . . . Now, to my thinking, them that is strong in any of God's gifts is meant to help the weak,—be hanged to the facts!"[55]

Though we discover that, despite some outward "sternness," Mr. Carson eventually not only recognizes the necessity of a relationship between masters and men governed "by the ties of respect and affection, not by mere money bargains alone" but acts upon it through "improvements . . . in the system of employment in Manchester,"[56] the charting of the course which has led to such convictions is, unfortunately, left to our imaginations.

It is perhaps because *Mary Barton* was most effective in suggesting the realities of an experience which Mrs. Gaskell's sympathy and close knowledge could authenticate—the trials of John Barton—that she was accused of exclusively presenting the workman's point of view. That point of view is not neglected in *North and South*, but she also tries to deal more realistically with the assumptions and basic values of someone in Carson's position and to accomplish what she had failed to do in Carson's case, trace the possible evolution of the convictions of a political economist toward an acceptance of interventionist principles. The difficulties of such a task would be made abundantly clear in her second attempt to deal with the conflicts between capital and labor.

II *North and South* (1854–55)

When Mrs. Gaskell returned to a consideration of social conflicts in *North and South*, many factors made her appraisal different from that of *Mary Barton.*

Her view of the essential requirements for sound relations between capital and labor had not changed; she most probably "succeeded better . . . than in 'Mary Barton' " in conveying "her sincere wish to be fair to both masters and men,"[57] because her emotional involvement with the miseries of the poor had lost some of its immediacy. Such increased detachment may have been effected not only by improved labor conditions and a rise in economic prosperity after the "hungry forties" but by a general reactionary tendency to which, as Cazamian points out, other writers were also responsive:

> The tone of philanthropic literature is no longer the same after 1850. A new timidity has deeply affected the most ardent apostles of interventionism; the imaginative impression left over from the Paris revolution, the vague sentiment that moderation was necessary after such excesses, the fear of awakening an imperfectly extinguished conflagration—all these more or less consciously directed good will towards prudent solutions. Mrs. Gaskell had not escaped these general influences.[58]

Undoubtedly, the desire to "correct the intransigence of her first prescriptions" and to confound "accusations of partiality"[59] were also meaningful factors to anyone as anxious as she to avoid prejudice and above all to refrain from inciting class against class. But her striving for impartiality in *North and South* is not as significant as the fact that an altered frame of mind—a muted emotional commitment to the deprived—made objectivity possible. After all, the urge to be fair had also impelled her in *Mary Barton* and yet, as we have seen, her sympathy with the workers' plight offset her attempts at detachment—to the detriment of artistic coherence.

The greater technical proficiency which she brought to her fourth major work also accounts for a qualitative change in approach. The sheer experience of writing had enabled her in *Cranford* to develop her latent powers as a humorist and in *Ruth* to refine her descriptive abilities and to harness her narrative talents to the devising of a more coherent plot.[60] Even literary influence may have inspired a greater sophistication in treating fictional characters and situations; the reviewer of *Blackwood's* suggests that Charlotte Brontë's example is evident in Mrs. Gaskell's depiction of the passionate lovers in *North and South* (and incidentally illumines the prejudices against which a Victorian novelist had to contend):

> . . . here are still the wide circles in the water, showing that not far off is the identical spot where Jane Eyre and Lucy Snowe, in their wild sport, have been casting stones; here is again the desperate, bitter quarrel out of which love is to come; here is love itself, always in a fury, often looking exceedingly like hatred, and by no means distinguished for its good manners or graces of speech.[61]

Though the critic mournfully raises the question—"Shall all our love-stories be squabbles after this?"[62]—post-Strindbergian readers may find the lovers' contentions rather tame. Yet, after *Mary Barton* and *Ruth*, they will appreciate the author's increased skill in depicting a romantic conflict. She has indeed in *North and South* progressed far beyond the artifices of melodrama and sentimentality which mark the relationship between Mary Barton and her two lovers, Harry Carson and Jem Wilson or between Ruth and her seducer, Mr. Bellingham.

That Charlotte Brontë's more emancipated view of woman's role in society influenced Mrs. Gaskell's conception of her heroine's behavior in a romantic situation (and indeed in her role as a social critic) seems plausible. After all, Mrs. Gaskell admired not only Charlotte's writings but her character, as eloquent a testimony to feminine potentialities as her art. Mrs. Gaskell's bolder conception of a romantic heroine in *North and South* may also have been the natural culmination of the increased assertion of her own individuality fostered by her literary success.

One thing is clear: however much indirect or direct influence her contemporary exerted (there are a few significant similarities between *Shirley* (1847) and *North and South*),[63] Mrs. Gaskell chose to treat her social theme in a manner which suggests both a decline in her emotional commitment to social justice and an increase in her artistic proficiency. Indeed, in this case the two phenomena are closely related.

We have seen that *Mary Barton* was in essence two novels: a social document testifying—mainly through John Barton—to the tragic aspects of social destitution, and a more conventional romantic story dealing with Mary's relations to her two lovers. Though Mary's emotional involvements were connected with her father's tragedy, they were neither a central element nor even a contributory cause of his downfall; romance (the staple of fiction) and social analysis were largely kept apart. *North and South*, on the other hand, owes its artistic coherence to Mrs. Gaskell's decision to make the central love story also the focal point for the confrontation of social views, an approach largely made possible because she no longer felt the pressing need "to give some utterance to the agony" of the "dumb" toiling masses. Being less engaged, she could not only assess social problems with greater restraint but could explore the vicissitudes of romance in the very context of such problems. She could afford a heroine who would not embody the views of the "care-worn men" but function as a more objective observer of the social scene while dramatically projecting some of the attitudes and personal convictions of the author. Since justice could more easily be done to the masters, such a melodramatic reconciliation of adversaries as she had depicted in *Mary Barton* was no longer called for. She could now suggest a resolution of differences not through the impulse of *caritas* alone but through the mellowing influence of romantic feelings.

While a lessened social commitment allowed romance at the heart of social commentary, romance itself assumed greater significance than in *Mary Barton* by being so directly related to social conflicts. Mary Barton's infatuation with Richard Carson showed no social consciousness beyond the desire to escape destitution (there is only the merest suggestion that she rebels against her father's hatred of the rich), and her eventual acceptance of Jem's poverty was merely a factor of her love. But the emotional relationship of Margaret Hale, the heroine of *North and South*, and John Thornton, the master manufacturer, is deeply affected by their social convictions. Their romantic feelings modify and are in turn influenced by those temperamental prejudices and intellectual views regarding social questions which lead to many contentions before a final understanding. Thus Thornton's early infatuation with Margaret Hale promotes his gradual conversion to her social views, while Margaret's progressive recognition of Thornton's ability as a manufacturer and her increasing sympathy with some of the aims and principles of industrialism help her to acknowledge her love for him.

Since Mrs. Gaskell is no longer intent on dramatizing the tremendous gap between poor and rich, she has not made the social contrast between her romantic adversaries as sharp as that between the two social enemies in *Mary Barton*—John Barton and Mr. Carson. The conflict between Margaret and Thornton is thus much subtler and embraces a far wider range of issues. The prestige which Thornton's wealth confers upon him is offset by his lack of cultivation; Margaret Hale's means may be more moderate, but she has had the leisure to become a lady in manners and education. Thornton's pride in the city of Milton-Northern (Manchester) is a measure of his insularity but also of his insight into the promise of industrialism; Margaret's fondness for rural life has survived a London education, and yet her ignorance of the industrial North initially beclouds her judgment. The sources of conflict between them are therefore not only—as in *Mary Barton*—basic disagreements regarding the relations of workmen and masters in industrial areas, but also contrasting views on the respective attributes of urban and rural cultures (with their opposing emphases on progress and tradition, material achievement and mental and spiritual growth).[64] Even the particular merits of the masculine principles of severity, self-reliance, and authority, and of the feminine instincts of tenderness, dependence, and conciliation are brought into contention.

Since Mrs. Gaskell's basic impulse in this novel is clearly towards moderation, adjustment, compromise, she not only shows that such contrasting viewpoints are amenable to correction and alteration under the impetus of emotional attraction but suggests from the beginning that they are not diametrically opposed. Because the protagonists also share certain inclinations, the possibility of a resolution in which sentiment is the final solvent of differences seems very authentic. For it is sentiment rather than reason which—as in *Mary Barton*—triumphs over strife, with the difference that the feeling is more particularized since romantic love plays an important part in reconciling the ways of master and workman, of North and South, of man and woman. Such a difference is well exemplified in the union of the two protagonists which, it has often been noted, enshrines the resolution of larger conflicts.

North and South is thus in many ways a broader, more coherent, more balanced and temperate exploration of contrasting views on social issues than *Mary Barton*. Both a gain and a loss of impact are, however, implicit in such an approach. The author's social and moral lesson deals more justly with opposing viewpoints, and her romantic protagonists have grown in stature and authenticity, but she has forfeited a certain emotional apprehension transcending social issues. For her greater objectivity inhibits that instinctive perception of the complexities and paradoxes of the human condition which her emotional involvement with human suffering had earlier liberated. That "passion which, almost willy-nilly, informs *Mary Barton*"[65] and which, as Kettle does, one misses in *North and South*, promoted not only a genuine psychological insight into the anguish and delusions of such men as John Barton but, through him, suggested many a "mysterious problem of life"—injustice, deprivation, suffering—which sympathy can alleviate but not entirely resolve and which puzzles others besides a bewildered and tormented workman.[66] The dilemmas and uncertainties characteristic of man's fate loom less large in *North and South* now that Mrs. Gaskell is no longer so personally involved with "the tragedy of a poor man's life."[67] Without an immediate emotional experience to spur her to greater insights, she is not tempted to transcend the more limited, more pedestrian, more comfortable view of the human condition which a lessening of social conflicts, the more conservative temper of the time, and her instinctive cautiousness would encourage. Since she is no longer challenging the social order, as she had done to a certain extent both in *Mary Barton* and *Ruth*, all larger challenges are also left in abeyance. Her social message is essentially valid (though, as we shall see, her greater desire for impartiality leads to some serious flaws in her arguments), and her control over structure and characterization has increased. Yet the novel does not have the same impact on one's imagination and feelings as *Mary Barton* and indeed as *Ruth*, despite the more evident weaknesses of these works.[68]

That such a temperate approach to social questions might indeed, as Cazamian points out, heighten the general appeal of *North and South*—and its effectiveness as a social document promoting good will[69] is undeniable. But that very moderateness seriously diminished its potentialities as a work of art. Indeed, as we have already suggested, an instinctive diffidence in challenging conventional assumptions about the social order (connected with the pious impulse to preach conciliation and resignation) tends to counteract in all three of her social novels that wider and bolder vision of the inequities in human relations and destinies which she was capable of entertaining. As Charlotte Brontë had indirectly suggested to her, she was much too dependent on the opinions of those around her to give her imagination and intelligence (in our terms, her power of empathy and her impulse to question) free rein.[70] Specifically hampered by her circumscribed upbringing and her position as a Unitarian minister's wife, she was also generally victimized by the uncontions of Victorian society whose power she had not sufficient independence to resist. Nor can that power be underestimated: the narrow-mindedness of some contemporary critical judgments impels us to admire the extent to which such a timid writer was actually willing to challenge her public.

In the more muted tones of *North and South*, not only the central conflict of social views but subsidiary dilemmas lack dramatic power or significant moral implications. The phenomenon is striking because these secondary problems reflect Mrs. Gaskell's fascination with a challenging subject already approached in *Mary Barton*: conflicts of conscience in which divided loyalties make a commitment to truth excruciatingly difficult. The dilemma of Mary, who might have to reveal a father's crime or by keeping silent condemn her innocent lover, at least provided an exciting interlude of suspense. An unfortunate decision in a different clash of loyalties plays a very significant moral role in *Ruth*. But in *North and South*, as we shall see, Mr. Hale and later Margaret Hale herself face problems of conscience which at first appear very critical, yet ultimately have no far-reaching dramatic, moral, or psychological effect on them.

As in *Mary Barton,* the father of a family in *North and South* is early confronted with an important problem whose resolution may have serious and extensive repercussions. For Mr. Hale, the Anglican pastor of Helstone, finds that he can no longer reconcile his duties with his religious doubts, but must seek a new vocation as tutor which will bring uncertainty and discomfort to his wife and daughter—indeed remove them from a southern village to a northern city where they will have to live very modestly in an alien environment. Perhaps because of her personal acquaintance with such a conflict,[71] Mrs. Gaskell succeeds in conveying Mr. Hale's initial anguish in moving terms; she even suggests that happiness is inexorably forfeited when one must sacrifice the well-being of loved ones to the well-being of a clear conscience. And yet as the novel progresses, we realize that despite the emphasis placed on this upheaval, Mr. Hale's spiritual crisis does not have significant reverberations; it merely provides an appropriate circumstance for bringing the cultures of South and North together and initially helps to clarify the strength, independence, and power of sympathy of his daughter Margaret Hale. For it is to her and not to his weak, complaining wife that Mr. Hale has first divulged his secret; she has the task of breaking the dismaying news of departure to the self-indulgent mother who is dissatisfied with her confined life but equally reluctant to change her ways.

We are not totally unprepared for Margaret's uncommon qualities. At the very beginning of the novel, in the London scenes, her stately beauty, her maturity, and her adventurous spirit point up the superficiality and the lack of imagination of her merely pretty cousin Edith. Somewhat later her rejection of Henry Lennox's marriage proposal reveals both discernment and self-possession. Now her courageous acceptance of her father's decision (though she does not share his religious convictions) contrasts with her mother's thoughtless, almost comically irrational peevishness. Like her father she draws a curious comfort from the negative aspects of the future; if she must lose her cherished Helstone, so "like a village in a poem—in one of Tennyson's poems," a dreary manufacturing town is the best possible alternative:

Discordant as it was—with almost a detestation for all she had ever heard of the North of England, the manufacturers, the people, the wild and bleak country—there was this one recommendation—it would be different from Helstone, and could never remind them of that beloved place.[72]

Though the family emergency obviously dramatizes the strength and self-reliance of Margaret Hale, it seems at first as if Mr. Hale's conflict of scruples must significantly determine the working out of the author's theme. But affirmation rather than diffidence is to be the keynote of the Milton-Northern experience; Mr. Hale's spiritual problems are accordingly left in abeyance. Indeed, much to our surprise, his imagination welcomes the material achievements revealed by his new home much before Margaret's conversion to the potentialities of industrialism:

After a quiet life in a country parsonage for more than twenty years, there was something dazzling to Mr. Hale in the energy which conquered immense difficulties with ease; the power of the machinery of Milton, the power of the men of Milton, impressed him with a sense of grandeur, which he yielded to without caring to inquire into the details of its exercise.[73]

It is Margaret rather than her father who is now concerned with scruples, though not, as in his case, in the matter of religious practices: it is her social conscience which has been aroused. Yet even as Mrs. Gaskell suggests why Margaret's initial reaction to Milton-Northern differs from Mr. Hale's, the qualitative difference between *Mary Barton* and *North and South* already becomes apparent. The concern with social justice seems muted: the victims of the social order are now considered "exceptions," unfortunate by-products of the splendid march of capitalistic enterprise:

But Margaret went less abroad, among machinery and men; saw less of power in its public effect, and, as it happened, she was thrown with one or two of those who, in all measures affecting masses of people, must be acute sufferers for the good of many. The question always is, has everything been done to make the sufferings of these exceptions as small as possible? Or, in the triumph of the crowded procession, have the helpless been trampled on, instead of being gently lifted aside out of the roadway of the conqueror, whom they had no power to accompany on his march?[74]

The contrast between her earlier and her present approach to social problems is most clearly seen in Chapter X, where the first confrontation of the social views of her protagonists—Margaret Hale and John Thornton—takes place. It reveals how wide a berth the author is prepared to give to the attitudes of the masters while still expressing, if less forcefully, the convictions with which Job Legh had challenged Mr. Carson in *Mary Barton*.

But preceding sections of the novel already anticipate the altered approach which will be so evident in Chapter X. That personal feelings will play an important part in the conflict of social values is suggested in the very first meeting between Margaret and Thornton. Though Margaret's aloof and self-possessed manner when she first encounters Thornton reflects her basic strength and integrity, Thornton not only gets, as strangers invariably do, an "impression of haughtiness" from "the short curled upper lip, the round, massive, upturned chin, the manner of carrying her head, her movements, full of soft feminine defiance,"[75] but assumes that he is a personal object of scorn. Such sensitivity is not wholly unfounded in view of Margaret's earlier prejudiced statement to her mother on the subject of tradesmen (while she was still unaware that she would have to leave her rural home):

"I don't like shoppy people. I think we are far better off, knowing only cottagers and labourers, and people without pretence."

"You must not be so fastidious, Margaret, dear!". . . .

"No! I call mine a very comprehensive taste; I like all people whose occupations have to do with land; I like soldiers and sailors, and the three learned professions, as they call them. I'm sure you don't want me to admire butchers and bakers, and candlestick-makers, do you, mamma?"[76]

The form which Thornton's annoyance takes, however, shows

that positive feelings toward her play an important part in his sense of wounded *amour-propre*:

He almost said to himself that he did not like her, before their conversation ended; he tried so to compensate himself for the mortified feeling, that while he looked upon her with an admiration he could not repress, she looked at him with proud indifference, taking him, he thought, for what, in his irritation, he told himself he was—a great rough fellow, with not a grace or a refinement about him.[77]

Margaret's reaction (conveyed to her parents) is also intriguingly ambiguous. Her initial impression of him, though still affected by her prejudices—Thornton is "not quite a gentleman; but that was hardly to be expected"—is modified by her temperamental affinity to the qualities of "resolution and power" reflected in his countenance. Yet her final assessment is not devoid of condescension: "Altogether a man who seems made for his niche . . . sagacious, and strong, as becomes a great tradesman."[78]

Mr. Hale's admonition to his daughter that the term "tradesman" is inappropriate since the manufacturers of Milton "are very different" also prepares us for that first exchange of social views in Chapter X in which the heroic attributes of the masters will be suggested. But the stage is not yet fully set for that exchange. If Margaret's reservations concerning social conditions are to be really convincing, they cannot merely be the result of early prejudices. So, before the discussion takes place, she meets and talks to "two of those who, in all measures affecting masses of people, must be acute sufferers for the good of many," the "careworn" (a significant recurrence of the characteristic adjective in *Mary Barton*) workman Nicholas Higgins and his sickly daughter Bessy. It is in this first direct experience of Margaret with a crucial aspect of the alien North that a possible coming to terms of two contrasting cultures is almost immediately suggested; Higgins comments that "North and South has both met and made kind o' friends in this big smoky place." Margaret's discoveries in this encounter are not extensive: there are only intimations that Bessy is deathly ill, that Higgins endures his personal tragedy with a touching dignity, and that he takes a commendable pride in his humble status—fearing possible patronage. Nevertheless, she has had a personal insight into poverty which will validate her arguments in the oncoming discussion with Thornton. Her attraction to the "resolution and power" of Thornton will have to contend not merely against her snobbish contempt for "all who have something tangible to sell,"[79] but against an incipient knowledge of the difficulties of the deprived.

Against the background of these previous experiences, the discussion in Chapter X meaningfully illustrates the difference in tone, temper, and emphasis between *North and South* and *Mary Barton.* In the exchange between Thornton and Hale (Margaret joins the discussion later) Thornton's commitment to Northern ways is predicated not on a sober, business-like evaluation of the possibilities of trade (such as Mr. Carson presents to Job Legh in *Mary Barton*) but on the challenges to man's inventiveness which industry represents. Likewise, Mr. Hale's reaction to the scientific progress exemplified by industrial inventions implies romantic attributes in the destiny of a master. Being told of "the magnificent power, yet delicate adjustment of the might of the steam-hammer," suggests to him "the wonderful stories of subservient genii in the Arabian Nights—one moment stretching from earth to sky and filling the width of the horizon, at the next obediently compressed into a vase small enough to be borne in the hand of a child."[80]

While industry offers a general challenge to scientific invention, it also presents, as Thornton makes clear, an opportune personal challenge to each individual of exercising "this imagination of power" when it is needed. Thus not only is the inventor of the steam hammer able "to mount, step by step . . . to higher marvels still," but after him others can wage "the war which compels, and shall compel, all material power to yield to science."[81] It is this emphasis on the inspiring opportunities for personal achievement offered to the intrepid by industry that marks the more optimistic turn of Mrs. Gaskell's thought. For by inference she is validating those very arguments advanced by W. R. Greg in criticizing *Mary Barton*: that all workers had possibilities of improvement given the necessary initiative and self-restraint. She had not denied such opportunities in *Mary Barton*: the not ignoble Mr. Carson was a self-made man, and Barton's accusation that Carson had made his fortune merely by exploiting the downtrodden was viewed as a distortion induced by bitterness. Yet, faced by an emotionally affecting spectacle of destitution, the direct suggestion that self-restraint might have enabled Barton to rise with equal effectiveness must have seemed both unfair and unrealistic; she could do no more than suggest that Barton was perhaps too carefree during good times.

When Margaret is led to enter the discussion between Thornton and Hale it is, interestingly enough, not because the question of the relationship between masters and men has been raised but because the advantages of the North have been exalted in contrast to the deficiencies of the South—a clear instance of the author's broader perspective on social questions in this novel. Moreover, the element of personal feelings is also unmistakably present in the contention that follows, for in Thornton's contemptuous reference to "What you call more aristocratic society," there lurk traces of the personal annoyance recently felt at Margaret's "haughtiness," just as in her reference to "the gambling spirit of trade" there are reminders of her temperamental dislike of "shoppy people."

Margaret's intercession in favor of the South seems at first a restatement on broader lines of the view expressed by Mrs. Gaskell in *Mary Barton* (and even stressed in her Preface to the novel). Provoked by Thornton's satisfaction in "belonging to . . . a district—the necessities of which give birth to such grandeur of conception," by his proud assertion that he "would rather be a man toiling, suffering—nay, failing and successless—here, than lead a dull prosperous life in the old worn grooves of what you call more aristocratic society down in the South, with their slow days of careless ease," she answers impetuously:

"You are mistaken. . . . You do not know anything about the South. If there is less adventure or less progress—I suppose I must not say less excitement—from the gambling spirit of trade, which seems requisite to force out these wonderful inventions, there is less suffering also. I see men here going about in the streets who look ground down by some pinching sorrow or care—who are not only sufferers but haters. Now, in the South we have our poor, but there is not that terrible expression in their countenances of a sullen sense of injustice which I see here."[82]

Yet Margaret's argument, formidable enough in the context of *Mary Barton*, is not allowed to stand. Indeed the "inexpressible gentleness" with which Thornton reacts to it has a purely personal source—"he saw that he had really hurt her." An elaborate disquisition follows in which, as Thornton attempts to enlighten Margaret about the North, he counters many of the general objections that could be raised against the industrial system (thus he maintains that the tyranny of cotton manufacturers has been checked by the need for manpower, causing "the battle" between masters and men to be now "pretty fairly waged") before answering her explicit accusations. That defense (so reminiscent of Greg's position in his attack on *Mary Barton*) transcends Mrs. Gaskell's own convictions, yet it becomes evident later that she accepts some of its premises. He tells Margaret that for him the term "battle between two classes" is extremely relevant insofar as:

". . . prudent wisdom and good conduct are always opposed to, and doing battle with, ignorance and improvidence. It is one of the great beauties of our system, that a working-man may raise himself into the power and position of a master by his own exertions and behaviour; that, in fact, every one who rules himself to decency and sobriety of conduct, and attention to his duties, comes over to our ranks; it may not be always as a master, but as an overlooker, a cashier, a book-keeper, a clerk, one on the side of authority and order."[83]

Though Margaret is not won over by this intellectual, abstract argument, she will, appropriately enough, be moved by the personal nature of his final argument. For to justify his opinion that "unsuccessful" workmen are not his "enemies" (as she in "haughty disapproval" had suggested) but rather "their own," he relates his own struggles after his father's ruin, and the success achieved through the ability "to despise indulgences not thoroughly earned." Such personal abnegation somewhat softens the severity of his final assertion that the "suffering" glimpsed by Margaret in the faces of Milton workmen "is but the natural punishment of dishonestly-enjoyed pleasure, at some former period of their lives," and that "self-indulgent, sensual people" do not deserve his "hatred" but only arouse his "contempt for their poorness of character."[84]

That Margaret has been somewhat mollified is first suggested at the end of Chapter X, when she regrets her failure to notice until too late that Thornton wishes to shake hands with her. In the next chapter we discover that one inroad has been made on her attitude; she is beginning to lose her early prejudices against tradespeople because of the personal appeal of Thornton's honest and modest confession of his "shop-boy" beginnings. (Interestingly, it is the older generation, exemplified by the two mothers of the protagonists, which is guilty of false pride: Mrs. Hale in being shocked at Thornton's humble past and Mrs. Thornton in first assuming that Margaret will eagerly marry her son for his money and later condemning Margaret for not appreciating Thornton's greatness.) Moreover, Margaret is not prepared to reject Thornton's accusations of the workers' "careless, wasteful improvidence," but only to condemn him for failing "to think it his duty to try to make them different—to give them anything of the training which his mother gave him, and to which he evidently owes his position, whatever that may be." As she informs her father that "I do think Mr. Thornton a very remarkable man; but personally I don't like him at all," there seems as much overcompensation in her protestations as in those of Thornton at the close of the previous chapter: "A more proud, disagreeable girl I never saw. Even her great beauty is blotted out of one's memory by her scornful ways."[85]

Another striking instance of the change in Mrs. Gaskell's viewpoint since *Mary Barton* is evident in her handling of the threat and actuality of a strike in Milton. Initially this impending crisis allows her to reassert a central concept of *Mary Barton*: since alienation and not economic discontent *per se* is the greatest source of social conflict, that conflict can only be resolved if the masters transcend their economic role to assume a responsibility for their fellow men's well-being sanctioned not by economic but by spiritual considerations. As in *Mary Barton* this whole approach rests on the question of the master's reluctance to reveal to their workmen the economic hardships which make it impractical for them to accede to labor's demand for higher wages. When Margaret suggests that such a show of confidence be made,

Thornton's countering argument, "Do you give your servants reasons for your expenditures, or your economy in the use of your money?" impels her to state those principles with which *Mary Barton* had made us familiar:

". . . there is no human law to prevent the employers from utterly wasting or throwing away all their money, if they choose; but . . . there are passages in the Bible which would rather imply—to me at least—that they neglected their duty as stewards if they did so."[86]

As the whole question of the kind of responsibility which a master should assume for his workers is then elaborately discussed by Thornton, Margaret, and Mr. Hale, the author tries to do greater justice than in *Mary Barton* not only to the master's assessment of the merits and prerogatives of leadership but also to his arguments against too great an interference in the personal lives of his men. The argument for the independence of workmen from masters is not unfamiliar to us: Mr. Carson in *Mary Barton* has suggested its value as attested by "facts" only to have Job Legh maintain that "them that is strong in any of God's gifts is meant to help the weak,—be hanged to the facts!" That the basic tenor of the discussion has changed in *North and South*, however, is shown as Thornton reveals himself committed to both these views, though in somewhat different terms. Through Thornton, the author has introduced additional considerations which negate a resolution of the conflict as simple as that suggested by Legh—"be hanged to the facts!" is no longer the impulse. Indeed we begin to suspect that Mrs. Gaskell herself is somewhat overwhelmed by the complexities of the problem when viewed less abstractly.

Though she was prepared in *Mary Barton* to accept certain limitations in the workers—the result of material and cultural deprivation—she did not clearly suggest that the Christian responsibility "to help the weak" through succor and sympathy also implied a parental responsibility to exercise authority over those whose childish immaturity made them unable to guide themselves. Yet now she partially accepts that view, and the conflict between her leanings to *paternalism* and her desire to defend the workman's right to *independence* is compounded by her abiding commitment to Christian solidarity in *brotherhood*.

However much Thornton, Margaret, and Mr. Hale may differ in their conception of the quality and scope of a master's duty, they share the assumption that the worker's mental and psychological limitations still require not just the "help" Job Legh had suggested but some kind of authoritative guidance. As Thornton defends himself against Margaret's charge that he perhaps wants to keep the workmen in "a blind, unreasoning kind of obedience," he reveals a recognition of responsibility toward them and not the kind of indifference characteristic of Carson before his personal tragedy. Because the workmen are immature, he feels the appropriateness of a "wise despotism," of "the unfailing laws of a discreet, firm authority" so helpful to "children and young people." He would no doubt agree with Job Legh that "them that is strong is meant to help the weak" but wants that strength expressed in a "constitutional monarchy" in which his decision and reasons are unchallenged. Thornton's sense of responsibility makes the conflict between his views and those of the Hales very different from that between Carson and Job Legh, the more so since neither Margaret nor Mr. Hale challenges his conception of a parental role. Both merely want him to be more indulgent to the workers' inclinations to assert themselves in the industrial relationship with the masters. Mr. Hale's suggestion that "a wise parent humours the desire for independent action, so as to become the friend and adviser when his absolute rule shall cease" implies an acceptance of that "absolute rule" as long as it shall be needed.[87]

How to reconcile the need to foster independence in the workers with the Christian impulse to become actively involved with their lives—now that she acknowledges the master's position of leadership and authority is the author's central dilemma. She does not, however, seem fully aware of the contradictions growing out of her new position. Thus, when Thornton opposes the argument that Christian solidarity entails a deep involvement in every aspect of the worker's life by claiming that such involvement would curtail their independence, what was originally Carson's argument in *Mary Barton* now carries a very different weight. The opponents seem to have changed places. It is the Hales, who have accused Thornton of wanting "unreasoning obedience" and urged him to foster "the desire for independent action," who want him to assume greater responsibility for the decisions and behavior of his workers. It is Thornton, the "constitutional monarch," who wants to put limitations on his paternalistic influence. Despite his illiberal contention that "independent action" is intolerable "during business hours," his reluctance to supervise his workers' lives seems impressively humane:

"And I say, that the masters would be trenching on the independence of their hands, in a way that I, for one, should not feel justified in doing, if we interfered too much with the life they lead out of the mills. Because they labour ten hours a day for us, I do not see that we have any right to impose leading-strings upon them for the rest of their time. I value my own independence so highly that I can fancy no degradation greater than that of having another man perpetually directing and advising and lecturing me, or even planning too closely in any way about my actions. He might be the wisest of men or the most powerful—I should equally rebel and resent his interference. I imagine this is a stronger feeling in the North of England than in the South."[88]

When Mr. Hale questions whether this prevalent "feeling" in Northern England may not arise "because every man has had to stand in an unchristian and isolated position, apart from and jealous of his brother-man: constantly afraid of his rights being trenched upon," we are momentarily back in the world of *Mary Barton*, in which alienation is the central source of social conflict. Yet the workman Nicholas Higgins encountered by Margaret has already demonstrated an instinctive pride in his privacy that is not just the result of living "in an unchristian and isolated position." So that Thornton's reiteration of his point rings perhaps more truly than the author fully intends:

"Given a strong feeling of independence in every Darkshire man, have I any right to obtrude my views of the manner in which he shall act, upon another (hating it as I should do most vehemently myself), merely because he has labour to sell and I capital to buy?"

Margaret's answer, when we compare it with Job Legh's to Carson, clearly reflects the tentativeness of the author's present point of view and her inability quite to resolve what the true role of the master should be:

"Not in the least . . . because of your labour and capital positions, whatever they are, but because you are a man, dealing with a set of men over whom you have, whether you reject the use of it or not, immense power, just because your lives and your welfare are so constantly and intimately interwoven. God has made us so that we must be mutually dependent. We may ignore our own dependence, or refuse to acknowledge that others depend upon us in more respects than the payment of weekly wages; but the thing must be, nevertheless."[89]

Though Mrs. Gaskell is eager to state that the relationship between masters and workmen should transcend considerations of capital and labor (Margaret is not even disturbed by her ignorance of "whatever" these mutual "positions" are), she cannot deny that the *human* dependence which she wishes the employers to acknowledge is a direct factor of the *economic* dependence of the two classes engaged in capitalistic production. Margaret urges Thornton to undertake the responsibility of a man to other men and yet cannot help viewing that responsibility in terms of the "immense power" of a master over his servants. Paradoxically, it is Thornton who seems to end up with the humane rather than the capitalistic point of view, since he does not wish his "immense power" to be a direct influence in his relations with his workers but rather the more indirect and personal power of the example he can set by his own forthrightness and honesty.

Some conflicting views are, of course, consciously presented by the author in preparation for an eventual reconciliation, but such contradictions as we have noted are not so easily justifiable. The viewpoint on Christian brotherhood and solidarity enshrined in *Mary Barton* not only does not easily harmonize in *North and South* with her leanings to paternalism but indeed cannot survive without perpetrating contradictions far greater than some of the contrasts she consciously wishes to present in her dialogue between Thornton and the Hales. It is, therefore, not surprising that her handling of this whole question gives rise to certain impressions of her characters not consciously intended. While she still means Margaret to be largely the apostle of a democratizing Christian spirit, she provides sufficient evidence for Kettle's contention that "Margaret's sympathy with the workers . . . is essentially aristocratic or at least paternalistic in quality; one can imagine her cheering on the Young England Movement."[90] She still wishes to stress the final Christian dependence of all men, but since this conviction is now qualified by her admiration for the individualism not only of the master Thornton but of the workman Higgins, the following comment by V. S. Pritchett seems pertinent even though Mrs. Gaskell herself might not have assented to it:

At first Margaret sees only the mutual hatred of the relationship [of Thornton and his workmen]; then she perceives that both sides like hating. It is a sort of independence with them, a sport, an animal instinct which on both sides seeks, not moral solutions, but a master.[91]

In attempting to do scrupulous justice to the positions and viewpoints of both masters and workmen—and to show her heroine brought to a similar fairness of judgment—she had of course set herself an extremely difficult task. The exercise of a far greater objectivity than in *Mary Barton* undercuts the possibilities of dramatic tension in her handling of the threat of a strike. As, mainly through the heroine's successive visits to the households of Nicholas Higgins and Mr. Thornton, we are introduced to the problems which the incipient strike presents for both workmen and masters, the impact of one point of view is inevitably attenuated by contact with contrasting arguments. The emotional potential of the conflict has also diminished because of a modified view of the workers' plight. It is true that Margaret's conversations with Higgins' ailing daughter seem to bring us back to the world of *Mary Barton*. Bessy's pathetic yearnings to escape from the weariness of her sickly state "to the land o' Beulah" are movingly suggested; her descriptions of the factory responsible for that dreadful suffocation from cotton "fluff" in her lungs appallingly testify to industrial evils; indeed, her evocation of hardships in the present strike (as she speaks of some of her father's visitors) directly recalls passages in *Mary Barton*:

"Some spoke o' deadly hatred, and made my blood run cold wi' the terrible things they said o' th' masters—but more, being women, kept plaining, plaining (wi' the tears running down their cheeks, and never wiped away, nor heeded), of the price o' meat, and how their childer could na sleep at nights for th' hunger."[92]

But in Nicholas Higgins, who rejects his daughter's "dreams and . . . Methodee fancies" for the necessary work waiting to be accomplished in this world, who is contemptuous of Southern laborers as a "pack of spiritless, down-trodden men," who looks forward to the "honest up and down fight" one can wage with an "oud bulldog" like Thornton, we have a very different man from the tormented, brooding John Barton, perishing slowly through his alienating sense of injustice. Like Barton, Higgins has a fighting spirit, but is totally devoid of morbidity; he is realistically determined to act through the Trades Union "when we're put upon,"[93] but is not likely to succumb to irrational violence (his friend John Boucher who does so is portrayed as a misled weakling, not a tragic figure).

If the workers' difficult position before the strike does not evoke the pity and indignation aroused in *Mary Barton*, concern for them is also lessened by suggestions of the equally critical predicament of the masters. As Thornton views the "approaching turn-out" he sees in it only one result: "the forethought of many anxious hours was thrown away, utterly wasted by their insane folly, which would injure themselves even more than him, though no one could set any limit to the mischief they were doing." That this assessment is selfless and honest is shown by his dismay at the behavior of other masters who have dishonestly raised the false hopes of higher wages now inciting the workers. Nor are we allowed to forget the grandeur of the masters' transcending aims which atones somewhat for their obduracy in business relations. Though she has been "painfully occupied" with the plight of the poor, Margaret cannot remain immune to the fascination of the masters' world when she attends Thornton's dinner party:

She liked the exultation in the sense of power which these Milton men had. It might be rather rampant in its display, and savour of boasting; but still they seemed to defy the old limits of possibility, in a kind of fine intoxication, caused by the recollection of what had been achieved, and what yet should be. If, in her cooler moments, she might not approve of their spirit in all things, still there was much to admire in their forgetfulness of themselves and the present, in their anticipated triumphs over all inanimate matter at some future time, which none of them should live to see.[94]

Thornton is not even denied those qualities of sympathy and understanding which Carson only demonstrated under the stress of great personal suffering. On a previous occasion Margaret, surprised to hear Thornton speak of Mrs. Hale's illness in a "grave and tremulous voice," had found it difficult to "reconcile those eyes, that voice, with the hard, reasoning, dry, merciless way in which he laid down axioms of trade, and serenely followed them out to their full consequences." Now, however, the author distinctly suggests not only that Thornton is capable of emotions but that the restraint which he exercises upon them in his position as master is admirable. Hale's comparison of Thornton with Boucher (whose intense fit of despair has led the Hales to relieve his destitution), minimizes the workmen's problems while paying tribute to the master's fortitude; he feels that Boucher's claims of "utter distress" were perhaps exaggerated because of his "passionate, demonstrative nature," while Thornton probably "is . . . of an exactly opposite nature—a man who is far too proud to show his feelings."[95]

Not only is the dramatic potential of a clash between masters and workmen curtailed by their more evenly weighted claims, but the reconciliation of these claims has become far more difficult. Therefore, in the latter part of the novel (beginning with the actual strike), it is the romantic involvement of Thornton and Margaret which is made to provide much of the excitement and—along with such mollifying personal experiences as the death of Bessy Higgins, of Mrs. Hale, and of John Boucher—to carry much of the burden of the theme of reconciliation.

In the climactic scene of the march against Thornton's factory to protest his hiring of Irish scab labor (Mrs. Gaskell here exhibits her narrative power in portraying the imminent danger of mob violence and its dramatic eruption) she is again attempting to straddle two viewpoints. Although we see the terrifying scene from the vantage point of the Thornton household anxiously awaiting an uncertain fate, made more ominous by the breaking of the front gate, we also sense that Thornton's arbitrary importation of labor warrants the "yell" of the workers, like "the demoniac desire of some terrible wild beast for the food that is withheld from his ravening." Thornton himself "drew back for a moment, dismayed at the intensity of hatred he had provoked."[96]

Margaret's very presence in the house (although accidental, for she has come to fetch a water bath for her sick mother and has been trapped by the emergency) adds that romantic dimension which already affected the tenor of previous discussions on social questions. But it is her intercession in the ensuing conflict and the ultimate effect of her interference which most clearly show the growing importance of the protagonists' personal feelings in resolving larger contentions. For Thornton mainly responds to Margaret's appeal that he avert the soldiers' interference and deal directly with his enraged workmen ("Speak to your workers as if they were human beings. Speak to them kindly.") because his personal admiration for her makes him sensitive not only to his pride ("go down this instant, if you are not a coward")[97] but to her impassioned pity. And Margaret's horrified realization of the vulnerable position in which her humanitarian impulse has placed Thornton is compounded by her (as yet unacknowledged) personal involvement with his safety.

In a different context, Thornton's refusal, as he confronts the mob, to yield to their shouted request that the "Irish blackguards be packed back again" might seem the mere hard-heartedness of a stubborn master. But the obduracy of the violent mob involves our emotions, like those of Margaret, with the master's personal courage in a very dangerous situation:

Her eye was on the group of lads who had armed themselves with their clogs some time before. She saw their gesture—she knew its meaning—she read their aim. Another moment, and Mr. Thornton might be smitten down—he whom she had urged and goaded to come to this perilous place. She only thought how she could save him. She threw her arms around him; she made her body into a shield from the fierce people beyond.[98]

In this case Margaret's impulse of charity for the downtrodden workers has hardly been vindicated as an agent of reconciliation since it has led to such unfortunate repercussions. Indeed Margaret will later reflect that though "it was not fair" for Thornton not to attempt at first "to bring them to reason," yet "it was worse than unfair for them to set on him as they threatened."[99] Neither side in the struggle can be exonerated, but sympathy seems more heavily weighted on the side of authority, order, and rule; we have moved far away from the basic approach to social conflicts in *Mary Barton.*

Through the vicissitudes of the dramatic scene, its social implications are far less evident than the romantic impact of Margaret's impulsive self-sacrifice in taking the blow intended for Thornton. Indeed, the effect of this action on the already susceptible Thornton is such as to leave no room in his heart for anything but personal feelings. After the riot dies down, he carries Margaret's insensible body back to the house and, though she has only been slightly hurt, he irrationally anticipates the worst in a most passionate utterance:

> "Oh, my Margaret—my Margaret! no one can tell what you are to me! Dead—cold as you lie there, you are the only woman I ever loved! Oh, Margaret—Margaret!"[100]

Thus, even as it dramatizes a general social conflict, the climactic riot scene suggests the triumph of personal affinities and private loyalties over deep-rooted principles on social questions. Each of the protagonists initially demonstrates an allegiance to certain convictions and is then impelled to sacrifice that allegiance and his personal safety for the sake of an emotional dependence on another human being. (Margaret's reluctance in her "maiden pride"—the author is bowing to Victorian convention—to countenance for a while this romantic motive for her dramatic interference actually enhances the reality of her unconscious impulses.) Though the principle of emotional dependence is an essential part of Mrs. Gaskell's social teachings, so much emphasis is placed here on its *romantic* significance that its *social* implications are barely perceptible.

Up to the moment of this scene, the larger social conflict between masters and men had managed to keep its prominence, for the more formal relationship between the two protagonists expressed itself most naturally in such intellectual discussions of social conditions as we have previously considered. Now that she has revealed the full force of their emotional involvement, the author is tempted to pursue the romantic aspects of her story, thus forestalling the necessity to come fully to grips with complex social problems. The larger consequences of the clash we have just witnessed are accordingly neglected in favor of its personal reverberations; immediately after the mob scene, we become aware that Thornton's involvement with his economic role is no longer the main preoccupation of his existence:

Mr. Thornton remained in the dining-room, trying to think of the business he had to do at the police-office, and in reality thinking of Margaret. Everything seemed dim and vague beyond—behind—besides the touch of her arms round his neck—the soft clinging which made the dark colour come and go in his cheek as he thought of it.[101]

In many of the following chapters, Mrs. Gaskell's emphasis on the romantic tribulations of the protagonists almost precludes a consideration of the social conflicts which previously had such climactic repercussions. Her depiction of the contending emotions of the lovers before their final union is again not inappropriate to the novel's social context, even if the sources of contention are no longer conflicting social views (but mainly Margaret's haughty reluctance to accept Thornton's love). After all, pride will eventually yield to the positive force of sentiment in the social as well as the romantic conflict. It is only the extent to which the author pursues this aspect of the story and her manner of treating it which are questionable. The social dimensions of the novel are dwarfed when greater effort is expended on the intricacies of romantic misunderstandings than on the complexities of the larger misunderstanding between capital and labor. As Mary Barton's exciting pursuit of Will Wilson shifted the reader's attention from the central conflict, so the private problems of Thornton and Margaret overshadow the public problems which their relationship had up to now dramatized. This limitation was noted by the reviewer of *Blackwood's* who, if he somewhat overstates his point because of his general objection to contending lovers, nevertheless points to a real weakness in the author's approach to her subject:

There is one feature of resemblance between Mrs. Gaskell's last work and Mr. Dickens' *Hard Times.* We are prepared in both for the discussion of an important social question; and in both, the story gradually slides off the public topic to pursue a course of its own. *North and South* has, of necessity, some good sketches of the "hands" and their homes; but it is Mr. Thornton's fierce and rugged course of true love to which the author is most anxious to direct our attention; and we have little time to think of Higgins or his trades-union, in presence of this intermitting, but always lively warfare going on beside them.[102]

As in *Mary Barton*, the author yields to the temptation of melodrama to heighten the uncertainties of the lovers' eventual conciliation. That pride should stand in the way of two passionate and self-reliant people seems very plausible (even though in Margaret a Brontëan spirit of self-assertion is weakened by a rather meretricious coyness and reticence in deference to Victorian prudery). The method chosen to show the conquest of such a feeling lacks psychological subtlety, however. The inclinations of the moralist impel the author to show pride vanquished only after a painful process of humiliation and the instincts of the storyteller lead her to rely mainly on dramatic events to make that process possible. Thus Margaret will be humbled by being put in the position of telling a lie (as in previous novels there is some justification for it, since she is protecting her proscribed brother who has secretly returned from exile to see his dying mother). Because the belief that she has fallen in God's eyes is at times less painful to her than her degradation in the eyes of Thornton who knows her lie (and worse, suspects her of protecting a secret lover by it), she is led to realize her true feelings for him. Even this situation has interesting possibilities, since mortified self-pride as well as an honorable reluctance to lose Thornton's regard seems to be causing Margaret's discomfort. However, the author neglects the pursuit of the subtle problems she has raised in favor of much sanctimonious concern with Margaret's breach of the truth, an attitude hard for us to accept in view of the attenuating circumstances. The striking events which precede and follow Margaret's fall from virtue also overshadow more complex psychological considerations; the realities of romantic passion cannot really assert themselves amidst a profusion of melodramatic devices. Margaret's brother is recognized by an informant in the railway station; a scuffle ensues before the brother escapes; the informer soon dies, perhaps as a result of that struggle; Margaret denies her presence at the station to protect her brother; and finally a coroner's inquest clears the brother in time to allow Thornton (the magistrate in this case!) to save Margaret most generously from a testimony which would be a second lie. Sensational happenings such as these can hardly authenticate the psychological conflicts of Margaret and Thornton, supposedly provoked by their strong, assertive personalities.

Of course Thornton will also, like Charlotte Brontë's Rochester, have to endure a chastening of his pride before the relationship can be successfully resolved (though Mrs. Gaskell had considered bringing about his financial ruin through a fire which would destroy his factory, she settled on less spectacular means).[103] As he had saved Margaret from public moral humiliation, she will in turn rescue him from economic failure through her fortuitous receipt of a legacy. Here again it is not the concept of purgation but the form it takes that is objectionable—the author relies too heavily on the machinery of plot to sustain her theme.

Even more than in *Mary Barton* not larger issues but personal considerations and circumstances—private trials, individual shocks to the conscience—effect solutions to social conflicts. Thus the death of his beloved daughter Bessy makes Nicholas Higgins amenable to the sympathetic intercession of Mr. Hale. Not only is Higgins' new instinct to seek consolation in religion strengthened, but he is now led to accept those tenets of political economy before so harshly presented to him as to seem merely a rationalization for social injustice. The suicide of Boucher—in a sense a victim of the harsh demands of the Union to which he could not discipline himself, particularly with a needy wife and children—also leads Higgins to soften his pride and obduracy to the masters by applying to Thornton for work to support Boucher's orphans and widow. (That the South as well as the North has its limitations has been made clear when Margaret convinces Higgins that he could not endure the rigorous life of a farm laborer but must remain in the relatively more comfortable position of an industrial worker.) Higgins' impulse of sympathy for the tragic victims of social conflict, expressed in his desire to support them by his labor, is at first rebuffed by Thornton; eventually, however, it finds an echo in the latter's own feelings, mollified as they have been by the experience of loving Margaret and being rejected by her:

> He tried not to be, but was convinced that all that Higgins had said was true. And then the conviction went in, as if by some spell, and touched the latent tenderness of his heart; the patience of the man, the simple generosity of his motive . . . made him forget entirely the mere reasonings of justice, and overleap them by a diviner instinct.[104]

Though the discussion of Higgins' working conditions still shows Thornton determined to be master and not to have Higgins' "brains" occupied in "meddling with my business," the elements of sympathy which have concurred to make that relation possible promise greater harmony and cooperation. The fulfillment is evident not only in concrete improvements by Thornton such as the establishment of a workers' kitchen in his factory but in his ultimate statement of his basic aim as a master: "My only wish is to have the opportunity of cultivating some intercourse with the hands beyond the mere 'cash nexus'."[105]

In keeping with the author's emphasis on the protagonists' romantic relationship, the alteration of Thornton's social views takes place before the resolution of his romantic problems which, as the true climax of the work, occurs in the last chapter of the novel. Undoubtedly the lasting emphasis on the vicissitudes of Margaret and Thornton's personal relationship is partially an escape from the necessity of coming to terms with the baffling problems of social conflict. Doing greater justice to the complexities of opposing viewpoints than in *Mary Barton* had, as we have seen, even heightened the difficulty of finding viable means to achieve harmony between capital and labor.

Both social novels demonstrate how much easier it was for her to present problems than to offer suggestions for their alleviation. Just as in *Mary Barton* she had rested her final hope for a resolution of conflicts mainly on the reactions of one particular man to another (Carson and John Barton; Carson and Job Legh), so in *North and South* she puts the whole burden of convincing us that human sympathy and cooperation can triumph over class conflicts upon the interaction of two individuals, Thornton and

Higgins, and two people at that who have always been essentially men of good will. Mrs. Gaskell lacks that wider vision capable of embracing in social solutions such petty greed and ambition in some employers and such intemperance and irresponsibility in some workers as she had depicted both in actions and attitudes at Milton (e.g., the false promises of the employers inciting the workers to strike, the behavior of Boucher). The very optimism of her solution could undoubtedly not have survived a fearless questioning of whether the baser impulses contributing to social friction could really yield to injunctions of selflessness and empathy.

Ultimately the limitations of her social vision can be traced to those ambiguous feelings about challenging the social order so evident in *Mary Barton.* The way in which these feelings hamper her attack on conventional social mores regarding the "fallen woman" in *Ruth* prepares us to understand more clearly why, after *North and South*, her third social novel, she did not choose ever again to explore the issues which had first put her in the public limelight and with which her name is still so often associated.

III Ruth (1853)

If Mrs. Gaskell's *Ruth* demonstrates, more clearly than her other works, those "fluctuations between fidelity to nature and compromise with convention"[106] which so often marred her artistic expression, so the many reactions of disapproval to her treatment of the "fallen woman" provide one dramatic clue to her ambivalence in criticizing the assumptions of her time. For if even such a tentative challenge to social attitudes as *Ruth* provoked shock and outrage, one can guess the enormous difficulties the author would have faced had she been more totally committed to tolerance. Though the limitations of her audience do not excuse her diffidence, they at least partially explain a tendency to temporize with her convictions.

A real effort of critical imagination is required nowadays to do justice to Mrs. Gaskell's intentions and artistic execution in *Ruth.* For our attitudes toward the "fallen woman" have so greatly evolved that we might minimize Mrs. Gaskell's courage and broad-mindedness in making a then proscribed topic the main subject of a novel. We might dismiss as ludicrous vagaries the manifestations of disgust and the accusations of immorality directed against a treatment of "sin" and redemption which strikes us as ethically above reproach—even rebuffs us by its consistent moralizing about sexual transgression and its pious insistence on the doctrines of repentance and expiation.

An awareness of the painful obstacles against which Mrs. Gaskell had to contend induces a certain self-consciousness about severely judging the work. It seems unfair to accuse her, from our vantage point, of a total lack of sophistication in treating her subject when many readers condemned her for being offensively worldly, to censure her timidity when she pursued her work knowing that certain reactions would deeply wound the self-conscious and reticent part of her nature.

That her own apprehensions were well-founded vindicates her courage in struggling against her specific fears and general diffidence. A paradoxical combination of decisiveness and acute sensitivity to criticism is evident in the letter to her sister-in-law in which she explains that she has "*forbidden* people to write, for their expressions of disapproval (although I have known that the feeling would exist in them) would be very painful and stinging at the time" and then goes on to comment:

> "An unfit subject for fiction" is the thing to say about it; I knew all this before; but I determined notwithstanding to speak my mind out about it; only now I shrink with more pain than I can tell you from what people are saying though I cld. do every jot of it over again tomorrow.[107]

"What people were saying" and indeed doing to demonstrate their disapproval (the term used by her personal friends was "deep regret") could indeed have tried the spirit of a much more worldly woman than the virtuous and proper minister's wife. We no longer wonder that she here compares herself "to St. Sebastian tied to a tree to be shot at with arrows" when, in another letter, we discover some specific reactions provoked by *Ruth*:

> I *have* been *so* ill; I do believe it has been a "Ruth" fever. . . . I

should never have left your last letter unanswered so long if it was not for that—but oh! I was so poorly! And cd. not get over the hard things people said of "Ruth." I mean I was just in that feverish way when I could not get them out of my head by thinking of anything else but dreamt about them and all that. I think I must be an improper woman without knowing it, I do so manage to shock people. Now *should* you have burnt the last ["1st" in *The Letters of Mrs. Gaskell*] vol. of "Ruth" as so *very* bad? even if you had been a very anxious father of a family? Yet *two* men have; and a third has forbidden his wife to read it; they sit next to us in Chapel and you can't think how "improper" I feel under their eyes.[108]

Such dramatic evidence of reactions far worse even than anticipated clarifies not only the reading audience's limitations but also reactions on Mrs. Gaskell's part which might otherwise seem absurdly inappropriate. For merely reading the text could hardly convince us that such public indignation and private agony might be provoked by a novel in which a young girl, seduced in absolute ignorance of sexual matters, is thereafter never allowed to escape the reproaches of her conscience and can find only in a self-sacrificing death the final expiation.

The author's acute sensitivity had of course already been tried by the narrow-mindedness and conventionality of some criticisms of *Mary Barton.* Though in that novel, she had often counteracted —even at times contradicted—her emotional commitments by a more measured approach to social conflicts, she had not escaped accusations of partiality, troubling mainly because they seemed to cast doubt upon her virtue, not of course in provoking immorality in that instance but—to her a very "WICKED" impulse —in arousing social strife. When one realizes how much she had in *Ruth* tried to justify conventional views on sexual transgression, and yet found that she had to part with her "'*respectable* friends' up and down the country,"[109] the extent of her emotional reaction becomes fully understandable.

Yet, though many factors thus appeal to our critical indulgence in judging what may rightly be called Mrs. Gaskell's second social novel, the force and truthfulness of a work of art cannot of course in the final analysis be assessed in terms of the obstacles against which it had to contend. That prudery and—what Emile

Montégut in discussing *Ruth* finds so central to the English temper[110]—*pharisaism* led many readers to conceive of Ruth's portrayal as the product of a "demoralising laxity"[111] suggests that the author had commendably challenged her public, but does not excuse the larger limitations of that portrayal.

Moreover Mrs. Gaskell was not totally victimized by conventionality. Not only did prominent literary and religious figures defend the book's purity of intention and spirit but—despite certain narrow-minded objections—several reviewers showed sympathy for the choice and the general treatment of the subject.[112] Most important of all, a far more sophisticated attitude towards the question was apparently tenable, even though still only a minority opinion. For if some readers thought Mrs. Gaskell outrageously daring, her convictions seemed rather less bold to some discerning minds: to her former critic W. R. Greg, who discussed her work along with that of other authors under the heading "False Morality of Lady Novelists," to Charlotte Brontë, whose pointed question "Why should she [Ruth] die?" adumbrated a significant weakness of the book, to George Eliot, who reacted against its melodramatic unreality by suggesting that the author "seems . . . to be constantly misled by a love of sharp contrasts —of 'dramatic' effects," to Arthur Hugh Clough who perceived not only her diffidence but the possible contradiction in asserting Ruth's extreme ignorance before and extreme guilt after her fall:

> . . . it [*Ruth*] is really very good, but it is a little too timid, I think. Ruth did well, but there is also another way. . . . I do not think she has got the whole truth. I do not think that such overpowering humiliation should be the result in the soul of the not really guilty though misguided girl, any more than it should be the judgment of the world.[113]

Such enlightened attitudes among critics and artists suggest a climate of opinion not totally repressive. The truth is, of course, that, beyond her reluctance to flout conventional attitudes, Mrs. Gaskell was influenced by her personal emotional commitment to social conventions. Indeed, "she had the whole spirit of her age against her," preventing her from viewing "closely and steadily" the phenomenon of "sexual irregularity,"[114] but she was loyal to that very hindrance even as she contended against it. As we shall see later, her commitment to certain religious principles presented in some ways an even stronger obstacle to an objective appraisal of her subject.

That she was prepared to challenge at least some of the assumptions of her contemporaries remains to her credit. Her very decision to deal with seduction in a detailed and restrained manner showed a willingness to transcend traditional literary approaches to this subject. For, as George Henry Lewes said in the *Westminster*, she had tackled

. . . a subject of the most delicate nature that can well be taken up; being one which has rarely if ever been looked fairly in the face; and one on which, of all others, it is rarest to hear a rational word spoken. The circulating libraries have furnished, and will continue to furnish, abundance of sickly sentimentality on this subject, wherein heroines strive to atone by consumption and broken hearts, for their lapse from virtue; or, if they do not take this "rose-pink" turn, present a frigid and barren morality, under which the luckless maiden if her mind be very much set upon re-entering the Eden of Respectability, lingers through the remainder of her life under a deadly weight of patronage and encouragement . . . a scarlet letter flaming upon her breast, attracting every eye; until one wonders how any being can be found able to live under such restoration to social amnesty![115]

Lewes went on to praise Mrs. Gaskell for the hopefulness of her view that those who have transgressed "may still redeem themselves if they will only rise and do honestly the work that still lies before them to be done." In showing Ruth's rehabilitation through the responsibility of honest labor (first as a governess and then as a nurse) and of bringing up her child,[116] Mrs. Gaskell was indeed eschewing the "rose-pink turn" of popular literature on the subject. But her emancipation from certain traditional attitudes consecrated in that literature is not as complete as one might at first assume; though she does not deem consumption to be *de rigueur* for her heroine, the principle of emotional mortification as an atonement for sin plays a very significant part in her idea of rehabilitation.

That she was not really liberated from conventional standards is already evident at the beginning of the novel in her handling of the circumstances of Ruth's seduction. Though Lewes also praised her for avoiding any "attempt to make a new line of action such as the world's morality would refuse to warrant," he did not seem fully aware of the relevance of this conservatism to what he, like Arthur Hugh Clough, justly saw as the central objection to the characterization of Ruth:

> The guilt . . . of Ruth is accompanied by such entire ignorance of evil, and by such a combination of fatalities, that even the sternest of provincial moralists could hardly be harsh with her; and this we think a mistake on the part of the authoress. Her position would have been stronger had Ruth been older, and had she more clearly perceived the whole consequences of her transgression. We think, for the object Mrs. Gaskell had in view, the guilt should not have had so many extenuating circumstances, because as it is, Ruth, although she has much to regret, cannot in her conscience have much to repent.[117]

Though Lewes deplored the emphasis on the "good qualities and good looks" of Ruth as an "attempt to interest and propitiate the reader by all manner of graceful accessories,"[118] he did not clearly see how much the total conception of Ruth's initial innocence was intended as a propitiation of a public opposed to any "new line of action"; her former critic Greg showed a much greater awareness of such an intention on her part.[119]

Yet even had she not so clearly wished to conciliate her public, a more realistic approach to Ruth's fall would have been far too demanding for her. A possible predicament is suggested by the critic of *The Gentleman's Magazine* who, feeling that Ruth "should have been less passive, more enkindled—more of the woman in short; ensnared from within as well as from without," yet cautiously admits that such a characterization would entail "objectionable draggings through dangerous mazes of sentiment and suffering, which a pure writer would of course much prefer shunning altogether."[120]

Such a consideration most probably influenced Mrs. Gaskell in determining how to achieve her double goal in challenging social prejudice against the fallen woman: to ask greater indulgence for her original error and to suggest her ultimate rehabilitation.

To show her heroine in the best possible light undoubtedly chimed in with her artistic intentions and her ethical and religious commitments. The creation of a more fallible passionate heroine would have made demands which her propriety, her limited experience, and, above all, the moral assumptions of her faith could not satisfy. Not only would a "pure writer" feel it a breach of taste to deal with the manifestations of sexual passion, but as an artist she would experience the handicap of having "grown up" in a society which "had made it a primary purpose to see that a respectable woman like her should know as little of the animal side of life as possible."[121] Most important of all, such a handling of her subject would have demanded a much greater tolerance on her part, since she would have had to condone not innocence betrayed under unfortuitous circumstances but the realities of passion in order to fulfill her goal of reconciling society to the fallen woman. Since her religious commitments led her to view sexual failings as transgressions against divine as well as human laws, it would have gone strongly against her convictions to demand understanding and forgiveness for one who had knowingly rather than ignorantly broken a divine injunction.

A much more realistic consideration may also have influenced her handling of the initial transgression. She was not ignorant of the concrete obstacles encountered in rehabilitating chronic sexual offenders, of as she put it in a letter "the difficulty of reclaiming this class, *after they had once taken to street life*."[122] The desire to show that rehabilitation was possible only if such a circumstance were avoided may well underlie the conception of a heroine capable from the start of inspiring the charity and understanding needed to keep her from the disastrous fate of prostitutes like Lizzie Leigh (in her first short story) and Esther in *Mary Barton*, who dies in utter destitution beyond rehabilitation by Jem and Mary.

She could not have fully foreseen the artistic problems arising from the choice of a wholly innocent heroine—especially that of convincing a discriminating reader not only of the reality of "sin" but, by inference, of the appropriateness of guilt, and the necessity of spiritual redemption and social rehabilitation in such a case. Had her heroine been less ignorant of sexual realities, the satisfaction that Mrs. Gaskell's friend, the Chevalier Bunsen, expressed over the appropriateness of Ruth's untimely death might (with some effort) be tolerated; given her faultlessness and protracted saintly atonement for a sin committed unwittingly, his statement that "*sie muste untergehen,*" that "Ruth *must needs* perish, but atoned and glorified" because "that is required by man's sense of the Eternal Laws of the World's order" is mere mystical twaddle.[123] Mrs. Gaskell's decision to kill off her heroine seems less the inexorable outcome of a coherent artistic conception (Charlotte Brontë had generously conceded it might be such)[124] than the product of conventional tendencies which offset larger impulses of tolerance.

All in all her original conception obscured rather than clarified her lesson of broad-mindedness and charity because of what Greg calls its "damaging and unfaithful inconsistency":

> If she designed to awaken the world's compassion for the ordinary class of betrayed and deserted Magdalenes, the circumstances of Ruth's error should not have been made so innocent, nor should Ruth herself have been painted as so perfect. If she intended to describe a saint (as she has done), she should not have held conventional and mysterious language about her as a grievous sinner.[125]

We might even go further than Greg and accuse her of also relying on "conventional and mysterious language" to convince us of Ruth's initial innocence. For when the dressmaker's apprentice is "delightfully happy" at the chance of an outing with a young gentleman (Mr. Bellingham) which will allow her to revisit the country home she left as an orphan and briefly to escape her shabby life, the author feels it necessary to comment:

> She was too young when her mother died to have received any cautions or words of advice respecting *the* subject of a woman's life—if, indeed, wise parents ever directly speak of what, in its depth and power, cannot be put into words—which is a brooding spirit with no definite form or shape that men should know it, but which is there, and present before we have recognised and realised its existence. Ruth was innocent and snow-pure. She had heard of falling in love, but did not know the signs and symptoms thereof; nor,

indeed, had she troubled her head much about them. Sorrow had filled up her days. . . .[126]

The author's timidity is evident in this circumlocutionary approach to the question of sexual passion. It would have been wiser and more natural to point out that Ruth had at least some acquaintance with "the signs and symptoms" of love, if none with the facts of life.[127] Intent on portraying her heroine as completely victimized she only allows her an eagerness "to value and cling to sympathy" in her pathetic loneliness. To show her as motivated by romantic love might imply a concomitant physical passion, implicating her in the seduction (which Bellingham will bring about after she has been discharged by her employer and can only turn to him).

And yet the refusal to portray Ruth as romantically involved with Bellingham negates some subtle touches which in the earlier depiction of the heroine had suggested a susceptible nature. Ruth's contempt for the "dismal, hateful, tumble-down old houses" of the decayed town in which she works; her yearnings for the freshness and freedom of the open air impelling her to look out the windows while the other seamstresses eat and chat during a rest period (or to rush out on errands in all kinds of weather); her very choice of a seat in front of a once-splendid panel of painted flowers which remind her of her former country home—all these reactions imply a temperament capable of emotional seduction at least by a show of kindness, particularly under romantic circumstances. When she, a mere seamstress, goes to a ball even if only to repair any damage to the ladies' dresses, the stage is set for a possible infatuation with a handsome and elegant young man. Not so much who he is but what he represents should be fascinating, since he forms part of that "joyous and brilliant whole" in the shire ballroom which has, earlier in the evening, given Ruth such imaginative satisfaction without concern for the identities of the participants:

. . . it was enough to gaze, and dream of the happy smoothness of the lives in which such music, and such profusion of flowers, of jewels, elegance of every description, and beauty of all shapes and hues, were every-day things.[128]

Up to this point Mrs. Gaskell has convincingly suggested Ruth's possible vulnerability to the romantic situation which soon confronts her, as Bellingham atones to Ruth for the rudeness of his dancing partner by giving a flower to the beautiful but humbly attired girl, present at the ball only to serve others. But the author mars her effect almost immediately by attempting to convince us that Ruth's interest in Bellingham is absolutely above reproach; that her emotions are not those of a woman toward a man; that she is unaware such emotions exist. Thus, Ruth's attitude to the gift is made to reflect absolute innocence, for when the more earthy Jenny, after admiring the flower, says "I wish it had some scent," Ruth replies: "I wish it to be exactly as it is—it is perfect. So pure!" And her dream of Bellingham giving "flower after flower to her" is proven innocent by its juxtaposition with an earlier dream:

The night before she had seen her mother in her sleep, and she wakened weeping. And now she dreamed of Mr. Bellingham, and smiled.

And yet, was this a more evil dream than the other?[129]

In keeping with her portrayal of a heroine immune even to romantic impulses (not to speak of sensual ones), the author soon suggests that Ruth's feelings toward Bellingham are strengthened not by his personal influence on her but by an admirable public act: as he dramatically urges his horse into the water to rescue a drowning boy, courage, selflessness, and care for all human need appear to complement the tact and generosity previously demonstrated to Ruth alone.

Unduly eager to suggest that Ruth will be victimized not by her own weaknesses but by Bellingham's, the author too quickly and blatantly adduces damaging evidence of an insensitivity, a selfishness, and a snobbery that strongly belie Bellingham's seeming altruism. She needed more such subtle clues to his callousness as the picture of Bellingham riding out of the water with the insensible boy, whom he does not encircle with a protecting arm, but "carried . . . across his horse" like a mere object (though even here she cannot resist explaining that Ruth "instinctively felt that the position in which he hung was not the most conducive to returning consciousness").[130] Instead she shows Bellingham in such an unpleasant light—complaining of the "stupid people" so slow in getting the doctor and the "stifling atmosphere" in the "horrible dirty place" which is the boy's home, and then obviously lending his purse to Ruth as a way of meeting her again—that it is hard for the reader to understand how even an unsophisticated girl could be blind to these unmistakable evidences of inhumanity. Yet such understanding would of course impair the picture of utter candor and trust which the author is as eager to sustain as she is to convey the limitations of Ruth's seducer.

Thus, until the final moment when Ruth, after the country outing, enters Bellingham's carriage thinking that they are driving back to her friends at the farm and is whirled away to London (the details of the actual seduction are omitted, and wisely so, for aside from the demands of propriety, the depiction of the fall of such a character would surely try the imagination of even the greatest writers), the emphasis is consistently thrown on those commendable attributes in Ruth which conspire to make her a helpless and ignorant victim of the Don Juanesque Bellingham. It may be "the union of the grace and loveliness of womanhood with the *naïveté*, simplicity, and innocence of an intelligent child" which has "something bewitching" for Bellingham; it is her commendable shyness which exercises a "spell" on the perverse young man, making him eager "to attract and tame her wildness, just as he had often allured and tamed the timid fawns in his mother's park."[131] It is her pious and loving desire to revisit her home and recapture its precious family associations which Bellingham exploits to get her consent to the fatal excursion. Unfortuitous circumstances also victimize her: her complete loneliness in the house on Sundays (deserted by an irresponsible employer) which makes Bellingham's proffered companionship particularly appealing, the departure of a sick friend who might have given her wise advice, and finally the callous behavior of her employer (Mrs. Mason) when she is discovered on the outing in the compromising company of Bellingham.

Ruth's reaction to the heartless insults of Mrs. Mason, who vulgarly casts aspersions on her reputation, is but the culmination of previous weaknesses in the author's handling of the character. Wishing at once to show the workings of a very scrupulous conscience and yet to sustain a picture of complete innocence, Mrs. Gaskell has earlier posited dim feelings of guilt in Ruth while having to deny any correlative for such self-castigation. After her first walk with Bellingham, Ruth had wondered why "she should feel . . . as if it were not right," since she owed no time to her employer and had not failed to go to church. Her self-questionings (and the author's comment on them) had already revealed inherent contradictions in the author's basic approach:

"If I had gone to walk with Jenny, I wonder whether I should have felt as I do now. There must be something wrong in me, myself, to feel so guilty when I have done nothing which is not right; and yet I can thank God for the happiness I have had in this charming spring walk, which dear mamma used to say was a sign when pleasures were innocent and good for us."

She was not conscious, as yet, that Bellingham's presence had added any charm to the ramble. . . .[132]

Even had she been conscious, the purity of her feelings should surely have secured her against the sense that she had "done" something "which is not right." And yet in this later scene, as Mrs. Mason dismisses her from work with the curt words: "Don't attempt to show your face at my house again. . . . I saw you, and your spark too. I'll have no slurs on the character of my apprentices. . . . I saw enough" (when all she could see was Bellingham holding Ruth's arm before he entered the inn), Ruth is overwhelmed not merely with grief, but with guilt:

It seemed to the poor child as if Mrs. Mason's words were irrevocable, and, that being so, she was shut out from every house. She saw how much she had done that was deserving of blame, now when it was too late to undo it.[133]

Not only is there no realistic basis for Ruth's self-castigation, but no consistent reaction to her acceptance of this guilt, since she proceeds to throw herself under the protection of the very person whose company has caused her to feel guilty. Such are the ambiguities which arise from the author's attempt to do justice both to the total innocence and the high moral scrupulosity of her heroine. To the last she cannot resist making us feel compunctions in Ruth which her total ignorance of evil cannot possibly warrant, such as the impulse to return to the farm to seek advice rather than accompany Bellingham to London by which she demonstrates an instinct for the virtuous choice. Bellingham alone is given the full responsibility for her fall, for he tricks her into the carriage going to that other destination—the wicked city —which marks her downfall.

Mrs. Gaskell's abiding tendency to exonerate her heroine leads to an even more bewildering treatment of her after her seduction and before that desertion by Bellingham which clarifies to her the full extent of her plight. Somehow the reader expects that the previous suggestions of guilty uneasiness in Ruth will be developed now that she has gone through the physical experience of passion, but Mrs. Gaskell does nothing of the sort. Such suggestions would of course be wholly inappropriate in view of Ruth's total ignorance. And so as we meet her again in the Welsh village where she has stopped with Bellingham, she shows no signs of the moral or psychological change which her fall should traditionally have brought about (one has but to think of little Emily's letter to Ham in *David Copperfield* to recall the usual treatment of such experiences) but is capable of rejoicing freely in the beauties of "that Alpine Country" of Wales of which Mrs. Gaskell was very fond and which she effectively describes:

> It was most true enjoyment to Ruth. It was opening a new sense; vast ideas of beauty and grandeur filled her mind at the sight of the mountains, now first beheld in full majesty. She was almost overpowered by the vague and solemn delight; but by-and-by her love for them equalled her awe, and in the nighttime she would softly rise, and steal to the window to see the white moonlight, which gave a new aspect to the everlasting hills that girdle the mountain village.
>
> . . . Ruth was up betimes, and out and away, brushing the dewdrops from the short crisp grass; the lark sung high above her head, and she knew not if she moved or stood still, for the grandeur of this beautiful earth absorbed all idea of separate and individual existence. Even rain was a pleasure to her. . . . She saw the swift-fleeting showers come athwart the sunlight like a rush of silver arrows; she watched the purple darkness on the heathery mountain-side, and then the pale golden gleam which succeeded.[134]

Though Ruth has been consistently viewed as totally innocent, the picture of her after her seduction enjoying with carefree delight the loveliness of her surroundings seems so striking a reversal of the traditional situation as to suggest a great sophistication in the author. Thus Annette Hopkins is led on to bestow a special commendation on this particular aspect of the heroine's portrayal:

> From the artistic standpoint these chapters give one the finest because most truly human, touches in the book: this permitting Ruth, while still living with Bellingham before the world's censure clouds her life, to revel like a wood sprite in the exhilarating atmosphere of these wild and lovely scenes.[135]

Had Mrs. Gaskell truly intended to picture Ruth as entirely victimized by a narrow-minded society whose pharisaism would not allow her to enjoy life without guilt, then such a depiction of her before the exercise of that tyranny would indeed be a masterful stroke "from the artistic standpoint." But of course the saintly expiation of Ruth will be posited on a complete acceptance not only of the judgment of "the world" but of the religious injunctions against sexual transgression. Indeed Mrs. Gaskell's commitment to religious standards of conduct will make it impossible for her to condemn social standards too harshly much as she might disapprove of some of the hypocrisy and bigotry that characterize them.

In the light of Ruth's future behavior—her noble endeavors to expiate her guilt—we realize that the seemingly bold portrayal results not from the author's negation of generally accepted standards, but from her inexorable commitment to her heroine's ignorance of what constitutes sin. Coming when it does, however, that portrayal dangerously undermines her future attempts to vindicate her heroine's possibilities of redemption. For the fact that a virtuous woman instinctively remains untroubled after sinning (in ignorance of course) casts a very dubious light on the necessity of guilt, an imperative Ruth will be *taught to feel* by social judgments and religious tenets (the latter conveyed by the ministrations of the sympathetic Reverend Benson) for a behavior that will be considered *inherently* sinful.

It becomes increasingly obvious that the author faced a difficult problem in regard to the kind of heroine she had conceived. With a lover who would have remained faithful, Ruth could hardly have been brought to believe in a sinfulness of which she was instinctively ignorant and which she could consciously apprehend only through the interpretations other people would put on her behavior. The rejection of Ruth by Bellingham, an absolute necessity therefore, is handled rather skillfully so as to suggest that the incompatibility of their temperaments, their intellects, their capacity to care for other people and for each other (unlike Bellingham, Ruth finds the mainspring of her existence in "feeling and thinking, and loving") made separation inexorable. Yet that rejection, it soon becomes apparent, is mainly a device to open the way for Ruth's realization of her guilt, and a means to enforce the reality of that guilt, since it is the first major concrete punishment which Ruth will have to endure for her transgression (she has already suffered minor castigations through the rejections of fellow guests at the inn).

Mrs. Gaskell was a sufficiently skillful artist, however, to realize that the only feelings Ruth could initially experience would be anguish at the loss of love. The beginning of such suffering is effectively suggested by the depiction of the long night Ruth spends outside the door of her sick lover (prevented from entering by his haughty, possessive mother who has come to nurse him and who will eventually, with her son's compliance, dismiss the girl). As she realizes that "earth has no barrier which avails against agony," the great poignancy of her torment is aptly conveyed through Mrs. Gaskell's insight into haunting states of misery (already demonstrated in *Mary Barton*), an insight which a personal experience of suffering (indeed in a similar Welsh setting at the time of her boy's death) had undoubtedly sharpened. That imaginative empathy is also evident as she depicts Ruth's reaction when her frantic attempt to overtake Bellingham's carriage has failed:

> She threw herself down on the ling by the side of the road, in despair. Her only hope was to die, and she believed she was dying. She could not think; she could believe anything. Surely life was a horrible dream, and God would mercifully awaken her from it? She had no penitence, no consciousness of error or offence: no knowledge

of any one circumstance but that he was gone. Yet afterwards—long afterwards she remembered the exact motion of a bright green beetle busily meandering among the wild thyme near her, and she recalled the musical, balanced, wavering drop of a skylark into her nest, near the heather-bed where she lay.[136]

The reality of an anguish not caused by guilt but by the denial of love is sustained through the suicide attempt that follows —an attempt only averted by an impulse of Ruth's "tender nature," the desire to be of help to the crippled Reverend Benson who has endured a painful fall—and through the long coma induced by despair into which she enters after he has convinced her to seek shelter with him. But the shift in appraisal has already been prepared through the suggestion that divine providence has saved her from self-destruction. The agent of that salvation is, appropriately enough, the very person who had already reproved her for her sinful life, not in the coarse manner of other guests at the Welsh inn expressing their worldly intolerance, but in a humble charitable fashion. For, before Ruth's desertion, when still ignorant of her specific fault, she had met the cruel, baffling insults of a little child "humbly and meekly," only to find herself mutely reproved by "the mild sad face of the deformed gentleman, who was sitting at the open window above the shop," when "his eyes met her glance with an expression of deep sorrow."[137]

Thus the Reverend Benson is from the beginning conceived as a representative not of the world's opinion but of the more merciful spirit of Christian forgiveness of sins and hope of salvation. That spirit will soon oppose the pharisaic limitations of the community of Eccleston to which Benson and his sister Faith will bring Ruth to reside. If that conception allows a more tolerant view of possible redemption, it also places a severer interpretation on her action, since it is viewed as a transgression against divine injunction rather than a violation of social mores. Because it is spiritual salvation rather than social rehabilitation which Benson will set as a goal for Ruth, her burden of guilt will be increased by her need to grapple with spiritual sin as well as social error.

Such harsher implications are not, however, immediately apparent in the minister's views, for what impresses one first of all is the great leniency toward Ruth arising from Benson's faith in divine mercy and providence. It impels him to interpret Ruth's approaching motherhood in a hopeful way by which Mrs. Gaskell resolutely sets herself against the traditional opprobrium visited by society on illegitimate children. At the outset, she dramatizes the unusual breadth of Christian charity and understanding in Benson, not by contrasting it with general bigotry but by opposing it to the opinions of someone sympathetic to his convictions but whose less sensitive nature is not immune to prejudice—his sister Faith Benson. When Faith refers to the coming child as "this disgrace—this badge of her shame!" her brother enjoins her:

> "Faith, Faith! Let me beg of you not to speak so of the little innocent babe, who may be God's messenger to lead her back to Him. . . . If her life has hitherto been self-seeking and wickedly thoughtless, here is the very instrument to make her forget herself, and be thoughtful for another. Teach her (and God will teach her, if man does not come between) to reverence her child; and this reverence will shut out sin,—will be purification."[138]

As Miss Benson expresses her doubt over the "questionable morality" of "rejoicing over the birth of an illegitimate child," Benson defends himself by clarifying his impulse: it is not to "rejoice" but to avoid possible "despair" in Ruth by "trying more than ever I did in my life to act as my blessed Lord would have done."[139]

So far the lines seem sharply drawn between the larger Christian view of human error and the narrow-minded condemnation by society of what it considers immoral behavior: "if man does not come between," Ruth may be able to achieve "purification" and consequent peace of mind. We soon discover, however, that Mrs. Gaskell is hampered in condemning social attitudes by her commitment not only to divine mercy but (as *Mary Barton* has taught us) to divine justice as well; that dilemma is appropriately revealed by the ambiguity of Benson's opinion on the adverse effect of social censure on unwed mothers:

> The world has, indeed, made such children miserable, innocent as

they are; but I doubt if this be according to the will of God, *unless it be His punishment for the parents' guilt*; and even then the world's way of treatment is too apt to harden the mother's natural love into something like hatred. Shame, and the terror of friends' displeasure, turn her mad—defile her holiest instincts; and, as for the fathers—God forgive them! I cannot—at least, not just now [*italics mine*].[140]

The last clause rings very forcefully—for on the subject of the world's double standard, Mrs. Gaskell's convictions are adamant. Later in the book, the picture of Bellingham looked up to by the community of Eccleston whose Parliamentary representative he has become etches in her contempt for such pharisaic distinctions between sinners as the world makes. But, the earlier suggestion that social opprobrium may possibly be a form of divine "punishment for the parents' guilt" shows that on the question of Ruth's guilt and of the necessity for expiation her vision is less clear and forthright. The very possibility that social condemnation reflects a divine retribution will make it progressively more difficult for her to challenge such manifestations of it as Ruth is forced to endure.

This ambiguous exercise of judgment on the social censure of "fallen women" informs her treatment of the lie which Faith Benson induces her brother to adopt in order to protect Ruth from the world's bigoted opinion. For the author's objection to social condemnation and ostracism leads her to sympathize with Miss Benson's plan to present Ruth as a widowed relative to the town of Eccleston instead of frankly publishing her state and abiding by the social repercussions of that revelation. And yet not only a general commitment to the moral imperative of truthfulness but that specific sense of the salutary punishment in a social castigation perhaps divinely intended informs her eventual condemnation of that lie. It is therefore not surprising that this whole question of the merits of the Bensons' charitable lie should have aroused profuse and often contradictory comments from critics of the novel. Without pursuing all the fine shadings of critical reactions, it is easy to see that the author's intentions had not been clearly conveyed when we find reactions ranging from indignation that Mrs. Gaskell should have shown such a saintly character as Benson committing a deliberate lie to praise for her perception that a man of good will might have to violate his deepest convictions to avoid the worse evil of pharisaism.[141] Reflecting her own conflict with regard to the role of social condemnation of sexual transgression, her treatment remains indeed ambiguous to the last.

The essential nature of that conflict should not be an unfamiliar phenomenon to us. For in *Ruth*, just as in *Mary Barton*, Mrs. Gaskell's human impulses of pity and indignation clash with her striving not to question divine justice, whose ways of "punishment for the parents' guilt" and indeed of forgiveness for that guilt transcend man's knowledge. If her instinctive sympathy is mirrored in Miss Benson's pity for "what [the child] will have to struggle through and endure," should its illegitimacy be published to a bigoted world, just as inevitably her religious convictions commit her to Benson's pious objection to the lie because there is a more important "opinion" to consider than that of man—one that may well require public opprobrium as an effective expiation of sin:

"She must strengthen her child to look to God, rather than to man's opinion. It will be the discipline, the penance, she has incurred. She must teach it to be (humanly speaking) self-dependent."[142]

And that commitment soon leads the author to suggest that, in granting his sister's wish, Benson has made the wrong choice, however touching his impulse to commit a lie "not for his own sake" (as a protector of Ruth) but "for the little helpless baby, about to enter a cruel, biting world." She deems that choice "the pivot, on which the fate of years moved; and he turned it the wrong way." While she condemns lying *per se* as a corrupting agent on the conscience, she is more specifically reproving the failure to rely on heavenly justice that it implies: "He forgot what he had just said, of the discipline and penance to the mother consisting in strengthening her child to meet, trustfully and bravely, the consequence of her own weakness."[143]

Such an appraisal of Benson's action unfortunately weakens the entire conception of that genuine rehabilitation and redemption which takes place in Ruth *before* the town discovers her past and ostracizes her. How are we to reconcile the condemnation of Benson's protective lie with our sense that, precisely because Ruth is sheltered for years from social opprobrium, she can develop emotionally and intellectually in the peaceful, kindly, and tolerant household of the Bensons and consequently fulfill her duties to her hosts and to her child in such a generous and saintly fashion. We shall see that Mrs. Gaskell was to a certain extent aware of such an inconsistency, for Faith Benson later defends their action on exactly those grounds—only to be censured by her brother. Since it is quite evident that the Reverend Benson is the central spokesman of the author, we must abide by his opinion.

But Mrs. Gaskell's conviction that the Bensons have erred in hiding Ruth's unmarried state has even wider repercussions on the treatment of her theme. For if the true course of action in such cases be indeed to transcend worldly opinion, then the very goal Mrs. Gaskell has set for herself in attacking that opinion loses its relevance. And if the world's judgment is essentially immaterial, why must Ruth strive so hard to court its approval after her disgrace is revealed? Why is she given the hard burden of proving herself to the society which shuns her—even under the dangerous conditions of the cholera epidemic that will cost her her life? The truth is of course that, as the novel proceeds, the author's initial intention of challenging social attitudes to sexual transgression becomes progressively blunted. She is increasingly led to view ostracism of the "fallen woman" not as an unfortunate consequence of social bigotry but as an appropriate expiation of sin, one of the most efficacious means of promoting purgation and ultimate redemption.

A greater, more fully conscious artist than Mrs. Gaskell might, in handling the whole question of the protective lie, have sustained a subtle tension between the conflicting alternatives in this complex moral problem of how to secure human frailty against social consequences when the demands of absolute justice also have to be satisfied. We have but to think of Conrad's "The Secret Sharer" to realize that it brings to a not so dissimilar problem as that posed in *Ruth*—the dilemma of coping with the conflicting demands of abstract justice and concrete emotional needs—a wealth of psychological subtlety and a total consciousness of possible choices lacking in Mrs. Gaskell's treatment. It is typical of her that she should be bold enough to conceive of the alternative suggested by Faith Benson and to make it seem so appropriate in the light of social bigotry that some critics condemned her for condoning the lie. She is indeed even able to view it in a humorous light, since she shows Miss Benson carried away by her own inventiveness in providing a respectable past for Ruth and the garrulous, eccentric maid Sally won over in her own quaint way to a subterfuge which initially offended her self-righteousness. But it is also characteristic of Mrs. Gaskell's social diffidence and pious abnegation that from the start she should question the behavior to which she is emotionally committed and eventually show the devastating consequences it entails. To the last she does not entirely renege on her impulses, for Faith Benson (who has been consistently shown as a lovable, generous person) feels no regret for her action and defends it very appropriately, but that such regret is in order is abundantly made clear by the comments of her more sensitive, far more praiseworthy brother:

"I did very wrong in making that false statement at first."

"No! I am sure you did not," said Miss Faith. "Ruth has had some years of peace, in which to grow stronger and wiser, so that she can bear her shame now in a way she never could have done at first."

"All the same it was wrong in me to do what I did."

"I did it too, as much or more than you. And I don't think it wrong. I'm certain it was quite right, and I would do just the same again."

"Perhaps it has not done you the harm it has done me."

"Nonsense! Thurstan. Don't be morbid. I'm sure you are as good—and better than ever you were."

"No, I am not. I have got what you call morbid, just in consequence of the sophistry by which I persuaded myself that wrong could be right. I torment myself. I have lost my clear instincts of conscience. . . . I grope where formerly I saw. Oh, Faith! It is such a relief to me to have the truth known, that I am afraid I have not been sufficiently sympathising with Ruth."

"Poor Ruth!" said Miss Benson. "But at any rate our telling a lie has been the saving of her. There is no fear of her going wrong now."

"God's omnipotence did not need our sin."[144]

The very judgment passed on the lie by calling it "our sin" is perfectly in keeping with Benson's basic judgment of Ruth's original fault. For, as we have suggested, his merciful view of her plight evident in his sanctioning of her motherhood and his assertion of her child's innocence does not preclude, indeed entails, his conception of her behavior as a *sin* rather than a social transgression. Thus it is mainly through the medium of religion that Ruth, previously unaware of her error or at most sensing some social disapproval during her stay in Wales, first becomes conscious of her wrongdoing. The revelation is sudden but lasting. At the first Sunday service after her arrival in Eccleston, Benson's reading of a chapter produces the following effect on Ruth:

And so it fell out that, as he read, Ruth's heart was smitten, and she sank down, and down, till she was kneeling on the floor of the pew, and speaking to God in the spirit, if not in the words, of the Prodigal Son: "Father! I have sinned against Heaven and before Thee, and am no more worthy to be called Thy child!"[145]

That such initial self-mortification should overcome Ruth, after her recent emotional agony at being abandoned, is not inappropriate. But the author continues to stress this penitential mood in Ruth—a mood which eventually makes her fearful of offending God by loving her child too much[146] and invests her with the sense of a permanent ineradicable "stain." That emphasis seems to put harsh limits on the possible scope of her redemption, limits difficult to reconcile with Mrs. Gaskell's basic message of tolerance and other aspects of her portrait of Ruth. Despite certain venial faults (discouragement makes Ruth's concentration on household tasks initially difficult until she is rebuked by the commonsensical, assertive Sally) she behaves faultlessly while her child is growing, lavishes great care and tenderness on him, remains faithful to the moral tenets of the Benson household, indeed subordinates her maternal love to the responsibility of earning money as a governess in the household of Benson's most important parishioner, the self-satisfied and patronizing Mr. Bradshaw. Yet when Ruth has seemingly redeemed herself and deserves a free mind and a calm spirit, we are given an insight into her moral and psychological state which reveals that she has never been allowed to drop the heavy burden of penitence. Even as she is proving her virtue by rejecting Bellingham who, through coincidence, has returned into her life and is tempting her once again, she demonstrates that this virtue has brought her no peace:

"Listen to me! . . . . When I said that I was happy with you long ago, I was choked with shame as I said it. And yet it may be a vain, false excuse that I make for myself. I was very young; I did not know how such a life was against God's pure and holy will—at least, not as I know it now; and I tell you the truth—all the days of my years since I have gone about with a stain on my hidden soul—a stain which made me loathe myself, and envy those who stood spotless and undefiled; which made me shrink from my child—from Mr. Benson, from his sister, from the innocent girls whom I teach—nay, even I have cowered away from God Himself; and what I did wrong then, I did blindly to what I should do now if I listened to you."[147]

Such a self-appraisal fits in most appropriately with the author's comment concerning Ruth which, despite its softer concluding words, rings harshly in our ears:

His laws once broken, His justice and the very nature of those laws bring the immutable retribution; but, if we turn penitently to Him, He enables us to bear our punishment with a meek and docile heart, "for His mercy endureth forever."[148]

Such a conception of punishment makes it difficult to credit Benson's hopeful views on error expounded to his spiritual adversary, the pharisaical Bradshaw, who obviously errs in seeking to abide by a justice that "is certain and inflexible" instead of one "tempered with mercy and consideration." Bradshaw, who has just discovered Ruth's identity, has demonstrated that harsh commitment by throwing Ruth out of his house and answering her pathetic plea, "I was so young," with the cruel judgment: "The more depraved, the more disgusting you." As he now announces to Benson with great self-satisfaction that "The world has decided how such women are to be treated; and, you may depend upon it, there is so much practical wisdom in the world, that its way of acting is right in the long run," Benson answers: "I take my stand with Christ against the world." He goes on to say that "it is God's will that the women who have fallen should be numbered among those who have broken hearts to be bound up, not cast aside as lost beyond recall."[149] At that moment, if we recall Ruth's speech to Bellingham, it is hard to believe that Benson has abided by these noble ideals in his ministrations to Ruth through many years, that the "heart" of one who still revolts at "a stain on [her] hidden soul" has really been "bound up," that Ruth is not burdened by the fear that at least on earth (and perhaps in heaven) she is indeed "lost beyond recall."

The treatment of Mr. Bradshaw reflects similar inconsistencies. The tyrannical father whose inhuman righteousness and dogmatic materialism only succeed in arousing rebellious reactions of disobedience in his daughter and of dishonesty in his son is surely meant to present an ironic contrast to the virtuous and noble woman whom he considers hopelessly degraded.[150] Jemima Bradshaw's arrogance to her father, her neurotic suspicions of her intended husband's motives, her almost pathological jealousy of the attentions which this same man (whom she has rebuffed) pays to Ruth, contrast unfavorably with Ruth's unfailing patience, sweet temper, and self-effacement. And yet the author eventually whitewashes both Bradshaw and his daughter. His indignation when he realizes that the truth about Ruth has been hidden from him is justified by Benson's intense guilt about the deception. Even his very obduracy to his son's fault (the theft of money) shows at least the nobility of a consistent commitment to even-handed justice, and his emotion at the news that his son may have died in an accident grants him even the capacity for mercy. As for Jemima, her previous moral weaknesses seem forgotten as the author portrays the intense shock of an innocent girl upon discovering—she is the first to learn of Ruth's past error—the reality of sin in the universe embodied in "one . . . who had been stained with that evil most repugnant to her womanly modesty, that would fain have ignored its existence altogether." Even though we are told that her first reaction is to a certain extent the result of "a pharisee's dread of publicans and sinners, and . . . a child's cowardliness," there is no indication of ironic intent in the author's reference to Jemima's "pride of innocence," the vantage point from which Jemima reviews

Ruth's impeccable behavior while in the Bradshaw household and feels more merciful toward her:

Her horror of the wrong was not diminished; but, the more she thought of the struggles that the wrongdoer must have made to extricate herself, the more she felt how cruel it would be to baffle all by revealing what had been.[151]

The earlier situation has been reversed as we are asked to admire the intrinsic tolerance and generosity toward the sinner of the pure and innocent young girl, a girl who surely has no claim to judge others at all in view of the stubbornness, ill temper, and implacable hatred which had earlier raged destructively within her.[152]

We can, moreover, hardly feel that it costs Jemima much effort to be kind to Ruth when the latter's fault is discovered by the community, for Mr. Farquar (the man who, alienated by her bad temper, had found himself attracted to the gentle and unassuming Ruth) is now or will easily be secured to her affections; after all, a union with Ruth would now be unthinkable. As we watch the two young people planning their marriage (Farquar mentally heaving a sigh of relief that he has not actually proposed to Ruth) with the blessings of Jemima's parents, and the seeming approval of the author, we measure the extent of Ruth's permanent alienation from the possibility of such virtuous self-contentment. It is true that jealousy has taught Jemima something about the possibilities of evil in herself, but no permanent damage has been done to her, no "retribution" seems in store for her. As Jemima begins her joyous wedded life, Ruth enters the long road of a second expiation, the atonement to society for the evil she has committed and hidden so long from their judgment.

The justification for such a second expiation shows most clearly what we have earlier suggested, that the author is reluctant to contravene the world's standards lest she might seem to be judging too lightly a religious transgression. Benson's encouragement to Ruth in the second crisis of despair in her life—that which follows her confession of her sin to her child—when she is impelled to run away from the Bensons and her child lest they have to "share in my disgrace," is posited on the acceptance of "the world's judgment" as an appropriate penitence. His argument, already familiar to us, yet again points up the inconsistencies of the author's view, particularly since it is so out of tune with the spirit of Christian tolerance Benson has so recently demonstrated in defending Ruth against Bradshaw's denunciations:

". . . we have gone on falsely, hitherto. It has been my doing, my mistake, my sin. I ought to have known better. Now, let us stand firm on the truth. You have no new fault to repent of. Be brave and faithful. It is to God you answer, not to men. The shame of having your sin known to the world, should be as nothing to the shame you felt at having sinned. We have dreaded men too much, and God too little, in the course we have taken. But now be of good cheer. Perhaps you will have to find your work in the world very low. . . . perhaps . . . you may have to stand and wait for some time . . . all may turn aside from you, and may speak very harshly of you. Can you accept all this treatment meekly, *as but the reasonable and just penance God has laid upon you*—feeling no anger against those who slight you, no impatience for the time to come. . . . when He, having purified you, even as by fire, will make a straight path for your feet? [italics mine]."[153]

Such a view of Ruth's duties in meeting the world's judgment accounts for the author's inclination to condemn her heroine to an untimely death. It is true that she shows her finally successful in gaining the community's approval for her work among the sick during a cholera epidemic (that gratitude is indeed concretely expressed in a document from the town Board and a vote of thanks from the medical practitioners). Having stressed the relative insignificance of the world's judgment in the light of spiritual purification, she could only free her heroine completely from the incubus of transgression by convincing us that Ruth was not only socially rehabilitated but spiritually whole as well. By having Ruth die a saintly death—a fate somewhat humanized since she is stricken because she insists on nursing her former lover—the author evades the need for such a bold assertion. At the same time she satisfies the conventional social views of readers who would have balked at the portrayal of a heroine completely triumphing over her fault and sharing the prosperity and peace of mind of those who had never erred.

While it is true then that Ruth's death was "a concession to the storm that Mrs. Gaskell anticipated would break over the novel,"[154] it was also necessitated by her commitment to certain religious principles. That commitment made it just as difficult for her to challenge the social conventions of her age with regard to sexual behavior in *Ruth* as to condemn its social inequities in *Mary Barton.* In both cases the fear of challenging authority had its deepest roots in certain spiritual convictions regarding divine justice which ultimately supported a social status quo, much as other impulses asserting the primacy of Christian mercy, pity, forgiveness, and brotherhood tended to favor social change. It is not surprising that, other factors aside, the reforming fervor has ebbed in *North and South* and that personal issues become more prominent in it than basic social problems. Whether or not Mrs. Gaskell was conscious of her fundamental conflict of values, she wisely directed her artistic energies away from such *romans à thèse* as *Mary Barton, Ruth,* and *North and South* which had made demands upon her that her divided social conscience could not satisfactorily fulfill.

CHAPTER 3

The Humorist's Vision

ALTHOUGH Mrs. Gaskell certainly contributed to the understanding of social problems, her genuine artistic achievement is not her sympathetic exploration of industrial conflicts but her humorous appraisal of the whimsies and foibles of small-town life. The permanent popularity of *Cranford* rests largely on the subtlety of her comic vision while much of the praise earned by her last work, *Wives and Daughters,* is due to the humorous portrayal of its characters and their mode of existence.

The depiction of manners in a small English town was a task far more appropriate to Mrs. Gaskell's talent than the analysis of urban social conditions. For the subject precluded many of the difficulties she had faced when trying to analyze and resolve complex social and economic problems. As we have seen, the tension between her emotional leanings to social reform and her reluctance to challenge the existing order, between her impulse to arouse public indignation and her strivings toward moderation and objectivity, had often weakened her artistic expression.

Obviously, the transmutation of childhood recollections of country life into literature would be far less trying for a diffident writer attuned to the conventions of her age and almost as committed to preserving them as to pointing out their weaknesses. The subject of small-town manners indeed allowed both the celebration of a conventional mode of life and a criticism of its limitations—not, however, in the harsh terms provoked by threatening conflict (the workers' dangerous embitterment in *Mary Barton,* for example) but in that sly, whimsical and gentle manner of the humorist irresistibly provoking the indulgent "smiles and laughter" which are, as Mrs. Gaskell herself says, "not very far apart from tears."[1] Since the weaknesses of her provincial characters posed no such disturbing questions as the flaws of John Barton or Ruth, the failings as well as the virtues of these characters could freely evoke her affection and tenderness, and liberate that amused perception of the incongruities in human behavior which is at the heart of humor.

In a study of manners, her fine powers of observation could also more effectively endow her subject with universal dimensions than in an analysis of social conflicts. The specific and temporal nature of such problems as the conflicts between capital and labor and the plight of the "fallen woman" inhibited a more universal perception of human strivings and limitations. And whenever that larger perception (of necessity a tragic one) asserted itself in the social novels, significant factors operated, as in *Mary Barton,* to negate that assertion. But her study of provincial life, though depicting a mode of existence threatened by economic and social change, seizes through humor upon certain characteristics of circumscribed lives that forever transcend external alterations.

Thus, though the author's tragic vision of life lacked sharpness, her humorous appraisal of reality enabled her to generalize certain experiences with great accuracy and subtlety. If she never as an artist fully plumbed the universal implications of overwhelming passions and calamities, she did succeed, through that comic perception of human nature and existence which, as in Dickens, was an instinctive gift, in deducing some of man's inevitable impulses and actions from the spectacle of lives unthreatened by devastating feelings or circumstances. She was able to suggest that the human condition itself, viewed in the microcosmic setting of a small town, could at its worst be merely pathetic, at its best provoke a rich, indulgent laughter.

If the story of *Mary Barton* had matured in her mind "as imperceptibly as a seed germinates in the earth,"[2] surely the material for her provincial studies was if possible absorbed even more unconsciously, since her exposure to country life in the little town of Knutsford (the original of Cranford) took place during the impressionable childhood years. Her longing to experience again that simple and beautiful existence so different from her hectic life in an ugly industrial city is evident in her desire, expressed in a letter to her literary friends, the Howitts, "to be off" in springtime "into the deep grassy solitudes of the country, just like a bird wakens up from its content at the change of the seasons and tends its way to some well-known but till then forgotten land." Since, she whimsically concludes, she is "a woman instead of a bird," with "ties at home and duties to perform," with "no wings like a dove to fly away," she "must stay at home and content herself with recalling the happy scenes which your books bring up before me."[3]

The impulse to recapture a happy life through the written word eventually led her not to rely on the descriptions of others but to refashion for herself a world owing its charm not only to graceful scenery but to its inhabitants—that largely female society pursuing its quiet way without the ravaging cares and demanding responsibilities that would make a man's presence imperative:

> . . . whatever does become of the gentlemen, they are not at Cranford. What could they do if they were there? The surgeon has his round of thirty miles, and sleeps at Cranford; but every man cannot be a surgeon. For keeping the trim gardens full of choice flowers without a weed to speck them; for frightening away little boys who look wistfully at the said flowers through the railings; for rushing out at the geese that occasionally venture into the gardens if the gates are left open; for deciding all questions of literature and politics without troubling themselves with unnecessary reasons or arguments; for obtaining clear and correct knowledge of everybody's affairs in the parish; for keeping their neat maid-servants in admirable order; for kindness (somewhat dictatorial) to the poor, and real tender good offices to each other whenever they are in distress, the ladies of

Cranford are quite sufficient. "A man," as one of them observed to me once, "is *so* in the way in the house!"[4]

The author here of course exercises her kindly irony on the insular assumption that if a man cannot contribute to the practical comforts of life, he is only an encumbrance, but she also conveys the appeal of an existence idyllically free of the physical deprivation and mental anguish which made the Manchester workers so appallingly "care-worn." A world in which one can afford to fashion reality to one's taste without devastating consequences ("reasons or arguments" after all only impede the settling of questions in Cranford) or to negate it by tacit agreement (we shall see that poverty is never acknowledged) is truly the kind of world to which one might long "to fly away" from the "ties at home and duties to perform." Both its virtues and its weaknesses are on a modest scale, as are its satisfactions and its yearnings; there is nothing here to harden the heart or bewilder the mind, above all no materialistic negation of the bonds of sentiment between human beings—that focal cause of social conflicts. Thus, Cranford's "kindness . . . to the poor" if "somewhat dictatorial" is nonetheless genuine, and no such conflicting strivings as oppose labor and capital impede "the real tender good offices" mutually rendered by the Cranford inhabitants in cases of "distress."

Altogether then, provincial life was the subject upon which Mrs. Gaskell could successfully exercise her talents. Her sympathetic insight into human eccentricities and her tender precision in documenting pedestrian details of daily life combined to do justice to a mode of existence making no other demands upon her artistry. No such moral imperative as led to *Mary Barton* provoked the re-creation of that world. *Cranford* itself might have remained merely one paper for Dickens' *Household Words* (he paid her the tribute of using it to head the opening number of the magazine—December 13, 1851) had she not been encouraged to continue the work.[5] And yet, as critics have remarked, the finished work does not show signs of improvisation: if it is but a series of sketches, they are sustained by a uniform point of view. The absence of conflicting impulses secured a coherence in this imperfectly conceived work which the author failed to achieve in the more consciously planned social novels.

Dickens' approval may have furthered that impulse to recapture the past, but his initial request for a contribution from the authoress of *Mary Barton* did not, significantly enough, set that impulse into being. The inclination to memorialize the experience of her youth had already twice found means of expression. Two years earlier (in July 1849) "The Last Generation of England," a small essay anticipating material in the initial chapters of *Cranford,* had appeared in *Sartain's Union Magazine,* a Philadelphia publication; more important still, "Mr. Harrison's Confessions," in so many ways similar to *Cranford,* had been published in February, March, and April of 1851 and, as Ward solemnly puts it, "was therefore anterior in date of publication, and doubtless also in date of production, to 'Cranford,' of which a scientific literary biographer would very probably incline to classify it as a '*Vorstudie.*'"[6]

"Mr. Harrison's Confessions" (*1851*)

"Mr. Harrison's Confessions" is indeed a remarkably enlightening introduction to *Cranford,* for it not only anticipates Mrs. Gaskell's basic approach in that work, but also the Cranford setting, characters, and situation. Less subtle in approach and less whimsical in characterization, it enables us to assess the fruition of her powers in *Cranford* where a fine discrimination is unerringly at work to suggest the humor and pathos of provincial existence.

Like *Cranford,* "Mr. Harrison's Confessions" treats us to a picture of small-town life in which a self-sufficient society largely composed of widows and maiden ladies pursues a well-regulated round of tea-drinkings, card-playings, shopping trips, and outings, and indulges in its favorite pastime of gossip (mostly matrimonial conjectures). Specific characters in *Cranford* are already suggested: Miss Tomkinson, the Roman-nosed "grenadier" whose gruff appearance belies her kind heart is an appropriate predecessor for the assertive bluestocking Miss Deborah Jenkyns; busybody Miss Horsman anticipates Miss Pole.

Though Mrs. Gaskell handles the at once absurd and endearing attributes of the "Amazons" ruling the provincial world with far greater skill and diversity in *Cranford,* she already irradiates them with humor in this early story. Even here the Duncombe ladies' gossip is not seen as just a silly, or even malicious, way of filling up idle time in a society where little work is performed. As she will show more subtly in *Cranford,* such conduct has its whimsical, appealing side because it reflects some basic contradictions and incongruities in the nature of its inhabitants and thus documents that eternally humorous contrast between the dictates of reason and the claims of the imagination. We already witness in "Mr. Harrison's Confessions" the comic and touching spectacle of a society whose behavior is confined within exact rules and ceremonies but whose imaginative life transcends those restrictions, appropriating to itself all external events and performing upon them those distortions and magnifications which bring them into line with their (often unconscious) aspirations and apprehensions.

The town's ludicrous misunderstandings regarding the marital intentions not only of young Doctor Harrison, a newcomer, but of Mr. Morgan, the older doctor who prides himself on his knowledge of the town's ways, could easily have been merely a series of farcical *quid pro quos.* But the author's whimsicality enriches the comic situation by sometimes giving the silly pretensions of the town ladies a certain baroque charm. Thus Miss Tomkinson makes a stab at culture and sophistication by naïvely assuring the young doctor that "We have been all anticipating an Apollo . . . and an Aesculapius combined in one; or, perhaps I might confine myself to saying Apollo, as he, I believe, was the god of medicine!" Mrs. Bullock strives for exquisite taste by objecting to the chemical symbols in her husband's manual because "they give the page a very ragged appearance" and by praising her father's contempt for "variety" in books.[7]

The tendency of Duncombe residents to deny reality and yield to their imagination is charmingly suggested in the narrator's comments on the practice of calling the police:

"Now there was no police, only a rheumatic constable, in the town; but it was the custom of the ladies, when alarmed at night, to call an imaginary police, which had, they thought, an intimidating effect; but, as everyone knew the real state of the unwatched town, we did not much mind it in general.[8]

Yet the womanly dependence displayed here and in matrimonial aspirations that contrast so humorously with the ladies' generally self-sufficient behavior is not as subtly suggested as in *Cranford.* There is none of that naïve unconsciousness of motivations which lends ineffable pathos and sweet humor to Miss Matty Jenkyns' nervous exclamation upon hearing of an impending Cranford marriage: "Two people that we know going to be married. It's coming very near!"[9]

Part of the qualitative difference between the two worlds is due to the vantage point from which they are each observed. And the choice of narrator is not as skillful in the earlier work. In *Cranford*, Mary Smith's sympathetic (if intermittent) participation in the town's activities guarantees an intimate knowledge of its assumptions, while her sophisticated insight into its lovable absurdities (her greatest charm) allows her to view these foibles at an affectionate remove and exercise her humor and irony upon them. The very technique of depicting Duncombe life from the point of view of Harrison, a genuine outsider by virtue of being both a *man* and a stranger to the community, effects the kind of distance which precludes doing justice, whether seriously or humorously, to the point of view of a feminine society. The self-absorption of such a society, its self-satisfaction regarding rules and traditions—its whole ethos in fact—is so effectively celebrated in *Cranford* because Mary Smith is partially committed to it, yet unerringly senses its limitations. But the logical outcome of confronting Harrison—a dashing young doctor—with the society of Duncombe is that its mores are seen from an alien vantage point and that the emphasis falls on his plight as an eligible bachelor in a society of largely ineligible ladies.

The temptation to treat such a situation in a farcical manner is irresistible. That in "Mr. Harrison's Confessions," unlike *Cranford,* actions rather than the life of imagination are a frequent source of laughter is evident in the behavior of the ladies who do not merely dream of a changed status but embrace any opportunities to achieve their matrimonial goal. Thus Miss Caroline Tomkinson exploits her supposed ill-health to win Mr. Harrison's interest, and Mrs. Rose uses her position as house-keeper to further her mistaken hopes. The former's silly frivolity and selfishness, the latter's absurd malapropisms and coyness make them unsubtle subjects for laughter.

"Mr. Harrison's Confessions" is thus basically a comedy of *situations* rather than a humorous exploration of *character* and *temperament*. The ludicrous deductions which characters make from misinterpreted appearances are not such imaginative delusions as, for example, the wild suspicions of Miss Pole in *Cranford* regarding the true identity of the female tramp, but traditional farcical misunderstandings. Mr. Harrison, who loves Sophy, the charming daughter of the Vicar, is thought to be wooing Miss Caroline Tomkinson when he is in fact on his knees only to examine her heart with his stethoscope; he is believed to be courting Mrs. Rose because he gives her a sewing table, whereas he is merely trying to get rid of an unfortunate purchase.

The farcical aspects of Harrison's situation are heightened by his active part in his own victimization; after all it is he who, right after buying the table, has tantalized Miss Horsman, the town gossip, by suggesting that he is indeed beginning to furnish a household and has a specific lady in mind. And he unwittingly reinforces Mrs. Rose's mistaken hopes by going out of his way to absolve himself of dallying with someone else. This scene in which Mr. Harrison by trying to solve one problem lays the foundation for a new one (there are echoes in the situation of that famous imbroglio which eventually landed Mr. Pickwick in prison) is a good example of the author's farcical approach to romantic misinterpretations in her story. Blind to the meaning of Mrs. Rose's coyly keeping "the fire screen . . . as yesterday, between me and her," Mr. Harrison blunders on in his presentation of what he conceives to be a reasonable, obvious justification:

" 'The most unfortunate misunderstanding has taken place. Miss Tomkinson thinks that I have been paying attention to Miss Caroline; when, in fact—may I tell you, Mrs. Rose?—my affections are placed elsewhere. Perhaps you have found it out already?' for indeed I thought I had been too much in love to conceal my attachment to

Sophy from anyone who knew my movements as well as Mrs. Rose.

"She hung down her head, and said she believed she had found out my secret.

" 'Then only think how miserably I am situated. If I have any hope—oh, Mrs. Rose, do you think I have any hope'—

"She put the hand-screen still more before her face, and after some hesitation she said she thought 'If I persevered—in time—I might have hope.' And then she suddenly got up and left the room.[10]

Almost invariably actions and situations rather than character are exploited for laughter. Thus Harrison's ludicrous predicament of being romantically identified with *three* ladies (Mrs. Bullock has been pushing her daughter's claim) when he has merely heeded his superior's advice to be generally friendly is intensified by the bad reputation he owes to the mischievousness of his rowdy friend Jack. The latter's reckless conversation convinces the ladies that their new doctor has a prison record ("in Newgate for three months" is the Duncombe version) when in fact he has only once briefly appeared before a magistrate, and he compounds Harrison's romantic difficulties by secretly sending a valentine to Miss Caroline. The subtle handling of a practical joker in *Cranford* reveals the psychological poverty of a character like Jack, a mere tool to complicate the intrigue.

In keeping with the farcical mood, the depiction of characters is, as we have suggested, far less indulgent and affectionate: failings seem too often ridiculous mannerisms rather than endearing, psychologically convincing foibles. The mellow mood of *Cranford,* investing so many of the characters with lovable attributes, is absent here; even gossip is not always a harmless, amusing weakness but can be dangerously malicious; eventually assumptions are made about Mr. Harrison's character that are not entirely digestible through laughter:

". . . . I found that my practice was falling off. The prejudice of the town ran strongly against me. . . . It was said—cruel little town—that my negligence or ignorance had been the cause of Walter's death; that Miss Tyrell had become worse under my treatment; and that John Brouncker was all but dead, if he was not quite, from my mismanagement. All Jack Marshland's jokes and revelations, which had, I thought, gone to oblivion, were raked up to my discredit. . . .

"In short, so prejudiced were the good people of Duncombe that I believe a very little would have made them suspect me of a brutal highway robbery, which took place in the neighbourhood about this time.[11]

Eventually of course, in the tradition of farce, all the problems are ironed out, not without the assistance of a crop of marriages. Harrison wins the pretty and virtuous Sophy whose life he has saved by racing to a distant town to secure the necessary medicine. Mr. Morgan condescends to marry Mrs. Rose as an "efficacious contradiction" of rumors linking him with Miss Tomkinson, and Miss Caroline elopes with a rich and old tallow-chandler, having first convinced her sister that her hysteria at Harrison's supposed engagement to Mrs. Rose merely resulted from "eating pickled cucumbers."

Whereas the suggestions of pathos are in *Cranford* often an intimate function of the humorous vision of life, they are here barely perceptible in the harsher and more unsubtle atmosphere of farce; only Miss Tomkinson is sometimes touching in her selfless concern for her worthless sister. The intrusion of tragedy (the sudden death of little Walter, Sophy's appealing brother) seems therefore particularly inappropriate. In *Cranford,* where the whimsy so often has pathetic undertones, even the totally unexpected death of Captain Brown seems psychologically tenable.[12] Humor has widened the range of possible feelings and thus reduced the gap between tears and laughter.

Cranford (*1851–1853*)

The qualitative difference between "Mr. Harrison's Confessions" and *Cranford* is already perceptible in the early chapters of the latter, which deal with Captain Brown and his relationship to the world of the Cranford "Amazons." Like Mr. Harrison in Duncombe, the Captain encounters difficulties in being both a man and a stranger to the mores of a small town, but the nature of his problems immediately suggests a more meaningful confrontation of viewpoints. Whereas the negligence of Harrison's attire, his penchant for hunting, or the presence of novels among his medical books could alienate Duncombe, Captain Brown poses a far more subtle threat to Cranford not only because of his present occupation but, far more important, because of his basic sense of values. Besides being employed by the railroad, that dangerous emblem of change, he soon manages to outrage the Cranford sensibilities by violating their important convention that at least the appearance of gentility be always sustained. He challenges their social conspiracy to make "economy" invariably seem "elegant" while "money spending" is always "vulgar and ostentatious" by acknowledging that he is poor with a total lack of discretion, "not in a whisper to an intimate friend . . . but in the public street! in a loud military voice!" The town's peace of mind is appropriately disturbed:

> . . . if, in addition to his masculine gender, and his connection with the obnoxious railroad, he was so brazen as to talk of being poor—why, then, indeed he must be sent to Coventry. Death was as true and as common as poverty; yet people never spoke about that, loud out in the streets. It was a word not to be mentioned to ears polite.[13]

Whereas Mr. Harrison's acceptance by Duncombe takes the farcical form of an attempt to secure the eligible bachelor and is checked for a while by prejudice, the rapid and sustained reconciliation of the Cranford inhabitants to Captain Brown's offhand behavior asserts the reality of certain emotional impulses which transcend the dictates of convention in the Cranford world. Once the Captain is brought into informal contact with Cranford society—an opportunity given only because his masculine help is needed "to discover the cause of a smoking chimney" —his humanity negates the value of that society's strict adherence to the code of gentility:

> . . . Captain Brown walked upstairs, nothing daunted, spoke in a voice too large for the room, and joked quite in the way of a tame man about the house. He had been blind to all the small slights, and omissions of trivial ceremonies, with which he had been received. He had been friendly, though the Cranford ladies had been cool; he had answered small sarcastic compliments in good faith; and with his manly frankness had overpowered all the shrinking which met him as a man who was not ashamed to be poor.[14]

The conflict of spontaneous feelings with formal social directives is thus shown from the beginning as a significant phenomenon of Cranfordian behavior. As the story develops, the often incongruous confrontation and clash of the claims of emotion and the demands of convention is revealed as the focal element in Mrs. Gaskell's humorous vision of reality. When we recall that such conflicting pressures are evident in the author's serious handling of social problems, we begin to assess the kind of artistic liberation her humorous works afforded her. For they enabled her to relieve a private dilemma by projecting it in such comic terms as would suggest that it was both universal and not necessarily dismaying.

The endearing and touching aspects of this personal and pervasive human conflict are first suggested in *Cranford* through the confrontation we have already discussed. Its humorous implications become evident as Captain Brown's unconventional enthusiasm clashes with the firm principles of Miss Deborah Jenkyns, the most formidable proponent of "the strict code of gentility," in that well-known literary discussion in which the relative merits of Dr. Johnson and Dickens are so strongly contested.

On that memorable evening, Miss Jenkyns' patience has already been tried: she has had "to drown . . . by a terrible cough"[15] a reference by the Captain's daughter to a shopkeeping uncle, so as not to offend the aristocratic sensibilities of the Honourable Mrs. Jamieson, Cranford's most distinguished resident. When Miss Jenkyns is then asked point blank by Captain Brown whether the recent numbers of *Pickwick Papers* are not "famously good" her answer and the resulting discussion humorously point up the incongruous contrast not only between two different canons of taste, but between the different temperaments, sets of values, and styles of life which literary preferences for Johnson and Dickens imply. By successfully exploiting the connotations attached to the two authors' works, Mrs. Gaskell suggests in comic terms the larger clash between those principles of reason, order, moderation, and self-restraint which justify formality and decorum and those inclinations to cultivate the instincts and the imagination which negate their relevance. Miss Jenkyns' stubborn adherence to her own convictions adds the humorous dimension of a complete failure of communication, as her answer to Captain Brown obsessively negates any standards but her own:

> "I must say, I don't think they are by any means equal to Dr. Johnson. Still, perhaps, the author is young. Let him persevere, and who knows what he may become if he will take the great Doctor for his model?"[16]

When the Captain appropriately suggests that "It is quite a different sort of thing, my dear madam," her amusing insularity is further illumined as she retorts: "I am quite aware of that. . . . And I make allowances, Captain Brown."[17] And she proceeds to set a passage of *Rasselas* against the description of the Bath "swarry" in *Pickwick Papers* to vindicate Johnson's incomparable style—the model for her own correspondence. Whether or not the Captain (in a burst of comic exasperation reminiscent of Squire Western's reaction to Milton in *Tom Jones*) really delivers himself *"sotto voce"* of the comment "D——n Johnson!" as a final telling blow, remains a Cranfordian moot point: the possibility, however, appropriately concludes the debate along with evidence that the kind-hearted Captain tried "to beguile her into conversation on some more pleasing subject" while "she was inexorable."[18]

Even the "inexorable" Miss Jenkyns will of course find that compassion challenges propriety when tragedy strikes the Brown household. As we have said the Captain's death is not inappropriate in the atmosphere of *Cranford*; even the humorous connotations of his character are not negated by his tragic accident. His appealing eccentricity almost suggests a possible heroism; for the very selflessness which could assume the ludicrous form of helping a poor woman by transporting "with . . . grave dignity" her baked mutton and potatoes safely home could also lead him to sacrifice his life to save a child from being crushed by a train; humor allows a wide scope to manifestations of charity. Indeed excessive pathos is deliberately avoided by reference to an earlier humorous motif; we discover that the Captain has spent the last few minutes of his life perusing *Pickwick Papers*, news which Miss Jenkyns greets with an amusing mixture of sympathy and obduracy: "Poor, dear, infatuated man!"[19]

The realization that laughable incongruities can assert themselves in the midst of sorrow or serious hardships rarely deserts Mrs. Gaskell; Mary Smith's reaction to Miss Jenkyns' mourning bonnet testifies to it, for despite her sadness Mary cannot help being struck by the bonnet's grotesque resemblance to a "helmet."[20]

These early chapters of *Cranford* already reveal the ease and subtlety with which the author could encompass her characters' virtues and foibles and the simultaneously absurd and appealing attributes of their way of life. In successive chapters, as the author shifts her emphasis from Miss Jenkyns to her sweet and lovable sister Matty and the small circle of her frends who constitute Cranford society, her approach is essentially the same: she explores with indulgent humor the details of a conventional life and the effects of any intrusions upon it.

That the very conventions themselves often display an amusing (and touching) eccentricity enriches the humorous contrast they present to the challenging unconventional, worldly standards. Indeed, from the very beginning, old-fashioned behavior is not in itself so amusing as the peculiar mode of its manifestation. Thus the ladies' genteel "dismay" at Captain Brown's proclamation of poverty is so very whimsical an insularity because of their specific *manner* of cultivating gentility, by conspiring for instance to abet Mrs. Forrester's illusions of gracious living as she thrones over her guests at a tea party:

> . . . pretending not to know what cakes were sent up, though she knew, and we knew, and she knew that we knew, and we knew that she knew that we knew, she had been busy all the morning making tea-bread and sponge-cakes.[21]

As the work proceeds, that particular aspect of Mrs. Gaskell's humor becomes more evident. Almost invariably she heightens the comic dimensions of Cranford conventionality (already quaint because of its conservatism) by revealing how traditional attitudes toward social entertainment, economy, fashion, or politics have an irresistible tendency to abet all the personal quirks and private foibles of the apostles of gentility.

True, their eccentric behavior is sometimes humorous only in contrast to urban sophistication, as Mary Smith reminds us by pointed questions: "Have you any red silk umbrellas in London?" "Do you ever see cows dressed in grey flannels in London?" "Do you make paper paths for every guest to walk upon in London?"[22] But most often the humorous effect transcends such temporal circumstances. Universal incongruities and irrationalities of human behavior are celebrated as we witness the eccentric forms that Cranford principles assume when put into practice. That Miss Matty Jenkyns should choose to economize rather strictly on candles seems a not unreasonable, if somewhat rigid impulse of conservatism; it is the manifestations of that economy, however, which document human fallibility from the humorist's viewpoint:

They [the candles] were usually brought in with tea; but we only burnt one at a time. As we lived in constant preparation for a friend who might come in any evening (but who never did), it required some contrivance to keep our two candles of the same length, ready to be lighted, and to look as if we burnt two always. The candles took it in turns; and, whatever we might be talking about or doing, Miss Matty's eyes were habitually fixed upon the candle, ready to jump up and extinguish it and to light the other before they had become too uneven in length to be restored to equality in the course of the evening.[23]

When the desire to protect a new carpet takes the form of spending a whole afternoon "chasing the sunbeams" by changing "the position of . . . newspapers," it exemplifies the perennially humorous tendencies of human behavior to defy the dictates of reason.

The inventive exaggeration of Cranford assumes another amusing form as old-fashioned modes of dress become inspired grotesquerie. "Any number of brooches, up and down and everywhere" are, Mary Smith informs us, along with fashionable caps, an essential feature of Cranford attire. But this odd custom easily reaches absurd proportions. At Mrs. Forrester's gathering, Miss Matty, Mrs. Forrester, and Miss Pole muster "a greater array of brooches than had ever been seen together at one time since Cranford was a town." Mary Smith, who has kept a careful count, recalls the various geographical locations ("cap," "net-neckerchief," "collar," "front of her gown," "midway between her throat and waist," "point of her stomacher") of six of Miss Pole's brooches, adding: "Where the seventh was I have forgotten, but it was somewhere about her, I am sure."[24]

Even the political conservatism of the town (anti-French sentiment being, of course, a prominent feature) becomes ludicrously irrational when Cranford yields to a "panic" after robberies punctuate the departure of the mysterious magician Signor Brunoni. Applying to wider problems that imaginative resourcefulness which once enabled her to rescue the precious antique lace swallowed by her cat, Mrs. Forrester adumbrates the undeniable cause of Cranford's troubles:

> . . . her theory was this:—The Cranford people respected themselves too much, and were too grateful to the aristocracy who were so kind as to live near the town, ever to disgrace their bringing up by being dishonest or immoral; therefore, we must believe that the robbers were strangers—if strangers, why not foreigners?—if foreigners, who so likely as the French? Signor Brunoni spoke broken English like a Frenchman; and though he wore a turban like a Turk, Mrs. Forrester had seen a print of Madame de Staël with a turban on, and another of Mr. Denon in just such a dress as that in which the conjurer had made his appearance, showing clearly that the French, as well as the Turks, wore turbans. There could be no doubt. Signor Brunoni was a Frenchman—a French spy come to discover the weak and undefended places of England, and doubtless had his accomplices.[25]

Even more serious weaknesses than the concern with fashion, economy, or political intrigue assume that eccentric guise which arouses the humorist's instinct. Though Mrs. Gaskell sometimes treats snobbery in a lightly satirical manner (as in the scene in which Miss Betsy Barker, the former milliner, outdoes the Cranford ladies in subtle distinctions as to who is eligible to attend the tea party for the Honorable Mrs. Jamieson), she often views it as a whimsical irrationality rather than an objectionable prejudice. If a deft irony is expended on the town's contempt for ungenteel Mr. Hoggins, humor also illumines the tendency of Cranford snobbery to negate with absurd abandon the claims of reason and logic:

Mr. Hoggins was the Cranford doctor now; we disliked the name and considered it coarse; but, as Miss Jenkyns said, if he changed it to Piggins it would not be much better. We had hoped to discover a relationship between him and that Marchioness of Exeter whose name was Molly Hoggins; but the man, careless of his own interests, utterly ignored and denied any such relationship, although as dear Miss Jenkyns had said, he had a sister called Mary, and the same Christian names were very apt to run in families.[26]

If in the world of Cranford the irrational incongruously asserts itself in the very adherence to social attitudes formalized by tradition, on a richer and subtler humorous level, the impulses of heart and imagination conflict (as we have previously suggested) with conventional social dictates. Miss Jenkyns gives some proof of not being wholly immune to those emotional vagaries which, as they undermine man's strivings for dignity, propriety, measure, and order, make him such an appropriate subject for humor. Yet she most often adheres to those principles of moderation and restraint which assert the sovereignty of mind over heart, the triumph of reason over imagination. Her sister Miss Matty, on the contrary, exemplifies the struggle of the instincts against those rigidities of thought and behavior which impede the spontaneity of human feelings and relationships.[27]

It is Miss Matty's humble allegiance to her sister's principles, yet her temperamental inability to live by them, which makes her behavior so comic and touching. Her naïve, largely unconscious strivings to reconcile her own impulses and yearnings with social propriety arouse our sense of the moving and laughable incongruities at the heart of all human conduct. Thus, the unconscious indictment of social propriety implicit in the very expression of an allegiance to it lends pathos and whimsy to her comment when she visits her former admirer, Mr. Holbrook: "It is very pleasant dining with a bachelor. . . . I only hope it is not improper; so many pleasant things are!"[28] (An earlier suggestion that Miss Matty has indeed been victimized by propriety, since Miss Jenkyns probably prevented her marriage to the ungenteel Mr. Holbrook heightens the pathos.) Soon after, in a far lighter vein, the persistence of her sister's literary standards is suggested in Miss Matty's imperviousness to the beauties of Tennyson's "Locksley Hall" (she takes "a comfortable nap" during most of Mr. Holbrook's reading) and her imperfect assimilation of these standards in her attempted assessment of the poem:

"It is so like that beautiful poem of Dr. Johnson's my sister used to read—I forget the name of it. . . . I don't remember what it was about, and I've quite forgotten what the name of it was; but it was written by Dr. Johnson, and was very beautiful, and very like what Mr. Holbrook has just been reading."[29]

When Miss Matty does reject the demands of propriety, her triumph is touchingly selfless, but also humorous as it points up the conflict between her sophisticated heart and her limited social experience. Inspired by her visit to Mr. Holbrook with the desire to give others the emotional freedom denied to her, she decides to rescind her rule that servants should not have man-callers, yet is hardly prepared for the lightning swiftness with which her suggestion is accepted. Two contrasting assumptions regarding social behavior clash divertingly in the following dialogue between Miss Matty and her maid:

". . . perhaps, Martha, you may some time meet with a young man you like, and who likes you. I did say you were not to have followers; but if you meet with such a young man, and tell me, and I find he is respectable, I have no objection to his coming to see you once a week. God forbid!" said she in a low voice, "that I should grieve any young hearts!". . .

"Please, ma'am, there's Jim Hearn, and he's a joiner making three-and-sixpence a day, and six foot one in his stocking-feet, please, ma'am; and if you'll ask about him tomorrow morning, every one will give him a character for steadiness; and he'll be glad enough to come tomorrow night, I'll be bound."[30]

Mary Smith's final comment on this scene, "Though Miss Matty was startled, she submitted to Fate and Love," epitomizes Miss Matty's appeal. For though her allegiance to the demands of convention sometimes impedes a submission to the claims of love, the latter almost invariably win out. After all, it is Miss Matty who by temperament and experience eventually transcends social distinctions in Cranford through the opinion she hands down on the Hoggins question—at a time when the impending marriage of Lady Glenmire to the Cranford doctor is viewed as an appalling misalliance:

> ". . . Mr. Hoggins is really a very personable man; and as for his manners, why, if they are not very polished, I have known people with very good hearts, and very clever minds too, who were not what some people reckoned refined, but who were both true and tender."
>
> She fell into a soft reverie about Mr. Holbrook. . . .[31]

The humorous contrast between the principles of decorum and the impulses of imagination is nowhere better illustrated than in the repression we discover Miss Jenkyns to have exercised over Miss Matty's irrational fears. When the Cranford ladies are impelled to consider the great questions of "conjuration, sleight of hand, magic, witchcraft" upon the forthcoming visit of the magician Brunoni, Miss Matty's predicament in living up to her sister's expectations becomes evident:

> Miss Pole was slightly sceptical, and inclined to think there might be a scientific solution found for even the proceedings of the Witch of Endor. Mrs. Forrester believed everything, from ghosts to death-watches. Miss Matty ranged between the two—always convinced by the last speaker. I think she was naturally more inclined to Mrs. Forrester's side, but a desire of proving herself a worthy sister to Miss Jenkyns kept her equally balanced—Miss Jenkyns, who would never allow a servant to call the little rolls of tallow that formed themselves round candles "winding-sheets," but insisted on their being spoken of as "roley-poleys!" A sister of hers to be superstitious! It would never do.[32]

When the Cranford "panic" liberates the ladies' confessions of their most secret apprehensions, we find out that Miss Matty

> . . . ever since she had been a girl, . . . had dreaded being caught by her last leg, just as she was getting into bed, by someone concealed under it. She said, when she was younger and more active, she used to take a flying leap from a distance, and so bring both her legs up safely into bed at once; but that this had always annoyed Deborah, who piqued herself upon getting into bed gracefully, and she had given it up in consequence.[33]

Yet the triumph of manners over instinct has hardly been permanent. The persistence of imaginative impulses, once the formidable Miss Jenkyns no longer personally restrains them with standards of conduct which absurdly negate their existence, has led Miss Matty to allay her fears by a most ingenious contrivance—in part reminiscent of the Duncombe practice in "Mr. Harrison's Confessions" which we have mentioned earlier:

. . . she had told Martha to buy her a penny ball, such as children play with—and now she rolled this ball under the bed every night; if it came out on the other side, well and good; if not she always took care to have her hand on the bell-rope, and meant to call out John and Harry, just as if she expected men-servants to answer her ring.[34]

That endearing susceptibility which makes Miss Matty profoundly human explains why the black sheep of the Jenkyns family, "poor Peter" (as Miss Matty tenderly calls her brother), frequently made her his confidante in their youth, while he deflated the pomposity of his father and older sister by grotesquely imaginative pranks. In a much less subtle way, Peter Jenkyns' behavior also exemplifies the rebellion of instincts against social rigidities; Miss Matty's loving tolerance of him and his deep affection for her sustain the meaningfulness of those values which transcend social conformity.

Intriguingly enough, because Peter directly outrages convention instead of attempting, like Miss Matty, the bewildering task of reconciling its claims with personal inclinations—Mrs. Gaskell's own problem, as we have seen it in the social novels—the author feels it incumbent upon her not to exonerate him completely. She undoubtedly expects us to enjoy the impish tricks of her *enfant terrible*—whether, disguised as an impressive lady, Peter flatters his father's pride in his sermons, or, in Miss Jenkyns' attire, cradles what seems to be an infant (really a pillow) in his arms to the horror of passing inhabitants. But when the severe and public flogging by his father impels him to leave home forever, we are told not only of the father's anguished remorse at his severity but of the heartbreak of the mother who misses her boy. That Peter, as well as his father, has contributed to such devastating suffering (which indeed accelerates the mother's death) is undeniable, even if that responsibility is never again held against him when he reappears—as the Aga Jenkyns—in time to save Miss Matty from the poverty she is patiently enduring. Yet even then Peter's incurable imagination is only allowed to ridicule those whose behavior is clearly reprehensible. Thus, he is allowed to fool the snobbish and narrow-minded Mrs. Jamieson into believing that he actually once inadvertently "shot a cherubim" and to counter her dismay at the "sacrilege" by slyly pointing out that such laxity was the unfortunate result of his "living for a long time among savages—all of whom were heathens—some of them, he was afraid, were downright Dissenters."[35] He is also permitted to indulge his fancy to satisfy the thirst for exoticism which is such an endearing Cranford weakness; significantly enough he restrains himself only for Miss Matty and the rector.

Miss Matty's appealing innocence would indeed not make her what Peter feels Mrs. Jamieson to be—"fair game" for his outrageous distortions of the truth. As David Cecil says, she "is that most typical figure of the English eighteenth-century novelist—the childlike, saintly innocent . . . whose very virtues, when brought up against the unromantic facts of everyday life, contribute to make her ridiculous." Yet if "she is the lineal descendant of Parson Adams, Dr. Primrose and Uncle Toby,"[36] she also evokes memories of Don Quixote and of course of Mr. Pickwick, who figures so prominently in Captain Brown's cherished reading. Her conviction that, despite her own ruin, she must personally make good the losses incurred by customers of that now bankrupt Town and County Bank of which she had been a shareholder reveals her touching and absurd ignorance of those "unromantic facts of everyday life" (to use Cecil's terms) which are not beyond the comprehension of the wiser narrator:

It was evidently a relief to her to be doing something in the way of retrenchment, for, as she said, whenever she paused to think, the recollection of the poor fellow with his bad five-pound note came over her, and she felt quite dishonest; only, if it made her so uncomfortable, what must it not be doing to the directors of the bank, who must know so much more of the misery consequent upon this failure? She almost made me angry by dividing her sympathy between these directors (whom she imagined overwhelmed by self-reproach for the mismanagement of other peoples' affairs) and those who were suffering like her. Indeed, of the two, she seemed to think poverty a lighter burden than self-reproach; but I privately doubted if the directors would agree with her.[37]

Her scruples about competing with the town grocer by selling tea (the only source of livelihood now open to her), her conflicts between the desire to satisfy her customers' predilection for green tea and her conviction that it would disagree with their constitutions humorously testify to her entire ignorance of such expediencies as are the unfortunate if almost inevitable outcome of experience.

Like her comic predecessors, Miss Matty has no particular arts or graces to recommend her. But the larger grace of her incapacity to comprehend evil and her ability to forgive not only thoughtlessness but harshness makes her deficiencies in education and intellect humorous emblems of a larger innocence which transcends even as it make irrelevant circumscribed achievements: the ability to spell correctly, to give the right change, to cast accounts, to distinguish between "astronomy" and "astrology," and to accept the idea that the earth moves, an idea which caused Miss Matty to "feel so tired and dizzy whenever she thought about it."[38]

The subtle dimensions of innocence granted to Miss Matty make the conflicts, confusions, and paradoxes in her behavior the richest source of humor in the work. But other characters also testify to the permanence of those contradictions and incongruities which are the province of humor. Thus it is the very Miss Pole who had expressed her contempt for occult mysteries by claiming to explain all of Signor Brunoni's conjuring tricks with the help of the Encyclopedia who gives the clearest instance of her vulnerability to superstition. Though she has met with "withering scorn" the suggestion that "a lady all in white, and without her head" is given to appearing in Darkness Lane, her behavior on the way home from Mrs. Jamieson's belies such sophistication, for, as Mary Smith tells us, "she had breath for nothing beyond an imploring 'Don't leave me!' uttered as she clutched my arm so tightly that I could not have quitted her, ghost or no ghost." She bribes the porters to change their route, alleging only the selfless desire to give Miss Matty a smoother ride in the sedan chair, for "the pavement in Darkness Lane jolts so, and she is not very strong."[39] Later Miss Pole's delight in making mysteries overcomes her desire to be business-like in the "involved and oracular" missive (signed with "initials reversed, P.E.") by which she summons Mary Smith to the secret meeting in which the ladies plan ways of financially assisting Miss Matty.

Most Cranford ladies indeed exemplify the difficulty of restraining the life of the imagination. We have seen the eccentric manner in which they abide by traditional principles of conduct. They are also given to unconscious contradictions of these very principles. However committed to the advantages of singleness, to woman's superiority (after all, Miss Jenkyns, the former oracle of Cranford, "would have despised the modern idea of women being equal to men. Equal, indeed! she knew they were superior!"),[40] indeed to the irrelevance of men in the general scheme of things, yet, as the narrator points out with sly understatement, their behavior challenges their convictions:

> I don't know whether it is a fancy of mine, or a real fact, but I have noticed that, just after the announcement of an engagement in any set, the unmarried ladies in that set flutter out in an unusual gaiety and newness of dress, as much as to say, in a tacit and unconscious manner, "We also are spinsters."[41]

In chronicling Cranford's mode of life and the character of its inhabitants, Mrs. Gaskell had undoubtedly transcribed some of the actual realities of Knutsford; indeed for certain readers the particular appeal of the book lies in that authenticity of detail enabling one not only to identify Cranford streets and houses (even Mr. Holbrook's farm and the place where Miss Matty sold tea) with specific Knutsford landmarks but Cranford peculiarities of conduct with actual Knutsford eccentricities. Mrs. Gaskell herself told Ruskin of the work: "it is true too, for I have seen the cow that wore the grey-flannel jacket—and I know the cat that swallowed the lace that belonged to the lady that sent for the doctor that gave the. . . ." She even confided to him a real instance of Knutsford behavior that outdoes Miss Matty's comic concern about her rug: two Knutsford ladies "had just laid down a new carpet with white spots or spaces over it, and . . . had been teaching [their new maid] . . . to vault or jump gracefully over these white places, lest her feet might dirty them!"[42]

Her debt to Knutsford has repeatedly been stressed but readers have also testified to her success in characterizing a particular way of life not limited to England or indeed to Europe.[43] She herself felt that she would have been able to handle her characters successfully in a very different setting.[44]

But the achievement of *Cranford* transcended even its appraisal of any small-town life. The widespread and persistent appeal of the book which Ruskin loved, which entertained George Eliot and George Henry Lewes on their travels, and which Mrs. Gaskell herself termed "the only one of my own books that I can read again,"[45] is undoubtedly due to the author's ability to transmute the material of her early experience into art, as she perceived in the quaint way of life and attitudes so familiar to her the larger truths about human character and behavior which they endearingly illustrated.

"My Lady Ludlow" (*1858*)

The persistence of that inspiration which transfigured Knutsford life in *Cranford* is most dramatically evident in Mrs. Gaskell's crowning work, *Wives and Daughters* (1864–66). For, as we shall see later, though both the scope of her observation and the depth of her psychological insight have increased in that novel, her basic approach to provincial life has not really changed. She has never ceased to feel for the patterned, circumscribed way of life celebrated in *Cranford* the understanding and loving tolerance which allowed her effortlessly to do justice to the humor and pathos of its vicissitudes.

A story written seven years after *Cranford* already testifies to the continuing claim of this material on her imagination. It is true that in "My Lady Ludlow" (which, like *Cranford*, first appeared in *Household Words*—from June 19 to September 25, 1858) her emphasis has shifted somewhat; since her heroine is a member of the aristocracy, not a genteel rector's daughter like Miss Matty, she faces different problems in relating to the little community of which she is the most august member. And yet Lady Ludlow's basic conflict is not so different from that of *Cranford's* real heroine. For if only one has a title, both are "ladies" in the higher sense (Miss Matty, we have been told, is in contrast to the Honorable Mrs. Jamieson, "a true lady herself") and find the claims of this natural nobility often hard to reconcile with traditional allegiances.

Undoubtedly, Lady Ludlow's plight does not possess the timeless attributes of Miss Matty's dilemma. For she quite specifically represents both in her narrow-mindedness and generosity the weaknesses and strengths of an aristocracy whose way of life is on the wane. The constant clash between her resistance to change and her benevolent instincts documents a social more than a psychological phenomenon. Of course we have never been unaware of the threat of social change in old-fashioned Cranford; it is to a certain extent true that, as Paul Elmer More says, the "charm" of that book does "depend largely . . . on a feeling of unreality, or, more precisely, of proximity to the great realities of Manchester"; that the "grace" of *Cranford* "is of something that has survived into an alien age, and is about to vanish away."[46] Indeed Mrs. Gaskell's sensitive description of the decay into which the Cranford Assembly Rooms have fallen is a moving reminder of how much "grace" (and indeed grandeur) has already vanished. But, as we have attempted to show, the author's humorous vision often transcends her specific subject to suggest in the unsophisticated Cranford ways eternal human eccentricities, thereby endowing a transient way of life with timeless, universal attributes. She is less successful in "My Lady Ludlow," for, however humorous and touching the conflicts of "the high-bred and high-spirited, but at heart God-fearing and humble *châtelaine*"[47] are, those conflicts most often grow out of her particular social position, whereas Miss Matty's are the natural function of her basic temperament, whose sweetness, innocence, and diffidence would be tried by the demands of conformity in almost any social situation.

Given that qualitative difference, there are remarkable resemblances in Mrs. Gaskell's approach to the social viewpoints governing the worlds of Cranford and Hanbury. Here again flourish those class distinctions which nourished many a Cranford conversation, that religious intolerance of Dissenters which the Aga Jenkyns so slyly ridiculed in Mrs. Jamieson, that conservative suspicion and hatred of all things French which Mrs. Forrester so amusingly exemplified during the Cranford "panic." And even though Lady Ludlow is the most spirited exemplar of such attitudes, neither the members of her household nor the town's inhabitants are exempt from convictions which the author, as in *Cranford*, handles with light humor or irony through the medium of a narrator. Though not as subtly conceived as the at once "prim" and shrewd Mary Smith, Margaret Dawson is nevertheless lively and observant as she reminisces on her youth when, one of a select group of young ladies, she was educated in Lady Ludlow's household. Like Mary Smith, she chronicles her former sympathies with the assumptions of that world, even as she reveals its humorous limitations. Thus as she recalls Lady Ludlow's indignation at the news that a neighboring estate "was bought by a Baptist baker from Birmingham," she goes on to display the absurdity of her own prejudices at that time:

> "A Baptist baker!" I exclaimed. I had never seen a Dissenter, to my knowledge; but, having always heard them spoken of with horror, I looked upon them almost as if they were rhinoceroses. I wanted to see a live Dissenter, I believe, and yet I wished it were over. I was almost surprised when I heard that any of them were engaged in such peaceful occupations as baking.[48]

It is of course in Lady Ludlow that such conservative views assume their most whimsical form. For her, the wearing of one's "own hair" is a sinister repercussion of the French Revolution since "To be without powder . . . was in fact to insult the proprieties of life by being undressed. It was English sans-culottism."[49] Because she is suspicious of widespread education as "levelling and revolutionary," she will not hire servants who can write; young Harry Gregson's boast of having read a letter before delivering it to her provokes a lengthy tale of woeful adventures during the French Revolution illustrating the dire results of educating the lower classes.[50] The Vicar Mr. Gray, who is eager to establish a Sunday school in the village, is accordingly a sore trial to her after the comforting presence of the former clergyman, Mr. Mountford, who, as the narrator informs us, "was true blue, as we call it, to the backbone; hated the dissenters and the French; and could hardly drink a dish of tea without giving out the toast of 'Church and King, and down with the Rump'."[51]

What the story documents is the humorous and touching way in which Lady Ludlow comes to terms with the threatening inroads of change upon those principles which are her way of life. Invariably, like Miss Matty, she triumphs over her deeply ingrained traditionalism through a kind heart.

Even her opposition to the Sunday school is eventually overcome as, almost in spite of herself, her natural feelings go out to the very people who had so uncomfortably challenged her. Her regard for her steward; her growing fondness for young Harry Gregson, his protégé (whom at some sacrifice she has helped financially after an accident); her increasing admiration and affection for the shy clergyman, Mr. Gray, whose courageous refusal to obey her has both outraged her pride and stimulated her liking—all these emotions triumph over her wish to assert authority by achieving a general subservience to conservative principles.

Though Lady Ludlow's apprehensions and prejudices sometimes possess the whimsy and absurd charm of private eccentricities rather than conventional snobberies, her capitulations to the dictates of the heart are viewed more often through sentiment than humor. Only one whimsical instance of true charity deserves to take its place with the best examples of the author's humor in *Cranford*; it is that in which Lady Ludlow's exquisite tact and tenderness triumph over her commitment to social graces as she rescues from public ridicule Mrs. Brooke, the wife of that same "Baptist baker from Birmingham" whose arrival in the community had so outraged her sensibilities. Margaret Dawson's correspondent describes for her the following scene at Lady Ludlow's tea party:

". . . all the parsonesses were looking at Mrs. Brooke, for she had shown her want of breeding before; and the parsonesses, who were just a step above her in manners, were very much inclined to smile at her doings and sayings. Well! what does she do but pull out a clean Bandana pocket-handkerchief, all red and yellow silk; spread it over her best silk gown. . . . There we were, Tom Diggles even on the grin . . . and Mrs. Parsoness of Headleigh—I forget her name, and it's no matter, for she's an ill-bred creature . . . —was right-down bursting with laughter, and as near a hee-haw as ever a donkey was; when what does my lady do? . . . She takes out her own pocket-handkerchief, all snowy cambric, and lays it softly down on her velvet lap, for all the world as if she did it every day of her life, just like Mrs. Brooke, the baker's wife; and when the one got up to shake the crumbs into the fireplace, the other did just the same. But with such a grace! and such a look at us all!"[52]

It is appropriate that this instance of Lady Ludlow's capacity to love (which puts to shame the coarser snobbery of those far less entitled to scoff at ill-breeding than she) should be recounted by Miss Galindo, the kind-hearted eccentric. From the moment this seemingly "queer, abrupt, disagreeable, busy old maid" appears on the scene (and she does so only halfway through the story), she brings with her direct reverberations from the Cranford world. Devoid of the aristocratic dignity and grace which make her august patroness Lady Ludlow a rather difficult subject for humor, Miss Galindo allows the author to illustrate with zest and whimsy those grotesqueries of behavior which distinguish the lovable Cranford eccentrics.

Nor is Miss Galindo, with her brusque frankness and outlandish generosity, a mere echo of such characters as Miss Deborah Jenkyns or Miss Pole. There is in her an added dimension of intelligence and self-consciousness which makes her both the subject of laughter and the conscious perpetrator of it. If she is, like Miss Jenkyns, committed to the proposition that women can do more than hold their own with men, she obviously enjoys her whimsical ways of abetting men's erroneous sense of self-importance. So that, when she undertakes, at the request of Lady Ludlow, the position of clerk to Mr. Horner, her attempts to allay his suspicions of womanly incompetence satisfy her playful instincts:

"I see he [Mr. Horner] can't find a fault—writing good, spelling correct, sums all right. And then he squints at me with the tail of his eye, and looks glummer than ever, just because I'm a woman—as if I could help that. I have gone good lengths to set his mind at ease. I have stuck my pen behind my ear; I have made him a bow instead of a curtsey; I have whistled—not a tune, I can't pipe up that—nay, if you won't tell my lady, I don't mind telling you that I have said 'Confound it!' and 'Zounds!' I can't get any farther."[53]

That her own eccentricities often imply some shrewd comment on human failings is evident when she describes a short-lived literary career, started by providing herself with "paper and half-a-hundred good pens, a bottle of ink, all ready," and abruptly terminated by "my having nothing to say, when I sat down to write." She finds the logic of that decision questionable, however, for, as she puts it, "sometimes, when I get hold of a book, I wonder why I let such a poor reason stop me. It does not others."[54] Even wholly absurd comments reveal some sharp power of observation turned to comic use. Thus she defends her assumption that Lady Ludlow's acquaintance, a retired captain in the navy, is the possessor of a wooden leg by indisputable evidence: ". . . sailors are almost always wounded in the leg. Look at Greenwich Hospital! I should say there were twenty one-legged pensioners to one without an arm there."[55]

Since Miss Galindo shares both Lady Ludlow's conservative principles (her objection to mass education takes the comic form of indignation that her little servant should be "seduced" from her daily work by the clergyman's attempts to save her soul) and her innate generosity of soul, but is more shrewd and realistic about the challenges of change, she serves as an appropriate mediator in reconciling Lady Ludlow to its demands. She herself has placed love above propriety by taking into her home the illegitimate child of a man she once hoped to marry (like Miss Matty, she has been condemned to spinsterhood by social prejudice). Her admiration for the Vicar's kind-heartedness has led to an emotional acceptance of his liberal views on education, an acceptance not without its effect on Lady Ludlow. It is Miss Galindo who, in her whimsical way, also reconciles Lady Ludlow to the final indignity of Captain James's marriage with the daughter of the Baptist baker. Of the actual choice made by the two partners she has this to say:

"Indeed, my lady, I have long left off trying to conjecture what makes Jack fancy Gill, or Gill Jack. It's best to sit down quiet under the belief that marriages are made for us, somewhere out of this world, and out of the range of this world's reason and laws. I'm not so sure that I should settle it down that they were made in heaven; t'other place seems to me as likely a workshop; but at any rate, I've given up troubling my head as to why they take place."[56]

How fully Lady Ludlow finally comes to share her opinion has already been demonstrated in the little scene described by Miss Galindo to Margaret Dawson. Both characters testify to the transcending power of human sympathy over social conventions, once again reasserting the author's central message not only in *Cranford*, of course, but in her social novels.

Though "My Lady Ludlow" lacks that sustained vision of human eccentricities and effortless control over plot and atmosphere which give *Cranford* its artistic coherence, it nevertheless provides another significant instance of the author's ability to make meaningful—especially through humor—those struggles and conflicts which do not take place in the dramatic arenas of the great world but in the confines of that provincial one whose secrets she had been able so early to discover.

Wives and Daughters (1864–66)

A frequently quoted tribute to Mrs. Gaskell's last work—*Wives and Daughters*—is that of George Sand who told Lord Houghton that the novel "could rivet the attention of the most *blasé* man in the world."[57] Undoubtedly such praise is meaningful, not only because of the critic's sophistication, but because in its general subject the novel would not seem appealing to very jaded tastes. Appropriately subtitled *An Every-day Story,*[58] it explores again the vicissitudes of provincial life in a manner very reminiscent of the works we have just considered. In the little town of Hollingford a society largely composed of spinsters and widows again pursues a well-regulated existence—highlighted by tea-drinking, card-playing, and shopping—indulges in gossip, discusses the latest fashions, and revels in social distinctions. The scope of her portrayal has broadened to include the landed gentry and resident aristocracy but her humorous appraisal of human foibles and eccentricities has not altered much since *Cranford.*

What George Sand may well have been commending is the psychological maturity Mrs. Gaskell displays in some of her characterizations. Even her heroine, Molly Gibson, though she possesses the standard virtues of young ladies in Victorian novels, has attributes of humor and insight which make her somewhat atypical. Her father, Dr. Gibson, though not sufficiently developed as a character, transcends the commonplace by his wit and intelligence. But no previous work prepares us for the psychological insight demonstrated here in her portrayal of two characters who profoundly affect the simple and tender relationship of Molly Gibson and her father: Hyacinth Clare Kirkpatrick—who becomes Molly's stepmother (Mrs. Gibson)—and her daughter Cynthia. What most surprises is the absence of a sustained moral judgment. To the last a reader familiar with Mrs. Gaskell's moral scrupulosity expects her to renege on her whimsical and witty appraisal of these ladies' foibles, but no consistent didactic impulse is ever asserted and, though the novel is incomplete, indications are that no final moral castigation was intended.[59] These two creations undoubtedly owed much of their sophistication to being essentially the product of the humorist's vision, a vision that had so richly informed *Cranford*, but now expressed itself with even greater variety.

The author's final maturity as an analyst of character is also evident in such minor characterizations as that of Lady Harriet, the intelligent and sophisticated daughter of Lord and Lady Cumnor. But this last novel hardly marks a turning point in her artistic career, for the scope of her inspiration and the extent of her craftsmanship remain limited.

The subject matter of *Wives and Daughters* would not in itself suggest a deficient inspiration. A very familiar and emotionally meaningful mode of life might well serve for a further artistic exploration of human behavior. After all, as Jane Austen has clearly demonstrated, such a subject is capable of having many subtle changes rung upon it if one exercises on the circumscribed universe and its inhabitants a penetration sufficient to suggest larger meanings. It is rather the persistence of certain standard themes, situations, and characters which reveals a limited inspiration. Thus Dr. Gibson and Molly exemplify that loyal and loving father-daughter relationship already explored in *Mary Barton, North and South*, "A Dark Night's Work," *Sylvia's Lovers*, and "Cousin Phillis." Despite some originality, Molly Gibson has the characteristic attributes of a certain type of young lady in her novels and stories. For, like Maggie Browne ("The Moorland Cottage"), Ruth, Margaret Hale, Ellinor Wilkins ("A Dark Night's Work"), and Phillis, she is basically serious, intelligent, patient, and sensitive, and, like these predecessors, is capable of empathy, forbearance, loyalty, and self-sacrifice. Even Molly's unusual stepsister Cynthia Kirkpatrick is partly an inspired reworking of another type of heroine in Mrs. Gaskell's works: the rather frivolous, coquettish, thoughtless, and immature young girl of which Mary Barton is the first sketch and Sylvia the most complex example up to this point (indeed the contrast between Mary Barton and Margaret Legh, between Sylvia and Hester Rose anticipates that presented by the two young girls in the Gibson household). Roger Hamley, the Squire's second son, clearly resembles Mr. Thornton of *North and South* in physical vigor, strength of will, intelligence, courage, and forthrightness. And, once again, the ways of the "Amazons" in the little town of Hollingford are exemplified in the kind of sisterly relationship already depicted in "Mr. Harrison's Confessions" and *Cranford*; although she brings whimsy and charm to the portrayal of the two Miss Brownings, the sheer repetition of the motif palls upon the reader.

Not only characters but familiar emotional situations confront us again. That Victorian convention, the heroine's protracted unawareness of being in love, had hardly enhanced the romantic problems in *Mary Barton, Ruth,* and *North and South*; in *Wives and Daughters*, Molly's persistent blindness to her feelings for Roger Hamley seems particularly meretricious in view of her basic self-awareness and sound judgment. Mrs. Gaskell still seems to be catering here to the public taste for maidenly coyness and to its predilection for romantic suspense. She is not being merely conventional in again introducing a dilemma connected with telling the truth (already a motif in *Mary Barton, Ruth*, "A Dark Night's Work," and *North and South*), for that question was very meaningful to her, but surely her thoughtful handling of Philip's prevarication in *Sylvia's Lovers* and her humorous treatment of Mrs. Gibson's mendacity in this novel should have sufficed without dragging in another predicament of that nature for Molly. Her conflict between the need to protect the reputation of her flighty stepsister by silence or secure her own by speaking up to defend herself (regarding her secret meetings with Mr. Preston to retrieve Cynthia's letters) neither illumines character nor enriches plot. It is not even significantly suspenseful, since her reputation is soon vindicated through Lady Harriet's public show of confidence in her. The whole situation seems to have been mustered to provide an amusing illustration of that delight in gossip which Hollingford shares with Duncombe, and to chalk up another item on the long list of Molly's virtues.

The author's artistic limitations are intriguingly revealed by the discrepancy between her sophisticated characterization and her unsubtle handling of plot. Her narrative ability is undeniably there, but that ability or courage to denote in actual behavior the inexorable results of certain psychological complexities of character (which she shows in *Sylvia's Lovers* and "Cousin Phillis") is rarely evident. Her subtle appraisal of human temperament makes more evident her failure to project the possible repercussions of complex personalities in the realm of human actions. Thus, what Mrs. Gibson and Cynthia feel and say invariably provides us with far greater insights into human nature than what they do; the same criticism applies to two other interesting characters, Dr. Gibson and Lady Harriet Cumnor. That mastery not just of character but of its manifestations in action which transfigures a story into a meaningful plot (so evident in Thackeray's treatment of Becky Sharp in *Vanity Fair*) remained beyond her reach. Not her last novel but *Sylvia's Lovers* and "Cousin Phillis" showed at least the potential for such an eventual emancipation of her talents; she unfortunately did not live long enough to realize it.

The very absence of sustained meaningful actions perhaps accounts for the sense that, despite its sound organization and general coherence,[60] *Wives and Daughters* is unduly drawn out and basically static. True, an exciting beginning introduces us not only to Molly Gibson but, through Lady Cumnor's annual party for the Hollingford ladies (which the little girl is privileged to attend as the doctor's daughter), to the female residents of the town, to the aristocratic Cumnor family who receive their respectful allegiance, and to the fascinating Hyacinth Clare, former governess to the Cumnor girls, who will figure significantly in Molly's life and already manages to affect her unfavorably. Nor are the series of events culminating in Dr. Gibson's proposal of marriage to Clare (as she prefers to be called by the Cumnor ladies) devoid of liveliness while the actual scene itself is a masterpiece of shrewd observation and subtle wit worthy of Jane Austen. Once the Gibson household settles down, however, and the emphasis shifts to the romantic involvements of Molly and her stepsister Cynthia, the story becomes much more conventional. There is the characteristic uncertainty about the romantic feelings of Osborne and Roger Hamley, the Squire's sons, who so often grace Mrs. Gibson's parlor, an uncertainty heightened by the knowledge that any entanglement would be considered a misalliance by the basically good-natured but narrow-minded Squire of Hamley Hall. When Osborne is disposed of as a prospective suitor for the girls (his secret marriage to a French governess, only discovered after his untimely death, will soften the Squire's pride), the attention is centered on Roger Hamley. In true storybook fashion, this younger son, originally the least promising of the two, proves to be the most reliable, the most loving, and the most gifted; he lacks the poetic talent which so aptly fits Osborne's languid, oversensitive nature, but excels in the scientific disciplines, a far more appropriate—since it is more solid and substantial—achievement for the hero of a Victorian novel.[61] He is undoubtedly the ideal suitor for Molly, whom he has consoled and advised in her despair at her father's remarriage; both are commonsensical, steady, honest, and loyal and already bound by deep emotional ties, since Molly helped to nurse Roger's mother during her illness and shares Roger's fondness for the kind-hearted but irascible Squire. Needless to say the inevitable is long delayed, since it is not the sober Molly but the flirtatious Cynthia who first wins Roger's heart. The rest of the novel is taken up with the smoothing out of all the obstacles (including two departures from England by Roger on scientific expeditions) which delay the achievement of a complete understanding between the deserving Roger and the virtuous Molly (all evidence points to their marriage as an appropriate conclusion to the work).[62]

Though brief and general, this outline of the problems and events in *Wives and Daughters* is not an unfair representation of the central action's main lines. And yet, significantly enough, in rehearsing that action, one finds oneself failing to consider the character most responsible for the novel's richness and psychological subtlety. For, as we have said before, the second Mrs. Gibson, beyond some meddlesomeness in alternately favoring the attentions of Osborne and Roger to her daughter (her natural interest in the eldest son-and-heir wanes when through eavesdropping she discovers his fatal illness) does not really distinguish herself by significant actions but by the verbal display of her ludicrous and fascinating personality. Like Mrs. Bennet in *Pride and Prejudice* and Mrs. Nickleby, who are to a certain extent her literary forebears,[63] she is a triumph of characterization through style, for she lives mainly through the words bestowed upon her and only intermittently through the appropriate actions and descriptive touches with which the author has thought fit to buttress her portrayal.

Because no other character in Mrs. Gaskell's works is at once so winning and so reprehensible, no other so clearly convinces us that her greatest artistic sophistication resided in her comic vision of those weaknesses, paradoxes, and delusions that eternally testify to human imperfection. For her art is least tendential when the spirit of humor is operative; only that spirit enables her to transcend didacticism, to free herself from those moral claims which restrained her artistic impulses in the social novels. *Cranford* had already testified to her capacity for imaginative freedom when a subject did not unduly try her moral scrupulosity, but none of the inhabitants of that idyllic world presented the kind of challenge offered by the creation of Mrs. Gibson. For it is no longer naïveté and kindly eccentricity but selfishness, vanity, and an insidious hypocrisy which are displayed in their most diverting and imaginative form. The basic liveliness and playfulness of Mrs. Gaskell's disposition, so often held in check by high standards of morality and conventional propriety as much a part of her as of her society, asserts itself in this work as never before. Only her correspondence, as we said at the beginning, adequately reveals up to this point the iconoclastic tendencies of her wit, irony, and humor. And if, mostly through her bold, frank, uninhibited servant girls, she had earlier poked fun at humbug and pomposity, she had not prepared us for the comic challenge to her most cherished values as failings she had always particularly castigated—selfishness, hypocrisy, and especially mendacity—are made a source of entertainment in her portrait of Mrs. Gibson. It is significant that in the same spirit she endows the more venial faults she had invariably reproved—frivolity, unsteadiness, thoughtlessness—with great charm in characterizing Mrs. Gibson's daughter Cynthia and reveals a playful tendency to substitute esthetic for ethical judgments in such passing comments as Roger's quip to Molly, "My sermons aren't long, are they? Have they given you an appetite for lunch? Sermons always make me hungry, I know," and Lady Harriet's injunction to Molly, worthy of Oscar Wilde in its witty impudence: "Tell the truth, now and evermore! Truth is generally amusing, if it's nothing else!"[64]

Much of her success in handling Mrs. Gibson lies in that deliberate avoidance of sentimentality and didacticism which, as we have just seen, enhances other portrayals. The comic portrait of this not wholly ill-natured but completely self-centered and frivolous woman is most effective, therefore, when the author relies on Mrs. Gibson's extensive, absurdly self-contradictory monologues to convey the humorous and ironical appraisal of a vain and hopelessly petty nature. Because Mrs. Gaskell's own descriptive comments veer toward moral judgments, they most often undercut the comic effect of the portrayal. Only at times does she manage to sustain that esthetic objectivity which guarantees her successful comic approach to character, as when, for instance, she wittily implies Mrs. Gibson's insincerity by commenting that "at eighteen she had been very proud of her blushes," and that "her words were always like ready-made clothes, and never fitted individual thoughts."[65]

If Mrs. Gaskell's own comments rarely illumine Mrs. Gibson's personality as effectively as does that lady's conversation, the actions devised for her do not, as we have said, subtly suggest her limitations. There are only rare instances of deft self-revelation such as the impulsive self-indulgence of Mrs. Gibson (then Mrs. Kirkpatrick) in eating Molly's untasted lunch and vanity in hiding her action even though she causes Molly great confusion and embarrassment. The scene near the conclusion of the novel which shows us Mrs. Gibson waving back a good-bye from the window to the departing Roger Hamley, obstructing Molly's last vision of him, coyly monopolizing his attention in the conviction that only she could warrant such a leave-taking indicates that Mrs. Gaskell's instincts could at times flawlessly document human failings through appropriate behavior. Most frequently, however, her character's vain and petty actions become meaningful only through the construction which that character's own glib eloquence puts upon them.

For the humorist's ability to capture the incongruous ramifications of Mrs. Gibson's "superficial and flimsy" nature and the deceptive "silkiness" of her temper through the spoken word almost never deserts her. It inspires her most telling points about her character's selfishness, insensitivity, lack of tact, and failure of reason. Securely ensconced in that solipsistic universe where self is the supreme authority, instinctively rejecting the impediments which logic and feeling might present to her plan for a comfortable and carefree life, Mrs. Gibson shadows forth in an endless and versatile flow of talk that eternally comic incongruity between appearance and reality, between the virtue she claims to possess and the human weakness which invariably asserts itself in the midst of her professions. Much of the portrait's power depends not on the unmasking of Mrs. Gibson's pretensions but on the imaginative form these pretensions assume. For their inventiveness asserts that dominance of the instincts over reason which (as we have seen in connection with *Cranford*) is so often the humorist's theme. Were Mrs. Gibson coldly and obviously deceitful, or tediously self-deluded, she would merely arouse loathing or contempt, but the inspired manner in which she toys with the truth, deceiving not only others but sometimes herself often makes her absurdly appealing. Whether she tries to achieve the upper hand by paying false tributes to values she finds meaningless or by defending her own dubious standards, her imaginative effrontery achieves that momentary triumph over logic and genuine feeling that is one of the primal sources of laughter.

Mrs. Gibson is, then, above all, like the fascinating Alfred Jingle of *Pickwick Papers*, an imaginative impostor; her pretensions persistently testify to the ingenuity, zest, and aplomb with which she manages to achieve her will under the most devious disguises. She is not, as we have said, above using against others principles irrelevant to her if she can thereby make petty objectives seem praiseworthy, and she brings to the task an artist's resourcefulness. Thus, when she wishes to get Molly out of the house so that she can monopolize the attention of her visitor, Lady Harriet, she finally hits upon an argument, at once convincing and calculated to redound to her credit: Molly is to go and see the Miss Brownings, formerly friends of her mother, for ". . . I would not have you break off old friendships for the world. 'Constancy above everything' is my motto, as you know. . . ."[66] When she then accounts for Molly's absence to Lady Harriet, her imagination first plays some variations on her inspiring theme and then adds those touches that will lend credence to the virtuous role which she has assigned to herself:

"Molly is gone out; she will be sorry to miss you, but she was obliged to go and see some old friends of her mother's whom she ought not to neglect; and I said to her, constancy is everything. It is Sterne, I think, who says, 'Thine own and thy mother's friends forsake not.' But, dear Lady Harriet, you'll stop till she comes home, won't you? I know how fond you are of her. . . ."[67]

With diverting technical skill, she rises to the difficulties of sustaining the image presented to the world. The dilemma in which Lady Harriet puts her on the subject of lying may at first seem insoluble, but Mrs. Gibson manages in the following dialogue to give the privileges of titled aristocracy their due (Harriet has just confessed to a lie) and still preserve the picture of her own perfect truthfulness, no mean achievement—especially at the moment when she is about to perpetrate upon her visitor the fraud of an "impromptu" lunch for which the most elaborate plans have been laid:

Lady Harriet was silent for a minute or two; then she said—"Tell me, Clare; you've told lies sometimes, haven't you?"

"Lady Harriet! I think you might have known me better; but I know you don't mean it, dear."

"Yes, I do. You must have told white lies, at any rate. How did you feel after them?"

"I should have been miserable, if I ever had. I should have died of self-reproach. 'The truth, the whole truth, and nothing but the truth,' has always seemed to me such a fine passage. But then I have so much that is unbending in my nature, and in our sphere of life there are so few temptations; if we are humble we are also simple, and unshackled by etiquette."

"Then you blame me very much? If somebody else will blame me, I shan't be so unhappy at what I said this morning."

"I am sure I never blamed you; not in my innermost heart, dear Lady Harriet. Blame you, indeed! That would be presumption in me."[68]

Thus does Mrs. Gibson's blissful oblivion regarding moral values enable her to glide smoothly over the complexities of ethical dilemmas and to create an image of herself which satisfies her sense of what one owes to appearances. As so often before, one suspects that she has momentarily succumbed to her own deception and is both perpetrator and victim of the imposture.

Indeed she is kept from seeming reprehensible by the comic power not only of her self-praise but of the lack of self-knowledge which that praise so often suggests. She has not really admitted to herself that wealth and status are her only index to personality when she exclaims "I do like that Osborne Hamley! What a nice fellow he is! Somehow, I always do like eldest sons." And when she is not paying lip service to values which leave her indifferent, the humorous contrast between her standards and the assumptions of others is heightened by the unconscious abandon with which she pursues her own viewpoint. Thus Dr. Gibson's hasty departure to the bedside of the dying Mr. Smith provokes the spontaneous outburst: "But, if this Mr. Smith is dying, as you say, what's the use of your father's going off to him in such a hurry? Does he expect a legacy, or anything of that kind?"[69]

In rare moments her inability to perceive the ludicrous contrast between her failings and the values she claims to admire even makes her seem absurdly touching. When Molly suggests that far from being, as Mrs. Gibson has said, "just the kind of weak young man to have his head turned" (by being lionized), Roger Hamley is "too sensible for anything of the kind," Mrs. Gibson in her typically illogical, weather-vane fashion adapts this comment to an invidious comparison between the young man and her late husband:

"That is just the fault I've always found with him [Roger]; sensible and cold-hearted! Now, that's a kind of character which may be very valuable, but which revolts me. Give me warmth of heart, even with a little of that extravagance of feeling which misleads the judgment, and conducts into romance. Poor Mr. Kirkpatrick! That was just his character. I used to tell him that his love for me was quite romantic. I think I have told you about his walking five miles in the rain to get me a muffin once when I was ill?"[70]

The incongruity of this self-centered and frivolous woman singing the praises of "warmth of heart" and "extravagance of feeling" is a familiar humorous element of her portrayal, but in this case she is not being totally insincere, since she finds romantic impulses indeed appealing though, unbeknownst to her, their value only inheres in satisfying her vanity. Her additional failure of perception—she is unaware that Mr. Kirkpatrick's demonstration of regard is grotesque—also suggests a certain vulnerability. Finally, if the at once ludicrous and touching gesture of the Reverend Kirkpatrick (and we might add, tragic, since we find out that it had fatal effects upon his health!) irresistibly points up the selfishness of the person who would countenance such an action, it also suggests her ability to call out such devotion—however eccentric—in another being. The humanizing power of humor is at work here to reconcile us to human frailty. By achieving a subtle blend of willful hypocrisy and deluded vanity, the author has succeeded in giving her character those complex dimensions which approximate the paradoxes and contradictions of the human temperament.

The humorous portrayal of human weakness in Mrs. Gibson would in itself have been a remarkable tribute to Mrs. Gaskell's psychological sophistication. Yet her achievement in suggesting the paradoxes of personality extended to another creation, a character which even more boldly challenges her conventional portraiture in its "infinite revelations of human nature."[71] How much the conception of Mrs. Gibson's daughter Cynthia marked a departure from the moral values embodied not only in her previous studies of young girls but in the depiction of her heroine Molly Gibson is made clear by David Cecil:

The Victorian standards in which she had been educated told her that Molly was indisputably better than Cynthia. And she was no more capable of questioning these standards than she was of flying. . . . But what are standards, however Victorian, against the lawless force of the sympathetic creative imagination? Mrs. Gaskell made Cynthia a living human being because she could not help it. And it is the dangerous power of people like Cynthia to win our hearts and set our moral principles by the ears.[72]

Henry James's cryptic statement that Mrs. Gibson was "less difficult . . . to draw than the daughter," accords with one's own feeling that the delineation of Cynthia's intriguing frivolity undoubtedly challenged the author's sophistication even more than the depiction of the hypocrisy and vanity of Mrs. Gibson. For Mrs. Gaskell's commitment to the frailty of her character is far greater in the case of Cynthia, who is never really made the butt of the author's humor, wit, or irony. Indeed Cynthia is herself endowed with that power of humorous discrimination which unerringly charts the devious progress of her mother's various impostures. Though James gives the author's objectivity perhaps somewhat more credit than it deserves, it is undeniably true that the force of the portrait, even more than that of Mrs. Gibson's, derives from what he calls "the author's own marked abdication of the authoritative generalizing tone which, when the other characters are concerned, she has used as a right," a self-effacement which gives the reader "a very delightful sense of the mystery of Cynthia's nature and of those large proportions which mystery always suggests."[73]

Once again, Mrs. Gaskell's descriptive touches are devoid of the subtlety which the character's self-revelations possess. The complexity of Cynthia's appeal is indeed belied by the sententiousness of an authorial comment on the nature of her fascination:

A woman will have this charm, not only over men but over her own sex; it cannot be defined, or rather it is so delicate a mixture of many gifts and qualities that it is impossible to decide on the proportions of each. Perhaps it is incompatible with very high principle; as its essence seems to consist in the most exquisite power of adaptation to varying people and still more various moods—"being all things to all men." At any rate, Molly might soon have been aware that Cynthia was not remarkable for unflinching morality. . . .[74]

Here too the action of the novel more often suggests the moral limitations rather than the psychological complexities of the character. Her emotional flightiness is illustrated by her ability to be (as she herself puts it) "off with the old and on with the new" with regard to three gentlemen. Her engagement to Roger is partly an attempt to reassure herself that she is not bound by the now distasteful prior engagement contracted at eighteen to the unscrupulous and ill-bred Mr. Preston; and she is in sufficiently good spirits during Roger's departure on a scientific expedition to lay the foundations for a third engagement to the barrister Mr. Henderson. In all three cases she is led on not by the vulnerability of her heart, but by the satisfaction her ego derives from the sympathy, interest, and praise of the gentlemen in question. Because she does not care to love so much as to be loved or to deserve regard as much as to receive it, the constancy of her involvement cannot be depended on. Roger Hamley's departure means for Cynthia the absence of gratifying daily tributes of respect and love, a specific loss which makes her that much more vulnerable to the attentions of Mr. Henderson. She cannot really assess the meaningfulness of an engagement to others because her basic commitment is to her own self.

Such egocentricity would seem to suggest a close resemblance to her mother in whom vanity is such an essential motivation. Yet the precise appeal of Cynthia's character—largely transmitted through her own words—is her ability to reject or transcend all her mother's flimsy values; indeed she thereby often provides the most illuminating criticism of Mrs. Gibson's deficiencies in the book. Avoiding the temptation of again exploiting vanity for humorous purposes, Mrs. Gaskell shows us through Cynthia that self-involvement can have psychological manifestations very different from an almost preposterous selfishness, and, most unconventional step of all, that it is not incompatible with generous instincts, psychological discrimination, and the graces of humor and wit.

Thus we are made to feel, for instance, that Cynthia is not merely (as the author at one time describes her) "one of those natural coquettes, who, from their cradle to their grave, instinctively bring out all their prettiest airs and graces to stand well with any man" but an eminently social creature who responds to most social relations as esthetic rather than moral challenges, flashing out her personality in its most complex and varied guises just as a painter shadows forth his best conception in his subtlest hues not necessarily to achieve any other aim than inspired self-expression. So Cynthia, as the author herself says, "exerted herself just as much to charm the two Miss Brownings as she would have done to delight Osborne Hamley, or any other young heir. That is to say, she used no exertion, but simply followed her own nature, which was to attract every one of those she was thrown amongst."[75] Such a lack of discrimination suggests, moreover, Cynthia's freedom from those foolish social distinctions which influence Mrs. Gibson in her attempts to impress (*she* would not seek to please those inelegant Hollingford spinsters but reserve her favors for the aristocratic Cumnor family and whichever of the two brothers Osborne and Roger would most likely be heir to the Hamley Estate).

Other aspects of Cynthia's nature also testify to the complexity and contradictoriness of the human psyche. We discover that though Cynthia pays no tributes to conventional standards of virtue and truth, she can be fearlessly honest, or untruthful for the most virtuous motives; and though she rejects sentiment, she can show great sensitivity to the feelings of others. If the inconstancy of her behavior ("off with the old love, and on with the new"), the erratic nature of her conversation ("she literally said what came uppermost, without caring very much whether it was accurate or not"), the impulsiveness of her efforts to attract ("she used no exertion, but simply followed her own nature")[76] seem instinctive leanings, she is nevertheless highly conscious in recognizing such frivolous tendencies.

Indeed the saving grace in her character is the self-knowledge which contrasts so dramatically with her mother's self-delusion and largely accounts for the qualitative difference between these two imperfect beings. Her ability to assess and publish her own faults (her failures in truth, love, and duty) reminds us that, in contrast to her mother, she is immune to those vices which are the special province of the humorist: hypocrisy and vanity. It is not surprising, therefore, that she is less a butt than a creator of humor in the novel.

Even that insistence on her inability to change which inevitably accompanies her confessions of weakness is much more the reminder that she is unpretentious than the evidence that she lacks moral fiber (one recalls by contrast her mother's tendency not only to hide weaknesses but to claim a nonexistent virtue). So, even more than such assertions as "I never seem to care much for anyone," "I never consider myself bound to be truthful; so I beg we may be on equal terms," ". . . I've often told you I've not the gift of loving . . . I can respect, and I fancy I can admire, and I can like, but I never feel carried off my feet by love for anyone," her admission that amendment is impossible testifies to an honest confrontation of her failings: ". . . it's no use talking; I am not good, and I never shall be now. Perhaps I might be a heroine still, but I shall never be a good woman, I know."[77]

Undoubtedly because Cynthia has authentic reasons for bitterness (her complaints of a lonely, rejected childhood are shown to be just criticism, not indulgent self-pity), her ability to view herself and others through the saving media of humor, wit, and irony seems a particularly worthy enhancement of her intelligence and insight. Her lively instinct to counteract sentimentality often serves her to poke fun at herself: thus her admission that she is only "capable of a great jerk, an effort, and then a relaxation," rather than "steady, every-day goodness" culminates in an absurd image: "I must be a moral kangaroo!" And when she has led the silly Mr. Coxe on to a marriage proposal, her comic impatience with this importunate lover rings like a parody of that willful selfishness so offensive in her mother and to which she senses herself also prone:

". . . it's born in me to try to make every one I come near fond of me; but then they shouldn't carry it too far, for it becomes very troublesome if they do. I shall hate red-haired people for the rest of my life."[78]

In a more thoughtful vein, she is capable of the bitter witticism: "I could worry myself to death, if I once took to serious thinking."[79]

Though she is not beyond seriously reminding Mrs. Gibson that she is deceiving herself and others, it is, as we have said, through wit and irony that Cynthia most often holds up to the light the absurd and reprehensible aspects of her mother's behavior, revealing in the process a sensitive and discriminating social conscience. She impudently echoes her mother's standards in an attempt to save Molly from Mrs. Gibson's matrimonial schemes: "I'm afraid Molly isn't properly grateful, mamma. If I were you, I wouldn't exert myself to give a dinner-party on her account. Bestow all your kindnesses upon me." In the same vein she proposes new challenges to her mother's deviousness after Mrs. Gibson has manipulated Molly's visit to the Brownings by bluntly reminding her that she too had better be gotten "safely out of the way" of the visiting Lady Harriet. When Mrs. Gibson prevents Molly and Cynthia from attending a small card party at the Misses Browning with the argument that "the girls are not out yet," because they have not as yet attended the Hollingford ball, Cynthia's comment to Miss Browning shows her indeed "always ready with her mockery to exaggerate any pretension of her mother's":

"Till then we are invisible. . . . We are so high in rank that our sovereign must give us her sanction, before we can play a round-game at your house."[80]

Her own lack of pretensions is sometimes conveyed through humor, as instead of impressing Osborne Hamley with her accomplishments, she blithely announces: "I don't know longitude from latitude now; and I'm always puzzled as to which is perpendicular and which is horizontal";[81] if she takes pleasure in exaggerating her defects for humorous purposes (to her mother's unqualified dismay), her exculpation for such behavior is, however, logically above reproach:

"I'm either a dunce, or I am not. If I am, I did right to own it; if I am not, he's a dunce if he doesn't find out I was joking."[82]

No amount of analysis can do full justice to the subtlety of the characterization. As James pertinently says: "To describe Cynthia as she stands in Mrs. Gaskell's pages is impossible. The reader who cares to know her must trace her attentively out."[83] If we but add to her attributes that utter lack of self-consciousness of great beauty which grows out of a very conscious recognition of its existence and that physical grace which makes her seem to be "moving almost, as it were, to the continual sound of music,"[84] the extent to which the author has invested a fallible human being with qualities which a more conventional portrait would have denied her are at least suggested.

The creation of Mrs. Gibson and Cynthia is Mrs. Gaskell's greatest achievement in *Wives and Daughters*. Yet she transcends the scope of her study of provincial life in *Cranford* and "My Lady Ludlow" by lively and versatile portraits of the landed gentry at Hamley Hall and of some members of the aristocratic Cumnor family. Lord Cumnor, that bumbling, hospitable, "old woman" of a gentleman; Lord Hollingford, his unpretentious, reserved son far more interested in science than in carrying out his social duties as prospective heir; and Lady Harriet, his younger daughter, are conceived with some measure of originality, especially the latter. Lively, tough-minded, as she herself says "a little impertinent," astute and totally unpretentious, Lady Harriet is as alive to the failings of her own class as to the weaknesses of the Hollingford residents: with a blend of wit and seriousness, she reveals her unconventional standards of nobility in contrasting Molly with "those Hollingford people":

". . . most of them are so unnatural in their exaggerated respect and admiration when they come up to the Towers, and put on so much pretence by way of fine manners, that they only make themselves objects of ridicule. You at least are simple and truthful, and that's why I separate you in my own mind from them, and have talked unconsciously to you as I would—well! now, here's another piece of impertinence—as I would to my equal—in rank, I mean; for I don't set myself up in solid things as any better than my neighbours."[85]

Her humorous praise of the Misses Browning—she points out that "one gets enough respect from them at any rate"—gently pokes fun at the obsequiousness of Hollingford residents and at her family's pride in such a tribute.

The distinctions between a landed gentry of long pedigree but now precarious financial position and an aristocracy whose splendid wealth and large property compensate for a rather recent vintage are skillfully conveyed. And if the portrayal of boorishness, ill-temper, ignorance, and narrow-mindedness in a country gentleman makes Squire Hamley a somewhat traditional characterization (there are certain faint echoes of Squire Western in it), the co-existence of these attributes with great honesty, loyalty, and an almost childish tenderness lends distinction to it. The author also at once enlivens and softens the portrait through humor. That the Squire, despite his limitations, is not unperceptive is conveyed through comic means, as in speaking to Mr. Gibson, he accurately assesses Mrs. Gibson's nature with a diverting combination of circumlocution and bluntness: "Madam your wife and I didn't hit it off, the only time I ever saw her. I won't say she was silly: but I think one of us was silly, and it wasn't me." Humor also most aptly conveys that mixture of obstinacy and tenderness so characteristic of Squire Hamley, for it best captures the ludicrous and touching reactions arising from the collision of a narrow mind with a warm heart. Thus the Squire's obstinate chauvinism clashes with his paternal love and pride in the following dialogue (initiated by the Squire's complaint that he has had great trouble understanding a review of a scientific article by Roger):

"I should have understood it better, if they could have called the animals by their English names, and not put so much of their French jingo into it."

"But it was an answer to an article by a French writer," pleaded Roger.

"I'd ha' let him alone!" said the Squire earnestly. "We had to beat 'em, and we did it at Waterloo; but I'd not demean myself by answering any of their lies, if I was you. But I got through the review, for all their Latin and French—I did; and if you doubt me, you just look at the end of the great ledger, turn it upside down, and you'll find I've copied out all the fine words they said of you: 'careful observer,' 'strong nervous English,' 'rising philosopher.' "[86]

Mrs. Gaskell's humorous picture of the eccentric mores of the little Hollingford town is not as inventive as *Cranford*; indeed, as we have previously said, she tends to rely too heavily on earlier inspiration. Nor is her comic approach as coherent and sustained as in *Cranford*, for it is not as consistently loving and tolerant; she is not so invariably amused by the devotion which the small-town residents bestow on the aristocracy (Lady Harriet's comment suggests how undiscriminating and fulsome it can be) or by their own attempts to be adjudged genteel. In the author's remarks on the significance of the Hollingford Book Society, we miss the gentle whimsy characterizing her descriptions of the Cranford conspiracy to cultivate gentility at all odds:

> Everybody who pretended to gentility in the place belonged to it. It was a test of gentility, indeed, rather than of education or a love of literature. No shopkeeper would have thought of offering himself as a member, however great his general intelligence and love of reading; while it boasted on its list of subscribers most of the county-families in the neighbourhood, some of whom subscribed to it as a sort of duty belonging to their station, without often using their privilege of reading the books; while there were residents in the little town, such as Mrs. Goodenough, who privately thought reading a great waste of time, that might much better be employed in sewing and knitting, and pastry-making, but who nevertheless belonged to it as a mark of station, just as these good, motherly women would have thought it a terrible come-down in the world, if they had not had a pretty young servant-maid to fetch them home from the tea-parties at night.[87]

Yet, despite this qualitative change in attitude (only perceptible intermittently) and her reliance on previous humorous devices, the author can still at times both recapture the golden mood of *Cranford* and find new whimsical ways of suggesting the eccentricity of her insular Hollingford residents. Mrs. Goodenough demonstrates that lively good nature and that gossipy meddlesomeness which we associate with Miss Pole, and she shares with Mrs. Forrester a quaint resourcefulness and a fear of and contempt for "the country where Robespierre and Bonyparte was born."[88] And though the relationship of the Misses Browning too closely resembles that of the Jenkyns sisters not to make us realize by contrast how much richer and more imaginative the earlier conception was, it has some touching and comic dimensions of its own, such as the elder Miss Browning's eccentric assumption that her middle-aged sister is too innocent to be exposed to the sordid realities of existence. Even Miss Browning's consistent self-righteousness becomes appealing as a quaint mode of protecting her sister from disillusioning experiences; she admits some weaknesses to Molly in private, with the following reservation: "It's as well Phoebe shouldn't know, for she thinks me perfect: and, when there's only two of us, we get along better if one of us thinks the other can do no wrong." Her self-assertion disarms criticism by its absurdity. We cannot reproach her for denying her sister direct access to the miniature brooches which are their prized possessions after Miss Phoebe herself has explained with endearing naïveté the reasons for such high-handed behavior:

> ". . . because they are so valuable, Dorothy always keeps them locked up with the best silver, and hides the box somewhere; she never will tell me where, because, she says, I've such weak nerves, and that if a burglar, with a loaded pistol at my head, were to ask me where we kept our plate and jewels, I should be sure to tell him; and, she says, for her part, she would never think of revealing it under any circumstances. (I'm sure I hope she won't be tried.)"[89]

Through such whimsical touches the author does not merely echo the inspiration of *Cranford* in treating secondary characters in the Hollingford scene. In view of the much wider scope of *Wives and Daughters*, it is perhaps not surprising that she did not expend as much care as in *Cranford* on her little society of spinsters and widows. Indeed, she was best able to sustain that scope by focusing on the household of a man like Dr. Gibson, whose professional status gave him a foothold in the worlds of the town as well as of the landed gentry and aristocracy.

And it is of course the Gibson household that is the center of all the life that flows through *Wives and Daughters*, partly through the intelligence of Dr. Gibson and the wholesome frankness and good sense of Molly, but mainly through the sheer power of Mrs. Gibson's and Cynthia's assertive self-involvement.

Just as, through her portrayal of Miss Matty, Mrs. Gaskell

transcended the circumscribed world of *Cranford* to apprehend some of the endearing universal attributes that redeem human nature, so in her creation of Mrs. Gibson and Cynthia she not only depicted the complicated and often contradictory aspects of two frivolous natures but, through them, suggested the paradoxes of all human frailty. For the first time she boldly confronted in the intriguing Cynthia the possibility that moral laxity and moral discrimination were not mutually exclusive.

In her praise of Mrs. Gaskell's last work, George Sand may well have had in mind the portraits of Mrs. Gibson and Cynthia which Thomas Seccombe has termed the author's "two subtlest divinations of womankind."[90] If nothing else, they testify to her transcendence of a rigid, traditional conception of the nature of morality and the purpose of art. They suggest her acceptance of human complexities and of the need to do justice to these with the freedom from didacticism which is the index of the true artist. Humor was above all responsible for that acceptance, for it is to her humorous perception of reality that she owed her nearest approach to an emancipation from restrictive conventions. Humor's mild iconoclasm provided the freedom which in turn made her greatest artistry possible.

CHAPTER 4

The Commemorative Impulse: *The Life of Charlotte Bronte*

THE SINGLE best-known work of Mrs. Gaskell, along with *Mary Barton* and *Cranford,* is *The Life of Charlotte Brontë* (1857), and for two significant reasons. While Mrs. Gaskell's literary stature has perceptibly declined, Charlotte Brontë's has remained such as to sustain interest in the subject matter if not in the author of the biography. Moreover, whatever its limitations, the work has the permanent distinction of having been the very first to reveal the highly dramatic life of a novelist whose books had been extremely popular but about whose life and character little was known and much conjectured.

Though the biography may thus owe its status to somewhat extraneous factors, its general validity and artistic merit have not been seriously challenged by subsequent scholarly and critical studies of the Brontës.[1] That Mrs. Gaskell could largely do justice to her subject is not surprising in view of certain specific talents and her personal knowledge of Charlotte Brontë. In addition to her skill in observation and description, her insight into certain aspects of character and intuitive apprehension of certain states of mind, and her fascination with regional customs and traditions, she was deeply committed to the moral values exemplified by the life she was depicting and painfully aware of the problems facing a woman who pursued an artistic career in the middle of the nineteenth century.

And just as the positive aspects of the biography reflect Mrs. Gaskell's characteristic attributes, so many of its weaknesses confirm those limitations previously noted which grow out of her reluctance to challenge conventional propriety. As in evaluating *Ruth,* however, one must consider the attitude of the reading public before condemning her diffidence and recall how severely the few instances of recklessness in the biography were denounced to realize her difficulties in handling the subject.[2] Though hardly as controversial as that of *Ruth,* it imposed a far greater responsibility. For she was not only seeking to pay tribute to a friend recently deceased but had been expressly requested to write the work by the Reverend Patrick Brontë, Charlotte's father, through the intercession of Charlotte's husband (the Reverend Arthur Nicholls) and at the initial suggestion of Charlotte's best friend (Ellen Nussey), in order to counteract erroneous and discrediting rumors and speculations.[3] Such restrictive conditions would only reinforce Mrs. Gaskell's innate reluctance to hazard the kind of absolute frankness that might seem a breach of confidence. Thus, even more than in *Ruth,* a certain tact and evasiveness would seem essential in special deference to the dead author and to those still living who had been most closely associated with her.[4] It is unfortunate that Mr. Brontë's request inhibited a plan of her own which she had earlier confided to her publisher George Smith, revealing her extreme reluctance to offend Charlotte Brontë's family and her recognition that only a certain time span would guarantee a proper treatment of the subject:

> Sometimes, it may be years hence—but if I live long enough, and no one is living whom such a publication would hurt, I will publish what I know of her, and make the world (if I am but strong enough in expression) honour the woman as much as they admired the writer. . . .[5]

Under such freer conditions, she might have brought to her subject, if not the psychological awareness of later critics, that witty common sense and shrewd realism often evident in her private correspondence relating to the Brontë family.[6] Indeed that correspondence provides the best clue to her self-restraint as a biographer—in the emendations which she introduces when quoting her own letters and the polite modifications and omissions of opinions and information initially conveyed to friends with a vivacity, a bold informality, and a humorous sophistication no mere reader of the biography would suspect.[7] A reader unaware of the scandal relating to her treatment of Branwell, which marred the reception of the work and made several deletions in a later edition a legal necessity,[8] and ignorant of other accusations from many sources that the author had tactlessly failed to understate information or recklessly distorted it,[9] would most likely complain of the general formality and diffidence of her approach. If informed of the work's reception he would wonder, as in the case of *Ruth,* at the great change of values time has brought about. As Naomi Lewis so aptly says of Mrs. Gaskell's work (in her review of another Brontë biography) after paying tribute to her "enthusiasm and audacity," her "relentless eye," and her "*rapport*" with her subject:

> But biography, however individual and bold, is conditioned finally by the age in which it is written; and today it is not the indiscretions that make us pause but the slant, the emphases, the conscious silences.[10]

One might add to this enumeration the intermittent apologies which seek to justify the relevance of seemingly peripheral material, lest the hardly flattering portraits of some of the people whose lives had been connected with Charlotte's be condemned as unwarranted intrusions upon privacy.[11] Awkward as these appeals may seem, however, the knowledge that they largely went unheeded to a certain extent justifies their presence in the text.

Given such restrictive conditions, the extent to which Mrs. Gaskell managed to produce a many-sided portrait not only of Charlotte but of the whole Brontë family and those closely associated with their lives is quite impressive.[12] Her very diffidence, though it may soften the impact of her revelations, never really impairs their significance; she often succeeds in striking a precarious balance between tact and frankness in her pursuit of what she believes to be the truth. This fascinating combination of pliancy to convention and stubbornness in adhering to her convictions—expressed in polite circumlocutions which only imperfectly hide her determination to be fully honest—is perhaps best exemplified in her discussions of the Reverend Carus Wilson (the original of the tyrannical Mr. Brocklehurst in *Jane Eyre*) and of the Reverend Brontë. She tries to show sympathy for Mr. Wilson, whose reputation Charlotte gravely injured by her fictional portrayal of conditions at the Cowan Bridge School (conditions which Charlotte believed had killed two of her sisters and ruined her own health), but her commendation of him is, to say the least, ambiguous: "So great was the amount of good which Mr. Wilson did . . . that I cannot help feeling sorry that, in his old age and declining health, the errors, which he certainly committed, should have been brought up against him in a form which received such wonderful force from the touch of Miss Brontë's great genius." In the same vein, a cryptic characterization of Mr. Wilson concludes by compounding Charlotte's relentless portrait much as its initial effect seems intended to soften it: "He was an energetic man, sparing no labour for the accomplishment of his ends, and willing to sacrifice everything but power," while a later passage, apparently seeking to do justice to other aspects of Mr. Wilson's nature, only succeeds the more in vindicating Charlotte Brontë's insight into his character:

> She saw only one side, and that the unfavourable side of Mr. Wilson; but many of those who knew him, assure me of the wonderful fidelity with which his disagreeable qualities, his spiritual pride, his love of power, his ignorance of human nature and consequent want of tenderness are represented; while, at the same time, they regret that the delineation of these should have obliterated, as it were, nearly all that was noble and conscientious.[13]

One can hardly be surprised at the indignation of Mr. Wilson's family upon the publication of the book.[14] That Mrs. Gaskell was not merely displaying her loyalty to Charlotte but expressing her own moral judgment of Mr. Wilson's role in superintending the school seems evident in her reactions to criticism; she instituted corrections but apparently refused to acknowledge herself in error. Her personal antipathy for the failings she mentions—"spiritual pride," "love of power," and "want of tenderness"—well exemplified in her portrayal of Mr. Bradshaw in *Ruth*—would naturally predispose her against the claims of those to whom she wryly referred in a letter as "the Carus Wilson clique."[15]

It is perhaps a tribute to Patrick Brontë's generosity of spirit (if not the indication of a satisfaction in being thought *outré*) that he showed no real rancor at Mrs. Gaskell's descriptions of his own eccentricity (while others were outraged at their tactlessness), the more so since the evidence adduced by her (and based largely on a servant's gossip) may well have been mostly unfounded. Just as remarkable is Mrs. Gaskell's bold approach to this material when we remember that Charlotte's father had not only commissioned the work but encouraged her in it ("No quailing, Mrs. Gaskell, no turning back") and been extremely cooperative in providing her with material in the form of personal recollections, correspondence, and even the unpublished manuscript of *The Professor*.[16] Though her portrayal of Mr. Brontë greatly softens the private opinion of him previously expressed in her correspondence,[17] it seems at times, as in the case of Mr. Wilson, to be paying the merest lip service to the demands of tact. She is quite prepared to maintain politely that he "spared nothing that offended his antique simplicity" in order to blunt the effect of such stories as those of the destruction of his children's bright boots or the slashing of his wife's silk gown, but is obviously unwilling to leave out any of the details of such eccentric behavior. Indeed, she makes no attempt to account for other such instances of an erratic temper as the venting of his ill humor in shooting off pistols, burning a hearth-rug, or sawing off the legs of chairs, beyond suggesting that he was asserting that "strong, passionate, Irish nature" which "was, in general, compressed down with resolute stoicism. . . ."[18] After such startling revelations of his lack of self-control, her elaborate concluding remarks culminating in an apology for introducing this material can hardly counteract the impression already created. They exemplify, however, her ability to understate—when she so chose—and her awareness of the difficulty of justly assessing these very complex personalities:

> His opinions might be often both wild and erroneous, his principles of action eccentric and strange, his views of life partial, and almost misanthropical; but not one opinion that he held could be stirred or

modified by any worldly motive; he acted up to his principles of action; and, if any touch of misanthropy mingled with his view of mankind in general, his conduct to the individuals who came in personal contact with him did not agree with such view. It is true that he had strong and vehement prejudices, and was obstinate in maintaining them, and that he was not dramatic enough in his perceptions to see how miserable others might be in a life that to him was all-sufficient. But I do not pretend to be able to harmonize points of character, and account for them, and bring them all into one consistent and intelligible whole. The family with whom I have now to do shot their roots down deeper than I can penetrate. I cannot measure them, much less is it for me to judge them. I have named these instances of eccentricity in the father because I hold them to be necessary for a right understanding of the life of his daughter.[19]

Mrs. Gaskell was undoubtedly sincere in doubting her capacity to evaluate not only Charlotte Brontë but those whose lives were so intertwined with hers as to make the biography of one family member incomplete without a consideration of the others. Yet, whether directly or indirectly, she could not avoid the tendency to "measure" and "judge" in her biography. If she did not indeed plumb the depths of her subjects, she nevertheless stamped upon the work her moral evaluation of Charlotte Brontë and her family. We need only remember that her initial impulse had been to pay tribute to the private virtues of a public figure, to "make the world . . . honour the woman as much as they admired the writer," to realize that, to a certain extent, her material would be made subservient to her desire to present Charlotte's life to the world as a moral exemplum. For better or worse the aim of arousing public respect and admiration for a worthy existence animates the biography; it has been aptly said that "the merits and defects of Mrs. Gaskell's achievement spring from just this fact; the *Life* is a friend's tribute to a friend."[20]

Such an intention could, of course, easily work against a fully rounded portrait. While Mrs. Gaskell's commitment to those principles of dutifulness and self-sacrifice glorified by her own works and steadily practiced by Charlotte Brontë would enable her to do justice to these admirable virtues, it might well override any reservations about Charlotte's weaknesses. Nowhere does she receive the ambiguous treatment given to Mr. Carus Wilson, Mr. Brontë, or Emily or Branwell Brontë. By consistently praising Charlotte's courage, selflessness, piety, and abnegation (such commendation is indeed the *leitmotif* of the work), Mrs. Gaskell runs the danger of making her main character so unreal as to forfeit our allegiance to her virtues.

This eventuality happily does not materialize because that very dedication which inspired the biography, though somewhat inhibiting, did not impair her eagerness to provide as many clues to Charlotte Brontë's intellect and emotions as the latter's own words could provide. She herself points out her strong "conviction . . . that where Charlotte Brontë's own words could be used, no others ought to take their place."[21] Although she carries that "conviction" to extremes, forcing the task of interpretation upon the reader by the scantiness of her critical comments on Charlotte's correspondence, her choice of that correspondence does not spare evidence of Charlotte's paradoxical nature—pious and doubting, ambitious and timid, yearning and self-denying, sentimental and mordantly witty. So ably has she selected her source material for variety of interest and emotional impact that the immediate effect is that of a carefully planned dramatic unfolding of character which yields an ever increasing understanding of its intriguing diversity.

Thus, though it is Charlotte Brontë who most often performs the work of illumination, it is to Mrs. Gaskell's credit that she realized the potential power of Charlotte's words to reveal the many facets of her nature. Indeed, though Charlotte keeps much of her mystery, the power and richness of her expression often vivify the restrained and limited appraisals of her biographer. Thus two arresting confessions to a friend of the neurotic self-doubt and self-contempt which at times overwhelmed her suggest the peculiar quality of what Mrs. Gaskell rather vaguely terms a "despondency," a "nervous disturbance":

Don't deceive yourself by imagining I have a bit of real goodness about me. My darling, if I were like you, I should have my face Zion-ward, though prejudice and error might occasionally fling a mist over the glorious vision before—but I *am not like you.* If you knew my thoughts, the dreams that absorb me, and the fiery imagination that at times eats me up, and makes me feel society, as it is, wretchedly insipid, you would pity and I dare say despise me.

I have some qualities that make me very miserable, some feelings that you can have no participation in—that few, very few, people in the world can at all understand. I don't pride myself on these peculiarities. I strive to conceal and suppress them as much as I can; but they burst out sometime, and then those who see the explosion despise me, and I hate myself for days afterwards. . . .[22]

And her vision of herself as a married woman counteracts Mrs. Gaskell's almost exclusive emphasis on Charlotte's seriousness, sobriety, reticence, and self-effacement:

I could not sit all day long making a grave face before my husband. I would laugh, and satirize, and say whatever came into my head first. And if he were a clever man, and loved me, the whole world, weighed in the balance against his smallest wish, should be light as air.[23]

If Mrs. Gaskell then considered mainly those aspects of Charlotte Brontë's nature most congenial to her own or most easily intuited, she compensated for omissions by presenting a great variety of source material. From the very beginning of the project, in fact, she had been far more clearly aware than Mr. Brontë and Mr. Nicholls that she had to shed light on all aspects of her subject's character and interest, as an excerpt from her first letter to Charlotte's best friend, Ellen Nussey, makes evident:

I told Mr. Brontë how much I felt the difficulty of the task I had undertaken, yet how much I wished to do it well, and make his daughter's most unusual character (as taken separately from her genius) known to those who from their deep interest and admiration of her writings would naturally, if her life was to be written, expect to be informed as to the circumstances which made her what she was. Both he and Mr. Nicholls object to this; Mr. Brontë not perceiving the full extent of the great interest in her personal history felt by strangers, but desirous above all things that her life should be written, and written by me.[24]

Her thoroughness in exploring every facet of her subject is displayed in this very letter. Its purpose is not only to get access to whatever material Miss Nussey has in her possession (Mrs. Gaskell informs her of an impending letter from Mr. Nicholls to "ask if you would allow me to see as much of her correspondence with you as you might feel inclined to trust me with") but to request a meeting with her (". . . recalling since, how often she has spoken of you to me, I should like very much to make your personal acquaintance if you will allow me") and to announce her intention of visiting Miss Wooler—Charlotte's beloved schoolmistress—and the parents of another school-friend, Mary Taylor, who had emigrated to New Zealand.

That "remarkable conscientiousness"[25] in garnering every variety of information on her subject (also displayed by visiting all the places where Charlotte had been) guaranteed a richness and versatility in approach which, like her handling of Charlotte's own correspondence, to a certain extent compensated for lacunae. She may not have used all the letters at her command, but she at least presented such representative ones as would illuminate character and attitudes in the Brontë family. Excerpts from a letter written by Charlotte's mother when she was engaged to Patrick Brontë, a letter from Branwell Brontë to Wordsworth asking him to evaluate his literary promise on the strength of an excerpt from a poem, a letter of Anne Brontë thanking friends for an invitation—such documents clearly reveal some of the attributes of those most closely associated with Charlotte: the simplicity and modesty of Mrs. Brontë, the self-assurance and intellectual sophistication of Branwell, the sweetness, courage, and resignation of Anne.

Though Mrs. Gaskell intended to reveal her subject's "most unusual character (as taken separately from her genius)" she was wise enough to realize that such a distinction could not be maintained. She did not guess its full import, but at least saw the relevance of presenting excerpts from that "curious packet . . . containing an immense amount of manuscript, in an inconceivably small space; tales, dramas, poems, romances, written principally by Charlotte, in a hand which it is almost impossible to decipher without the aid of a magnifying glass," so as to do justice to the early imaginative life and literary cravings of the Brontë children. Even Charlotte's "list of painters whose works

I wish to see" and her youthful evaluations of certain art works provoke comments from Mrs. Gaskell indicative of her concern with "genius" as well as with "character":

> Here is this little girl, in a remote Yorkshire parsonage, who has probably never seen anything worthy the name of a painting in her life, studying the names and characteristics of the great old Italian and Flemish masters, whose works she longs to see sometime, in the dim future that lies before her! There is a paper remaining which contains minute studies of, and criticisms upon, the engravings in "Friendship's Offering for 1829;" showing how she had early formed those habits of close observation, and patient analysis of cause and effect, which served so well in after-life as handmaids to her genius.[26]

Her desire to do justice to the writer as well as to the woman leads her to present a small poem of Charlotte's ("The Wounded Stag") "as a specimen of the remarkable poetic talent shown in the various diminutive writings of this time"[27] and—a very felicitous choice—to include two of Charlotte's French exercises when she studied at Brussels. Aside from demonstrating the impressive growth of Charlotte's facility in the language, these significantly reflect her abiding commitment to courage, initiative, selflessness, faith, and dutifulness (exemplified here by her two subjects, Pierre l'Ermite and her childhood hero, Wellington) and even anticipate her characteristic style, as her passionate utterance breaks through the restraints of the Gallic tongue.

Mrs. Gaskell's preoccupation with Charlotte as the artist is in fact never really absent. Thus, she connects the exciting stories of former Luddite riots which Charlotte would undoubtedly have overheard at Miss Wooler's school in Roe Head with the composition of *Shirley*, and she suggests the possible influence on *Jane Eyre* of a scandal involving a second marriage (also at Roe Head). Of course, in conveying Charlotte's experiences at the schools in Cowan's Bridge, Roe Head, and Brussels, her thorough exploration of those institutions—their physical appearance, their living conditions, their particular routine, the nature of teachers and students, the impact of immediate surroundings and of the characteristic traditions associated with these—inevitably sheds light on many aspects of *Jane Eyre, Shirley*, and *Villette*. Charlotte's early yearnings for an artistic career are documented by her correspondence with Southey asking his advice on the appropriateness of such endeavors. While Southey's discouraging if kindly reply illumines the pervasiveness of certain assumptions concerning a woman's duties, Charlotte's humble acceptance of any advice suggesting the danger of shirking such duties adumbrates her future conscientiousness in never cultivating her art at the expense of household needs.

In later chapters, drawing from Charlotte's correspondence, Mrs. Gaskell never neglects to convey the literary persona through Charlotte's comments on her own work and critical evaluations of other writers. Independence of mind and spiritual dedication to art are appropriately revealed in two closely connected statements: "I must have my own way in the matter of writing" and ". . . it is for me a part of my religion to defend this gift, and to profit by its possession." The quality of Charlotte's literary tastes and critical acumen is displayed in her effective characterization of Ruskin ("He writes like a consecrated Priest of the Abstract and Ideal"), her shrewd assessment of Tennyson's *In Memoriam* ("It is beautiful; it is mournful; it is monotonous"), her temperamental blindness to the merits of Jane Austen's *Pride and Prejudice* ("An accurate, daguerreotyped portrait of a commonplace face; a carefully-fenced, highly cultivated garden, with neat borders and delicate flowers; but no glance of a bright, vivid physiognomy, no open country, no fresh air, no blue hill, no bonny beck.")[28]

If Mrs. Gaskell managed to provide insights into the life of the artist, she was far more attuned to portraying the human aspects of the Brontë story. The pathos, drama, and tragedy in the life of this ill-fated family were particularly calculated to impress this biographer's imagination. The destruction of promise grimly exemplified in the degeneration and death of Branwell, the inexorable fulfillment of Charlotte's anxieties as Emily and Anne successively perished with talents unfulfilled and recognition unwon, her own endurance of torturing solitude and self-abnegation, and her early death—all these tragic manifestations were very meaningful to Mrs. Gaskell who was herself, as we shall see, impelled to explore in her short stories harrowing instances of loneliness, physical suffering, mournful bereavement and hard-won resignation in settings which often enhance the state of mind of the tragic protagonists.

Consequently she excels in conveying the personal drama of circumscribed lives and tragic deaths which the Brontë offspring endured and in doing justice not only to the impact of their immediate environment (Haworth parsonage almost surrounded by its grim churchyard) but to the possible influence of the picturesque region which had become their home. With that flair for evoking the *ambiance* and traditions of certain sections of England through suggestive narration and description, she implies some correspondence between the wildness, individualism, "self-sufficiency," and personal reticence of the Yorkshire people and some of the attributes of the Brontë family who had settled among them. She even intimates the impact of Yorkshire folklore on the lively imagination of the Brontë children, through the medium of their faithful maid, Tabby:

> No doubt she had many a tale to tell of by-gone days of the country-side; old ways of living, former inhabitants, decayed gentry, who had melted away, and whose places knew them no more; family tragedies, and dark superstitious dooms. . . .[29]

The fact that such a description easily applies to Mrs. Gaskell's own efforts as a storyteller suggests her understanding of the effect of such themes on youthful imaginations. It is precisely the attributes, not of the social novelist or humorist, but of the writer of sensational short stories which enabled Mrs. Gaskell to intuit the state of mind of the hypersensitive and highly imaginative Brontë children whose father was "not naturally fond of children," who soon no longer had the steadying influence of a mother, who "knew no other children . . . knew no other modes of thought than what were suggested to them by fragments of clerical conversation which they overheard in the parlour, or the subjects of village and local interest which they heard discussed in the kitchen," and who instinctively shunned the presence of others, for "their walks were directed rather out towards the heathery moors . . . than towards the long descending village street."[30] This empathy with the kind of imaginative life induced by such circumstances attunes Mrs. Gaskell especially to the peculiar quality of Charlotte's early inventiveness. Herself undoubtedly aware of the negative effect of too exclusively relying on one's imagination, Mrs. Gaskell could draw a subtle distinction between two aspects of Charlotte's work which also applies to her own, especially as a short-story writer:

While her description of any real occurrence is, as we have seen, homely, graphic, and forcible, when she gives way to her powers of creation, her fancy and her language alike run riot, sometimes to the very borders of apparent delirium.[31]

Her concern in this case, not merely with the incipient artist but with the general state of mind of a susceptible child, is evident in a more elaborate passage which sensitively suggests the influence of particular circumstances in shaping children's temperaments:

Life in an isolated village, or a lonely country-house, presents many little occurrences which sink into the mind of childhood, there to be brooded over. No other event may have happened, or be likely to happen, for days, to push this aside, before it has assumed a vague and mysterious importance. Thus, children leading a secluded life are often thoughtful and dreamy: the impressions made upon them by the world without—the unusual sights of earth and sky—the accidental meetings with strange faces and figures—(rare occurrences in these out of the way places)—are sometimes magnified by them into things so deeply significant as to be almost supernatural.[32]

It is her understanding of this hypersensitivity in Charlotte which enables her later in the book to convey very dramatically the peculiar state of mind to which Charlotte sometimes yielded at a trying period of her life—after helplessly witnessing the death of a once-admired brother, who eventually sought escape in drink and drugs from his wasted life and self-destructive passion, and watching her two beloved sisters gradually succumb to consumption. Left only with anguishing memories of the time when "they were all in all to each other," Charlotte endured a solitude that even the greatest strength of will and persevering endurance could not assuage, especially during "the lonely night":

No one on earth can even imagine what those hours were to her. All the grim superstitions of the North had been implanted in her during her childhood by the servants, who believed in them. They recurred to her now,—with no shrinking from the spirits of the Dead, but with such an intense longing once more to stand face to face with the souls of her sisters, as no one but she could have felt. It seemed as if the very strength of her yearning should have compelled them to appear. On windy nights, cries, and sobs, and wailings seemed to go round the house, as of the dearly-beloved striving to force their way to her. Some one conversing with her once objected, in my presence, to that part of "Jane Eyre" in which she hears Rochester's voice crying out to her. . . . I do not know what incident was in Miss Brontë's recollection when she replied, in a low voice, drawing in her breath, "But it is a true thing; it really happened."[33]

If Mrs. Gaskell's own temperament enabled her to intuit the quality of those haunting obsessions which sometimes overcame Charlotte, her shrewdness in assessing character and her powers of sympathy, assisted by her personal knowledge of Charlotte's reactions and attitudes, led her to do justice to aspects of Charlotte's nature different from her own. Very early she is aware of that "absence of hope" in Charlotte which circumstances were so unfortunately to vindicate and of its connection with her characteristic diffidence in social relations—a timidity alien to Mrs. Gaskell's outgoing, eminently social tendencies:

I am not sure whether Mr. Brontë did not consider distrust of others as a part of that knowledge of human nature on which he piqued himself. His precepts to this effect, combined with Charlotte's lack of hope, made her always fearful of loving too much; of wearying the objects of her affection; and thus she was often trying to restrain her warm feelings, and was ever chary of that presence so invariably welcome to her true friends.[34]

Though Mrs. Gaskell herself could not gladly have foregone household duties and the constant supervision of her children despite the inroads made on time available for writing, she was fully able to understand Charlotte's strong objections to the curtailment of her imaginative life by the often menial duties of a governess, and her failure to find compensation in the challenge of taking care of children:

This description of uncertain, yet perpetual employment, subject to the exercise of another person's will at all hours of the day, was peculiarly trying to one whose life at home had been full of abundant leisure. *Idle* she never was in any place, but of the multitude of small talks, plans, duties, pleasures, &c., that make up most people's days, her home life was nearly destitute. This made it possible for her to go through long and deep histories of feeling and imagination, for which others, odd as it sounds, have rarely time. . . . Yet all exercise of her strongest and most characteristic faculties was now out of the question. . . . to Charlotte it was a perpetual attempt to force all her faculties into a direction for which the whole of her previous life had unfitted them. Moreover, the little Brontës had been brought up motherless; and from knowing nothing of the gaiety and the sportiveness of childhood—from never having experienced caresses or fond attentions themselves—they were ignorant of the very nature of infancy, or how to call out its engaging qualities.[35]

If she was not as fully committed to her artistic career as Charlotte, she could not but approve of the former's spiritual dedication to her talent, so clearly shown in her conviction that "it [was] . . . a part of [her] religion to defend this gift and to profit by its possession" in bringing "pleasure to others." Later, in her own moments of doubt about the appropriateness of her career, Mrs. Gaskell would find solace in very similar ideas; the following defense of Charlotte in the biography resembles opinions expressed in Mrs. Gaskell's correspondence:

. . . a woman's principal work in life is hardly left to her own choice; nor can she drop the domestic charges devolving on her as an individual, for the exercise of the most splendid talents that were ever bestowed. And yet she must not shrink from the extra responsibility implied by the very fact of her possessing such talents. She must not hide her gift in a napkin; it was meant for the use and service of others.[36]

As we have said, any judgment of Mrs. Gaskell's biography must take into account the restrictive circumstances in which it was produced; there is no reason to believe, however, that these were solely responsible for some of the limitations of the biography. Large as Mrs. Gaskell's powers of sympathy were, and shrewd as her intuitions of character often proved to be, she lacked that brilliant insight and psychological sophistication which would have enabled her, under fortuitous circumstances, to explore her subject in great depth. That her taste and artistic restraint were also not unimpeachable is best demonstrated by her melodramatic diatribes against the woman she accused of having seduced Branwell. Yet even the following sentence preparing us for tragic events in the Brontë family too clearly reveals such weaknesses: "But the dark cloud was hanging over that doomed household, and gathering blackness every hour."[37] Moreover, despite her larger conscientiousness, she lacked the scholar's care for detailed accuracy; with very unfortunate results, she relied on the gossip of servants and put too much trust in the opinions of such a personally involved informant as Charlotte. As Clement Shorter has demonstrated, she did not quote with accuracy and was not above combining excerpts from several letters.[38]

Yet all in all, she produced a most human, lively, and coherent portrait of the popular "authoress of *Jane Eyre*" whose private life had heretofore remained a mystery. Regardless of the ultimate appropriateness of her aim to write "so that every line should go to its great purpose of making *her* known & valued, as one who had gone through such a terrible life with a brave & faithful heart,"[39] the following reaction of the *Westminster* critic among others suggests that she had certainly achieved that aim:

> What we are! how we live! what we make of ourselves! Other things are of light importance by the sight of these.
>
> And thus it is that the story of a life bravely spent has an unequalled charm for us. It nerves our courage, and shames our cowardice, and while teaching us little which can be expressed in words, works upon us like an invigorating atmosphere. . . . little as Charlotte Brontë knew it, she was earning for herself a better title than many a St. Catherine, or St. Bridget, for a place among those noble ones whose virtues are carved out of rock, and will endure to the end.[40]

CHAPTER 5

Moral Purpose, Melodrama, Mystery, and Idyl

MRS. GASKELL'S minor contributions to periodical literature show her peculiarly well suited to the demands of popular journalism. Her narrative skill is displayed in a variety of tales (moral exempla, love stories, tales of violence, terror, and the supernatural) calculated to satisfy the public taste for inspiration as well as for mystery, adventure, and exoticism. Her proficiency in light descriptive and expository prose is equally evident in many short essays on subjects of unusual interest or particular quaintness whose very titles ("Disappearances," "The Shah's English Gardener," "An Accursed Race," "An Italian Institution") often suggest exciting matter for a general audience.[1]

Though the novelist several times challenged public opinion, the journalist was basically in tune with her audience. She might at times find it burdensome to produce occasional pieces under a deadline and to satisfy the taste of a particular editor,[2] but on the whole writing short stories and essays must have been not only a financially rewarding but also a gratifying experience. She could explore in a different medium the central moral concerns of her novels; better still, she could find an appropriate outlet for certain imaginative tendencies repressed in more ambitious works. As Miriam Allott puts it: "A love of Gothic sensationalism, hinted at in the plots of her novels, lets itself go in the ghosts and murders and robbers, the blood and the revenge which crowd these tales."[3]

The author's fascination with mysterious, terrible, unnatural phenomena was of long date. We are told that "even when a girl she had a love for the supernatural, and, like Charlotte Brontë, found her sphere among her school friends in telling ghost-stories."[4] Her earliest work, the description of Clopton House, includes the brief but harrowing tale of Charlotte Clopton who, inadvertently entombed alive, was eventually discovered "indeed dead, but not before, in the agonies of despair and hunger, she had bitten a piece from her white round shoulder! Of course, she had *walked* ever since."[5] This youthful penchant for sensationalism suggests that while its prevalence in her short stories perhaps reflects a yearning "to escape from the ordinary and banal, the dimness and monotony of Manchester middle-class life,"[6] it is above all the natural expression of an extremely susceptible imagination.

It might seem paradoxical that a writer who demonstrates maturity and seriousness in her social novels, and a subtle sense of proportion in her humorous works, could devote so much time and talent to stories of strange curses and ominous hauntings, of harrowing acts of violence and morbid mental sufferings. Yet such inclinations are not wholly out of tune with the emotionalism so often expressed in the social novels and with the flair for grotesquerie evident in her comic exploration of provincial life.[7]

I *Pervasive Social and Moral Concerns*

A. EARLY STORIES (1847–50)

The prominence of sensational elements in her stories and essays tempts one to dwell almost exclusively on these aspects. But such emphasis would not do justice to the permanence of certain social and moral preoccupations evident in her tendency to explore in many stories important questions more elaborately treated in her novels. These stories also testify to the persistent meaningfulness of certain characters and situations (indeed of certain settings, since Knutsford, Manchester, and the landscapes of Wales, Lancashire, and Yorkshire recur in them). Admittedly, they likewise suggest the narrow scope of her inspiration.

Mrs. Gaskell's concern with the "fallen woman" (Esther) in *Mary Barton* and her consciousness in that novel of the striking contrast between Manchester and the countryside are also elements of "Lizzie Leigh" (1850), a melodramatic story of the eventual redemption—through the tragic loss of her illegitimate child—of a country girl ruined in the big city. The author's faith in the basic charity of humble people, so evident in *Mary Barton*, is already asserted in her earliest published story, "Libbie Marsh's Three Eras" (1847), which depicts the care and sympathy extended by simple workmen's families to an invalid boy on a country outing. That sympathy for resignation which informs Mrs. Gaskell's judgment of John Barton is expressed—in simplified and didactic form—in this story as the homely Libbie Marsh stoically accepts her lot in life; knowing that she will never get married, she settles down to a life of constructive work, not being like some who "hanker after what is ne'er likely to be theirs, instead of facing it out."[8]

The author's admiration for those strivings to live by the Gospel which John Barton could not realize is expressed in "The Sexton's Hero" (1847), in which a man who has earned public contempt for refusing to fight an opponent demonstrates by heroically sacrificing his life that his expressed reluctance "to quarrel, and use violence" was not "cowardliness" but a total commitment to Christian teachings. After his death, those he has saved from "the rushing tide coming up the bay"—the girl he once loved and the man who had humiliated him and supplanted him in her affections—discover in the Bible which the drowned man has left behind "many a text in the Gospel, marked broad with his carpenter's pencil, which more than bore him out in his refusal to fight."[9]

"The Heart of John Middleton" (1850) also exemplifies the principles of Christian charity demonstrated in *Mary Barton* as Mr. Carson forgives the murderer of his son. In this melodramatic tale of obsessive hatred and desire for revenge, a man whose wife has been crippled by protecting him from the violence of a jealous rival, eagerly seizes the chance of a reprisal when the culprit years later (now an illegally returned convict) unknowingly seeks shelter at his house. Only the charitable, deeply pious influence of his dying wife and his little child prevents him from betraying his guest to the authorities and enables him to forgive. In the realization "that it is better to be sinned against than to sin," he experiences the relief of losing "the burning burden of a sinful, angry heart."[10]

Most of Mrs. Gaskell's early stories indeed anticipate or enhance the central teachings of *Mary Barton*, for the conflicts she portrays are inevitably solved by the triumph of an altruistic love over the selfish strivings, the violent hatreds and destructive jealousies which alienate human beings from each other. Whether the approach is somewhat farcical, as in the Dickensian "Christmas Storms and Sunshine" (1848), didactic and sentimental as in the little Sunday-school tracts "Bessy's Troubles at Home" (1849), and "Hand and Heart" (1852), or melodramatic as in "The Well of Pen-Morfa" (1850), the ultimate message is the same: only through total selflessness and charity can one overcome petty envy, fulfill duties, promote the welfare of others, and conquer hatred and bitterness.

The most interesting and elaborate treatment of self-sacrifice in the early tales is found in "The Moorland Cottage" (1850), a story that most probably influenced George Eliot's creation of Maggie Tulliver in *The Mill on the Floss*.[11] Like Maggie Tulliver, little Maggie Browne is a "grave, imaginative, and somewhat quaint" child who is denied the love she yearns for by a "selfish, vain, and impatient" brother (who, like Tom Tulliver, rebukes his sister for clumsiness, belittles her abilities, and orders her about) and by a mother who (like Mrs. Tulliver) is flighty, superficial, and overly concerned with material comforts. Maggie Browne's self-consciousness, impulsive generosity, and loyalty (Maggie Tulliver's very qualities) are respectively demonstrated as she reproaches herself for awkwardness, is eager to make her own enjoyments subservient to her brother's pleasure, and feels sad at his departure for school. Unlike Erminia (the niece of Mr. Buxton, the prosperous landholder, who is "a little tripping fairy, with long golden ringlets, and a complexion like a china rose," Maggie with "her hair . . . cut short all round, her shoes [that] were thick, and clumped as she walked," and her faded dress, is indeed "a little brown mouse,"[12] as Mr. Buxton's son

Frank tenderly calls her. The contrast initially established between the two girls closely resembles that between Maggie Tulliver and her little cousin Lucy Deane.

The story of nobility and self-sacrifice does not, unfortunately, live up to its promise; though she has conceived an unstereotyped character, Mrs. Gaskell fails to develop it with George Eliot's moral subtlety and psychological sophistication. The grown-up Maggie Browne who, like Maggie Tulliver, now has a "style of beauty" that "makes her positively distinguished" is not, like her namesake, impelled by strivings alien to a commonplace world; neither the anguish which love causes her nor the conflict between love and loyalty to her brother is rooted in significant psychological difficulties. Characterization becomes subservient to a melodramatic plot as Maggie's worthless brother, by stealing money from Mr. Buxton, threatens her engagement to the worthy Frank Buxton; only if Maggie breaks her engagement will Mr. Buxton let her brother escape the authorities. Caught in a characteristic conflict of loyalties, Maggie shows integrity and selflessness in refusing to cancel her commitment to Frank and in deciding to accompany the proscribed Edward to America for a year. A fire on the ship, Edward's drowning, Maggie's rescue by Frank, who has secretly followed her, Mr. Buxton's conversion to their union because of Maggie's sisterly devotion—these are the unsubtle rewards of self-sacrifice; here are none of the tragic repercussions on a finely attuned nature conveyed in *The Mill on the Floss*.

"The Moorland Cottage" would not warrant such detailed discussion if it did not also intriguingly anticipate characters, attitudes, and situations in Mrs. Gaskell's later works. Maggie's relationship to the Buxtons and that of Molly Gibson to the Hamley family in *Wives and Daughters* are remarkably similar: each girl wins the love and confidence of the frail, saintly lady of the household, and each arouses in the master a conflict between genuine fondness and fear of a misalliance for his son. That spirited temper of Mr. Buxton and his lack of social graces, that profound admiration for his wife which makes him experience "in his innermost soul a wonder how one so saint-like could ever have learnt to love such a boor as he was," that susceptibility to her influence after her death which leaves him "as one distracted"[13]—all these elements prefigure the characterization of Squire Hamley, just as Mrs. Buxton's beneficent influence qualitatively resembles that of Mrs. Hamley. The portrait of a selfish and willful son and brother who causes his family great anguish and severely tries their loyalty anticipates that of Jemima's brother in *Ruth* and that of the violently destructive Benjamin Huntroyd in "The Crooked Branch" (1859). The faithful servant Nancy is "a type which the author was afterwards to take a particular pleasure in elaborating,"[14] the first in a long line of servants, both male and female, to whose devotion, forthrightness, insight, and racy humor (the latter best exemplified in Sally of *Ruth*) Mrs. Gaskell paid ample tribute.

B. LATER STORIES (1853–63)

As we have seen, many of the early stories (1847–50) enhance the significance of *Mary Barton*, while the most elaborate, "The Moorland Cottage," anticipates certain elements in succeeding novels. Though later tales do not so often show a relationship between the inspiration of the storyteller and that of the novelist, a few reveal distinct traces of such conjunction. We recognize in "Morton Hall" (1853) some of the pathos and whimsy of *Cranford*, while its concern with the downfall of a great house victimized not only by political conflict but eventually by the triumph of commercialism reflects that fascination with a disappearing way of life evident in *Cranford* and "My Lady Ludlow." The author's respect for the skill and self-sufficiency of the Manchester businessman (so obvious in *North and South*) governs her portrait of the brusque but kind-hearted Mr. Openshaw in "The Manchester Marriage" (1859).[15]

The story which best documents the persistence of certain themes is "A Dark Night's Work," an elaborate tale published very late in her career (1863). The conflict of loyalties confronting Ellinor Wilkins when her father, in a fit of violence, accidentally kills his agent, directly resembles Mary Barton's plight (whether personal loyalty justifies untruth is of course the very problem faced by the Bensons in *Ruth*, by Margaret Hale in *North and South*, and, to a certain extent, as we shall see, by Philip Hepburn in *Sylvia's Lovers*.) In both *Mary Barton* and "A Dark Night's Work," an innocent man is suspected of the crime, while the crime itself is somewhat attenuated by circumstances. Indeed both the guilty fathers are basically honest and well-meaning people whose finer impulses of generosity and idealism have been perverted by embitterment. While John Barton suffers from the callous indifference of another social class, the lawyer Mr. Wilkins is victimized by a more devious form of social ostracism, the snobbery of county families whose refusal to accept him allows him no scope for exercising his intelligence, his cultivation, or his artistic leanings. Like John Barton, Mr. Wilkins errs in not accepting the limitations of his position (he is one of those who, unlike Libbie Marsh, "hanker after what is ne'er likely to be theirs"). The peace of mind and integrity of both men are further weakened by the loss of a beloved wife; while Barton succumbs to a false idea of duty, Mr. Wilkins, "dissatisfied with his position, neglected to fulfill the duties thereof," turning for escape to drink as Barton does to opium. Personal weaknesses and unfortuitous circumstances in both cases culminate in a destructive act—Mr. Wilkins striking down the man whose devastating efficiency is a tacit reproach to his own weakness.[16]

Ellinor, the faithful daughter, resembles not only Mary Barton but Margaret Hale in being devoted to a weak father and in protecting a member of her family who has committed an act of violence. The haunting mental suffering she endures after her complicity in hiding the crime (she and the servant help Mr. Wilkins to bury the corpse in the garden) and particularly when years later the crime is discovered and the servant convicted of it, is qualitatively very similar to Mary Barton's torment when she seeks to find an alibi for Jem or to Margaret Hale's temporary distraction after she has lied to protect her proscribed brother.

"A Dark Night's Work" exemplifies of course another variation on the theme of self-sacrifice, so significant in the early stories (and also the central conception of the moving "Half A Lifetime Ago" [1855] and "The Half-Brothers" [1859]). Both the heroine and the faithful servant forfeit their peace of mind in trying to protect the person who claims their love and loyalty even after his untimely death. Ellinor, moreover, also sacrifices personal happiness to her conscience by suggesting to the ambitious and promising young lawyer whom she deeply loves that an obstacle to their engagement would entitle him to cancel it, while the servant Dixon is prepared to face execution to prevent his dead master's disgrace from being discovered.

The inexorable principle that "truth will out," so dramatically exemplified in *Ruth*,[17] is also made a focal turning point in this plot (the crime is discovered when both Ellinor and Dixon are away from home, helpless to prevent the surveying of the property). Though marred by a facile denouement—favorable circumstances forestall (as in *Mary Barton*) the need for a public revelation of the killing—the story shows some subtlety of characterization. The brooding, unstable, embittered, "sensually self-indulgent" Mr. Wilkins, the prematurely grave, generous, sensitive, tormented Ellinor, the self-contained, ambitious suitor whose "intellect" is "superior in strength to either affections or passions," the simple servant "as loyal and true and kind as any nobleman"[18] are handled with some of the analytic care and psychological insight that we associate with such late works as "Cousin Phillis" and *Sylvia's Lovers*.

II *Pervasive Melodramatic Elements*

Though, as we shall soon see, obsessive guilt, madness, violence, and terror are central elements in the tales of robbery, murder, supernatural appearances, and strange curses, many of the sober moral stories we have just considered are not exempt from such sensational phenomena. These suggest not only the persistence of Mrs. Gaskell's fascination with certain morbid states but of her tendency to exploit them for thrills and suspense. Thus in "A Dark Night's Work" she depicts the emotional impact of guilt on Mr. Wilkins and his daughter with extravagant emphasis. On the day after the catastrophe Mr. Wilkins' "cheek was livid and worn, and its healthy colouring . . . was all gone into the wanness of age. . . . He stooped, and looked dreamily earthward where formerly he had stood erect." Ellinor herself, overwhelmed by the "horrible tangle of events" falls "in a stupor, which they feared might end in delirium." Though tempted "to creep into her grave," she lives to confront the daily nightmare of repressed truth, perpetually conscious of the secret in the flower garden, of the "fatal oblong she knew by heart."[19]

In other stories of self-sacrifice the author exploits more blatantly the manifestations of mental disturbance. In both "The Well of Pen-Morfa" and "Half A Lifetime Ago" the sacrifices of the two heroines (Nest Gwynn and Susan Dixon) are given melodramatic intensity by the fact that both devote themselves to caring for an insane person; their predicament is indeed suggested in very similar sensational terms. Though the demented woman to whom Nest has given a home—to atone for her former harshness to her own mother—is most often docile:

> . . . there were times when Mary was overpowered by the glooms and fancies of her poor disordered brain. Fearful times! No one knew how fearful. On those days Nest warned the little children who loved to come and play around her that they must not visit the house. . . . On those days the sorrowful and sick waited in vain for the sound of Nest's lame approach.[20]

In complete secrecy, Susan Dixon, who has sacrificed her chance of marriage to take care of her idiot brother, undergoes intense suffering as his idiocy culminates in madness:

> It is true that occasional passers-by on the lonely road heard sounds at night of knocking about of furniture, blows, and cries, as of some tearing demon within the solitary farmhouse; but these fits of violence usually occurred in the night; and, whatever had been their consequence, Susan had tidied and redded up all signs of aught unusual before the morning.[21]

Thus instances not only of guilt and madness but of violent passions and the ugly crimes they provoke are present in stories not merely intended as thrillers. Other striking dramatizations of evil are to be found in the first section of "Morton Hall" and especially in "The Crooked Branch." The situation of a son prepared to kill his parents in order to rob them is exploited for pathos and horror as the loving parents are ultimately forced to testify against their only child. Not until the last scene is the son's abominable behavior fully revealed, as the father explains what broke his wife's spirit during her struggle with unknown robbers:

"My Lord Judge, a woman bore ye, as I reckon; it's a cruel shame to serve a mother so. It wur my son, my only child, as called out for us t' open door, and who shouted out for to hold th' oud woman's throat if she did na stop her noise, when hoo'd fain ha' cried for her niece to help. And now yo've truth, and a' th' truth, and I'll leave yo' to th' judgment o' God for th' way yo've getten at it."[22]

If the preceding examples suggest Mrs. Gaskell's susceptibility to morbid states of mind or pathological behavior, the stories basically written for sensational effects fully display it. But even these do not indicate any personal unbalance in the writer. She has herself in *Cranford* convincingly shown that a craving for fearful excitement is not incompatible with the most touchingly simple and serene natures. Miss Matty, we recall, "did not like to be outdone" when the ladies regaled each other during the "panic" with "such horrid stories of robbery and murder that [Mary Smith tells us] I quite quaked in my shoes."[23] What is evident is that Mrs. Gaskell is not only satisfying popular taste, but personal inclinations as well. However different her temperament may have seemed from Charlotte Brontë's, she shared with her an acute sensitivity to certain mental states and the power to project them, a restless imaginative urge to fathom feelings and behavior which arouse both apprehension and revulsion, and finally an instinctive tendency to credit the possibility of supernatural phenomena.

III *Tales of Terror*

Two "horrid stories of robbery and murder" that would undoubtedly have won the approval of the Cranford ladies are "The Squire's Story" (1853), based on the career of a highwayman who actually once lived in Knutsford, and "The Grey Woman" (1861), a classic Gothic tale which for sheer sustained excitement and suspense has no peer among her stories. The first story treats only the latter part of the highwayman's career: his purchase of a house near Barford [Knutsford], his acceptance by society, his elopement with the rich squire's daughter, his secret pursuit of a criminal career until he is unmasked as the culprit in a ghastly murder at Bath. Yet this short tale has interesting aspects in common with the second story, which chronicles the terrible deeds of a secret band of robbers in France. In both cases the highwaymen succeed in wearing the mask of gentility long enough to entice a woman to marry them; much is made of the element of deception—the frightening incongruity between appearance and reality—while enough is initially said to cast suspicion on these outwardly personable young men. As Mr. Higgins in "The Squire's Story" first appears in Barford, his cruelty is immediately hinted at:

"The gentleman was tall, well-dressed, handsome; but there was a sinister cold look in his quick-glancing, light blue eye, which a keen observer might not have liked. There were no keen observers among the boys and ill-conditioned gaping girls. But they stood too near, inconveniently close; and the gentleman, lifting up his right hand, in which he carried a short riding-whip, dealt one or two sharp blows to the nearest, with a look of savage enjoyment on his face as they moved away, whimpering and crying."[24]

And when, in "The Grey Woman," the beautiful miller's daughter from Heidelberg meets M. de la Tourelle in Carlsruhe, there are, in his appearance and manners, subtle suggestions of depravity and hypocrisy:

I thought I had never seen any one so handsome or so elegant. . . . His features were as delicate as a girl's, and set off by two little "mouches," as we called patches in those days; one at the left corner of his mouth, the other prolonging as it were, the right eye. His dress was blue and silver. . . . he tried German, speaking it with a kind of soft lisp that I thought charming. But, before the end of the evening I became a little tired of the affected softness and effeminacy of his manners, and the exaggerated compliments he paid me, which had the effect of making all the company turn round and look at me.[25]

The peculiar nature of the horror in each tale is, however, quite different. In "The Squire's Story" it resides in our sudden insight into the fiendish rationalizations of a terror-stricken conscience as the highwayman, obsessed with his murder of an old lady at Bath, relates it to someone as a piece of news he has overheard:

"People said she was a good old woman; but, for all that, she hoarded and hoarded, and never gave to the poor. Mr. Davis, it is wicked not to give to the poor—wicked—wicked, is it not? . . . . The wicked old woman never gave, but hoarded her money, and saved, and saved. Some one heard of it; I say she threw temptation in his way, and God will punish her for it. . . . she was nodding over her Bible—and that, mark you! is a sin, and one that God will avenge sooner or later—and a step came, in the dusk, up the stair, and that person I told you of stood in the room. . . . the old miser defied him, and would not ask for mercy and give up her keys, even when he threatened her, but looked him in the face as if he had been a baby. Oh, God!, Mr. Davis, I once dreamt, when I was a little, innocent boy, that I should commit a crime like this, and I wakened up crying; and my mother comforted me—that is the reason I tremble so now—that and the cold, for it is very, very cold!"[26]

"The Grey Woman," on the other hand, derives its thrills from the plight of its innocent young heroine who, against her instincts, has been convinced to marry the elegant proprietor of a château in the Vosges (really the headquarters of the *Chauffeurs*, a band of robbers given to "roasting the feet of their victims" to elicit information from them). When she flees the sinister castle after discovering her husband's identity and the grisly murder he and his accomplices have just committed, she embarks on a harrowing journey (to make matters worse, she is pregnant) with her devoted French servant, knowing all the time that her husband, who has vowed to kill her if she should find him out, is in pursuit. In depicting the narrow, breath-taking escapes of the hapless lady and her faithful Amante from the pursuing *Chauffeurs*, the author shows her flair for sustaining and progressively increasing suspense and for suggesting its harrowing effects on its victims. The full meaning of the story's title only becomes apparent at the close of it when, in a most chilling way, the impact of the ordeal on the lady is revealed. Having found some peace in her remarriage to a kindly doctor, she informs us that:

. . . when the dye [used to disguise herself] had once passed away from my face, my husband did not wish me to renew it. There was no need; my yellow hair was gray, my complexion was ashen-coloured; no creature could have recognized the fresh-coloured, bright-haired young woman of eighteen months before. The few people whom I saw knew me only as Madame Voss; a widow much older than himself, whom Dr. Voss had secretly married. They called me the Grey Woman.[27]

Even her former husband, passing below her windows "saw me, an old grey woman, and he did not recognize me! Yet it was not three years since we had parted, and his eyes were keen and dreadful, like those of the lynx."

Although the girl's plight is Mrs. Gaskell's main subject, her treatment of the chief robber far more subtly suggests the perverse nature of evil than in "The Squire's Story." For the attributes of delicacy, refinement, "effeminacy," which characterize M. de la Tourelle at the beginning, are no mere hypocritical mask for a rough, fierce, and brutal nature. The man in whose rooms a "sweet perfume . . . hung in the air," who has "scent-bottles of silver that decked his toilet-table" is no standard highwayman but a corrupt esthete who indeed delights in exercising his intellect as he indulges in cruel jests about the murder he has just committed:

He repeated some mocking reply of double meaning, which he himself had given to some one who had made inquiry. He enjoyed the play upon words, softly applauding his own wit. And all the time, the poor helpless outstretched arms of the dead lay close to his dainty boot![28]

This sinister combination of preciousness and savagery is only one of the many means by which in her short stories the author succeeded so well in purveying thrills and terror to her readers.

IV Tales of the Supernatural

Considering Mrs. Gaskell's early aptitude as a teller of ghost stories, it is surprising that she only produced one complete tale in that genre. "The Old Nurse's Story" (1852) is, however, acknowledged to be one of her finest efforts at creating mystery, suspense, and terror. It derives much of its effectiveness from its very conciseness and simplicity (it is being told to children) and from having a narrator whose basic common sense gives authenticity to the disquieting events in the old Furnivall Manor House near the Cumberland Fells where she has come to live with her little charge, the niece of Miss Furnivall. Like all successful stories of this kind, the tale is one of gradual discovery and initiation into strange mysteries; it achieves its impact through the sheer accretion of eerie circumstances and events. The forbidding "large, and vast, and grand" Hall whose east wing is never opened; the very aged "hard, sad" aunt and her "so cold, and grey, and stony" companion; the youthful portraits of Miss Furnivall and her older sister disclosing "scornful pride" as well as "beauty"—these disquieting aspects of a new life are but a prelude to the phenomenon of strange music heard "as winter drew on." Not only is the sound attributed by the servants to "the old lord playing on the great organ in the hall, just as he used to do when he was alive," but the organ itself proves, upon the nurse's inspection, to be "all broken and destroyed inside, though it looked so brave and fine."[29]

These ominous signs are tame, however, by comparison with the strange spell soon cast on little Rosamond, drawing her to follow a little girl (who leaves no footsteps in the snow) to the Fells, where a shepherd later chances to find her almost dead from exposure. That her claim of seeing the child and then meeting "a lady weeping and crying" who soon "smiled very proud and grand . . . and began to lull me to sleep" may be authentic is first suggested by Miss Furnivall's distraction upon hearing of it. It is made fully believable when the skeptical nurse herself sees the child, "dressed all unfit to be out-of-doors such a bitter night—crying, and beating against the window panes, as if she wanted to be let in," "beating and battering to get in, yet always without any sound or noise—with the dark wound on its right shoulder."[30]

As the nurse, through the agency of a fellow servant, is led into the secrets of the violent passions which have long since climaxed in tragedy—the fierce cruelty of Lord Furnivall, the implacable jealousy of his two daughters who, unknown to him, both loved the humble music master who had taught him to play the organ—the stage is set for the crowning conclusion to this tale of terror. It is a re-enactment of the tragic scene of former years when, after the envious Miss Furnivall had revealed her older sister's marriage to the music master and identified the offspring, the irate father had cast daughter and child out to die in the snow, having first inflicted with his crutch that "dark wound" still to be seen on the child. From the beginning of the final scene, as Miss Furnivall exclaims: "I hear voices! . . . I hear terrible screams—I hear my father's voice!" and Rosamond begs not to be restrained from joining the little girl ("I hear her; she is coming! Hester, I must go!") to the first climax when "a tall old man, with grey hair and gleaming eyes" who "drove before him, with many a relentless gesture of abhorrence, a stern and beautiful woman, with a little child clinging to her dress," issues "with a thundering crash" from the mysterious "east door," the atmosphere of terror is skillfully sustained. The impact of another world on the present is suggested by the hypnotic effect which her wretched, fierce ancestors exercise on the innocent descendant of the house: "she [Rosamond] was almost convulsed by her efforts to get away; but I held her tighter and tighter till I feared I should do her a hurt; but rather that than let her go towards those terrible phantoms." The tale of terror is then transformed into an eerie drama of conscience. As her father is about to reenact his violent blow, Miss Furnivall begs too late for the mercy she had once refused to show. The vanity of her repentance is revealed as she is confronted by "another phantom shape," her own "likeness . . . in her youth," full of "relentless hate and triumphant scorn":

> . . . and the terrible phantoms moved on, regardless of old Miss Furnivall's wild entreaty,—and the uplifted crutch fell on the right shoulder of the little child, and the younger sister looked on, stony, and deadly serene. But at that moment, the dim lights, and the fire that gave no heat, went out of themselves, and Miss Furnivall lay at our feet stricken down by the palsy—death-stricken.
>
> Yes! she was carried to her bed that night never to rise again. She lay with her face to the wall, muttering low, but muttering always: "Alas! alas! what is done in youth can never be undone in age! What is done in youth can never be undone in age!"[31]

While the impact of "The Old Nurse's Tale" is predicated on a complete acceptance of supernatural realities, a progressive ambivalence marks Mrs. Gaskell's treatment of the supernatural as she explores the repercussions of a curse in three stories: "The Poor Clare" (1856), "The Doom of the Griffiths" (1858), and "Lois the Witch" (1859). In "The Poor Clare" she already makes the magic elements subservient to a moral purpose and even provides a religious interpretation for supernatural manifestations. In the next two stories she handles such phenomena with progressive skepticism, though she is not wholly committed to a rationalist viewpoint. Indeed "The Doom of the Griffiths," and especially "Lois the Witch" (which deals with the Salem Witch Trials) intriguingly reflect the conflict between Mrs. Gaskell's imagination and her reason, in this case between her emotional identification with supernatural phenomena and her rational attempt to account for unusual phenomena in moral and psychological terms (particularly out of the humanitarian impulse to combat superstition). The tension between these two tendencies mars the coherence of both stories even as it shows a much more sophisticated handling of her material.

Because of certain basic similarities, the first two stories—"The Poor Clare" and "The Doom of the Griffiths"—can appropriately be considered together in assessing that progressive stress on moral and psychological rather than merely sensational aspects. Not that sensational elements are lacking, of course. The very settings are ominous, both landscapes (Northeast Lancashire and Wales) being appropriately gloomy and wild, with, in both cases, "ghastly" looking trees. Dreadful curses are pronounced as punishments for misdeeds: in "The Poor Clare" the fiery Bridget Fitzgerald dooms Squire Gisborne who has carelessly killed her little dog (the only possession of her beloved daughter who had left home against the mother's will) "to see the creature you love best, and who alone loves you—ay, a human creature, but as innocent and fond as my poor, dead darling— . . . become a terror and a loathing to all, for this blood's sake."[32] And the great Owen Glendower in "The Doom of the Griffiths" pronounces a curse upon the former friend who plotted his death that is all-encompassing in its destructiveness: not only will all his family "except the weakling in arms," come to "perish by the sword," but his "race shall be accursed":

Each generation shall see their land melt away like snow. . . . And when nine generations have passed from the face of the earth, thy blood shall no longer flow in the veins of any human being. In these days the last male of thy race shall avenge me. The son shall slay the father.[33]

In both cases the impact of the curse is as fearful as its threat and takes the form of painfully alienating a parent and child. The import of Bridget's curse is revealed in "The Poor Clare" by the appearance of a *Doppelgänger*, a climactic experience described here by the innocent victim Lucy Gisborne to the narrator (a young lawyer who has befriended her in exile):

"In the great mirror opposite I saw myself, and right behind, another wicked, fearful self, so like me that my soul seemed to quiver within me, as though not knowing to which similitude of body it belonged. My father saw my Double at the same moment, either in its dreadful reality, whatever that might be, or in the scarcely less terrible reflection in the mirror. . . . I was in my bed for days; and even while I lay there my Double was seen by all, flitting about the house and gardens, always about some mischievous or detestable work. What wonder that every one shrank from me in dread—that my father drove me forth at length, when the disgrace of which I was the cause was past his patience to bear."[34]

And in "The Doom of the Griffiths," while the curse is as yet unfulfilled, the knowledge of the fate which hangs upon them perpetually casts a shadow over the loving relationship between the two last representatives of the Griffiths family—Squire Griffiths and his little son Owen:

. . . Squire Griffiths told the legend, in a half-jesting manner, to his little son, when they were roaming over the wild heaths in the autumn days . . . or while they sat in the oak-wainscoted room, surrounded by mysterious relics that gleamed strangely forth by the flickering fire-light. The legend was wrought into the boy's mind, and he would crave, yet tremble, to hear it told over and over again, while the words were intermingled with caresses and questions as to his love. Occasionally his loving words and actions were cut short by his father's light yet bitter speech—"Get thee away, my lad; thou knowest not what is to come of all this love."[35]

The passages just quoted sufficiently demonstrate the sensational nature of the stories. Though qualitatively different (one depicts the manifestation of supernatural power; the other suggests the morbid feelings induced by a fear of its imminent assertion), both embody thrilling elements of terror, suspense, and mystery. A more serious purpose becomes evident in "The Poor Clare" when the emphasis falls not on the peculiar horror of the *Doppelgänger* phenomenon but on the great sinfulness of the curse itself. It is soon made clear that Bridget Fitzgerald's pronouncement of doom, for whose execution she has prayed to the saints, is a sacrilegious act, a religious transgression which entails retribution even in its fulfillment. She discovers that she has unknowingly pronounced a curse on her own grandchild (the offspring of that beloved daughter never heard of again), on "bone of my bone! flesh of my flesh!" As the Catholic priest, from whom she has sought help in atoning for her sin, explains to the narrator, "prayers" and "masses" cannot suffice either for her own absolution or the lifting of the curse:

"Her words of passion, and cries for revenge—her unholy prayers could never reach the ears of the holy saints! Other powers intercepted them, and wrought so that the curses thrown up to heaven have fallen on her own flesh and blood, and so, through her very strength of love, have bruised and crushed her heart. Henceforward her former self must be buried,—yea, buried quick if need be,—but never more to make sign, or utter cry on earth! She has become a Poor Clare, in order that, by perpetual penitence and constant service of others, she may at length so act as to obtain final absolution and rest for her soul."[36]

Like Nest Gwynn of "The Well of Pen-Morfa," Bridget finally finds redemption in a striking act of self-sacrifice, as in a time of war and famine in Antwerp, she saves her former enemy, Squire Gisborne, from death on the battlefield, and starves to death to preserve him from hunger. Her last words attest to the salvation she has gained: " 'She [Lucy] is freed from the curse!' said she, as she fell back dead."[37]

Though Glendower's curse in "The Doom of the Griffiths" is eventually realized, the author eschews a facile dramatic effect by emphasizing the psychological aspects of the somber tragedy.

As we have seen she does not stress the curse itself so much as the morbid fears it inspires, promoting the estrangement between a father and child which will precipitate the tragedy. The mutual rejections which punctuate their relationships are shown to have plausible emotional roots. When the marriage of his older sister leaves the home comfortless, young Owen's eagerness to return to school after the holidays is evident to "the mortified parent," while the abrupt announcement of his father's remarriage makes the young man feel outcast from a once loving relationship. Owen's loneliness after his stepmother has supplanted him in his father's affections only feeds his impassioned nature, making him "moody and soured; brooding over his unloved existence, and craving with a human heart after sympathy." At that stage the psychological effect of the curse on his nature grows, appropriately enough, in intensity; he is shown to dwell on the story of Oedipus "with the craving disease," for "with his consciousness of neglect, there was a sort of self-flattery in the consequence which the legend gave him."[38] He triumphs for a while over morbidity through a happy marriage and the birth of a child, but his father's destructiveness (he indirectly causes the child's death) awakens Owen's latent capacity for anger and violence.

The very fact that the final killing of father by son, in fulfillment of the curse, is accidental (the father actually attacks the son and in the ensuing struggle, falls into the water, fatally hitting his head against the side of a boat, before the son can save him) also shows Mrs. Gaskell's tendency to mute the supernatural element. Indeed she continues to probe the psychological effect of a consciousness of doom on the last scion of the Griffiths. She suggests that it is not actually Glendower's curse which paralyzes Owen with despair and distraction after the catastrophe but his own diseased conviction of its present efficacy and future power to destroy him. When the boat in which he had temporarily left his father's body is discovered to have "broken loose and disappeared," young Owen's will to live is finally shattered because he feels that his father "has revolted even in death" at his plan to promote "a certain reconciliation, so to say, by laying his father and his child both in one grave." That such a feeling is merely the product of a morbid state of mind is clearly suggested by the author: "This last event [the boat's unmooring], so simple and natural in itself, struck on his excited and superstitious mind in an extraordinary manner."[39]

Yet Mrs. Gaskell's attempt to explore the psychological rather than the supernatural aspects of her tragedy is never fully sustained. The sinister behavior of the wicked stepmother, the fiendish cruelty of her impish child, the grotesque violence of Squire Griffiths himself (who throws Owen's child with such "ungovernable rage" at the mother that it hits "the sharp edge of the dresser" and drops "on to the stone floor")—such extravagant elements are reminiscent of the more simple horror tales previously discussed. The following melodramatic announcement also strangely contrasts with the author's generally sophisticated approach to her theme: "But the curse was at work! The fulfilment of the prophecy was nigh at hand!" And after Owen, his wife and her father sail off to Liverpool, despite a mention of the realistic dangers of "stormy waters" which the older man must face alone since his son-in-law is distracted with guilt, the tale concludes in the ominous tones characteristic of horror stories that assert the triumph of supernatural forces:

> They sailed into the tossing darkness, and were never more seen of men.
>
> The house of Bodowen has sunk into damp, dark ruin; and a Saxon stranger holds the lands of the Griffiths.[40]

In "Lois the Witch," one of Mrs. Gaskell's most ambitious short stories, she earnestly sought to point up the devastating consequences of prejudice and mass hysteria on the lives of innocent people. Her painstaking efforts to achieve historical authenticity suggest the seriousness of her purpose; she not only based part of her story on the actual events in colonial Salem (as some resemblances in characters and situations show) but chose to quote part of Cotton Mather's speech at the trials and to include the final deposition of the Salem jury which twenty years later exonerated the victims of their persecution.[41]

In highly dramatic terms, she depicts the triumph of fear, malice, and irrationality over innocence and virtue as a young English orphan, Lois Barclay, who has come to reside with her uncle in Salem just before the witch-hunting, is victimized during the panic by the hysterical accusations of her "impish" young cousin Prudence Hickson, and is condemned and hung as a witch.

Mrs. Gaskell's intention of treating such a story in realistic terms is evident as she appraises the environmental and cultural factors which conspired to produce mass hysteria in Salem at that time, and suggests the psychological reasons for the enmity of the Hickson family against Lois once her uncle's death leaves her unprotected. In a strikingly evocative passage, the author indicates the significant influence of external "circumstances" in provoking the panic which for a while overtook the little community:

> Salem was, as it were, snowed up, and left to prey upon itself. The long, dark evenings; the dimly-lighted rooms; the creaking passages, where heterogeneous articles were piled away . . . and where occasionally, in the dead of night, a sound was heard, as of some heavy falling body, when, next morning, everything appeared to be in its right place (so accustomed are we to measure noises by comparison with themselves, and not with the absolute stillness of the night-season); the white mist, coming nearer and nearer to the windows every evening in strange shapes, like phantoms—all these, and many other circumstances: such as the distant fall of mighty trees in the mysterious forests girdling them round; the faint whoop and cry of some Indian seeking his camp, and unwittingly nearer the white men's settlement than either he or they would have liked . . . the hungry yells of the wild beasts approaching the cattle pens—these were the things which made that winter life in Salem, in the memorable time of 1691–2, seem strange, and haunted, and terrific to many. . . .[42]

And that such unfortuitous circumstances, in themselves capable of arousing fears and inducing delusions, were operating on already highly susceptible minds is emphasized in the author's comment on "the wild stories . . . of the wizards of her race" related by the Hicksons' Indian servant Nattee:

> We can afford to smile at them now; but our English ancestors entertained superstitions of much the same character at the same period, and with less excuse, as the circumstances surrounding them were better known, and consequently more explicable by common sense, than the real mysteries of the deep, untrodden forests of New Eng-

land. The greatest divines not only believed stories similar to that of the double-headed serpent, and other tales of witchcraft, but they made such narrations the subjects of preaching and prayer; and, as cowardice makes us all cruel, men who were blameless in many of the relations of life, and even praiseworthy in some, became, from superstition, cruel persecutors about this time, showing no mercy towards any one whom they believed to be in league with the Evil One.[43]

The Hickson family's allegiance to supernatural convictions during the panic is carefully viewed in psychological terms. Mrs. Hickson's superstition is not only the effect of hysterical delusions but the outgrowth of bigotry, selfishness, and distorted motherly love. She has always been antagonized by Lois' Anglican upbringing and has tolerated her only because of the soothing influence she could exercise over her mentally unbalanced son. To protect that son, she now allows the community of Salem, and even herself, to believe that Manasseh's mad ravings in defense of Lois at the trial are but another example of her bewitching influence on others. As for her daughters, mental instability inflates their petty strivings to irrational proportions: "if Lois had been a physician of modern times, she might have traced somewhat of the same temperament in his [Manasseh's] sisters as well —in Prudence's lack of natural feeling and impish delight in mischief, in Faith's vehemence of unrequited love." Both girls conspire to the destruction of Lois, the oldest daughter Faith out of jealousy (she thinks Lois her rival with regard to Pastor Nolan) and the younger, Prudence, through a pathological desire for attention. She, who eventually accuses Lois of being a witch, has been greatly impressed with the attention that the "grave ministers" as well as "many folk come from a distance" have paid to the hysterical children of Pastor Tappau, and muses aloud: "I wonder how long I might wriggle, before great and godly folk would take so much notice of me?"[44]

If such a realistic approach reflects the liberality of mind and commonsensical insight into some of the worst weaknesses of mankind already demonstrated by the author in her essay "An Accursed Race,"[45] the fact that she does not sustain such an approach suggests an incapacity to master her susceptibility to irrational feelings. Gerald Sanders' cryptic statement that "Mrs. Gaskell mars the story in places by linking the actual with the supernatural, a procedure in which she falls far short of the skill of Hawthorne,"[46] though quite accurately diagnosing the effect of such "linking," implies a consciousness of purpose, an artistic control over her material which the story simply does not bear out. Indeed no qualitative similarity between her intentions and Hawthorne's is apparent: the supernatural elements she introduces lack that symbolic force and provocative irony which give *The Scarlet Letter*, for instance, such subtle psychological dimensions.

And consequently, these supernatural elements vitiate the moral impact of her story, as the author seems to be paying allegiance to the very susceptibilities whose destructive effect she seeks to denounce. Her portrayal of Lois' tragic fate resulting from unfavorable social circumstances and inimical human influences is undercut by her suggestion that this fate is but the inexorable working out of a curse. Early in the tale, we discover that, as a child, Lois had been doomed by an old woman whom the townspeople attacked for witchcraft to endure a fate similar to her own: "Parson's wench, parson's wench, yonder, in thy nurse's arms, thy dad hath never tried for to save me; and none shall save thee, when thou art brought up for a witch."[47] Precisely those circumstances of being helpless, alone, alienated from all who might intercede of course characterize Lois' final predicament. Moreover, her ultimate fate is not only foreordained by the curse of some one suspected of supernatural powers (the very accuracy of the old woman's predictions unfortunately suggests that such suspicions were well-founded!) but also prophesied by the mad Manasseh who insists in his ravings that, should Lois refuse to be his wife, she is destined to "a violent death" which he has envisioned in a state "between sleeping and waking."

Such an implied threat might bear a natural interpretation if Manasseh, upon Lois' refusal, had plotted her death; however, the madman is the only one who pleads for her at the trial, though his ravings unfortunately confirm the audience's conviction that Lois has bewitched him. Taken together, the curse and the prophecy—those familiar elements of Mrs. Gaskell's earlier tales of horror—undermine the coherence of a most dramatic and incisive tale of the terrifying repercussions of man's irrationality. Once again, as in her handling of the social novels, what seems to be an unresolved conflict between contradictory tendencies in the author's nature deeply affects the quality of her artistic expression.

V *The Pastoral Romance*

It is not surprising that Mrs. Gaskell's art is most effective in "Cousin Phillis" (1863–64), which explores neither social and moral problems nor violent passions and supernatural terrors. The subject of a simple and tender love in an idyllic rural setting called upon powers over which the author had the greatest control: her ability to describe nature feelingly, her skill in recording with sympathy and imagination the homely details of simple but dedicated lives, and her insight into the basic emotions and secret yearnings fostered by a circumscribed existence.

Two short works which precede "Cousin Phillis" had particularly demonstrated her empathy with the beauty of nature and the appeal of a rustic life. The little essay "Cumberland Sheep-Shearers" (1853), which relates the expedition of a couple and their children—undoubtedly the Gaskell family—to witness the annual shearing of the herds, lovingly reflects a whole mode of life in its description of farm and yard and of the various steps in the "sort of rural Olympics" that sheep-shearing is. Even the element of a simple romance between two young participants is not missing from the spectacle in which the narrator (obviously the author) finds indeed "all the classical elements for the representation of life."[48] Though set in a very different landscape, her romantic little story, "Six Weeks at Heppenheim" (1862) also pays tribute to the beauty and simplicity of country life; another bucolic festival—the gathering of grapes—presents a pleasing picture of human endeavors carried out in harmonious surroundings.

Like Paul Manning in "Cousin Phillis" (and somewhat like the narrator in "Cumberland Sheep-Shearers") the narrator of "Six Weeks at Heppenheim," a young Englishman stranded by a severe illness in a little German village, becomes the sympathetic witness of the romantic difficulties of a young woman. If the servant girl Thekla does not bear much physical resemblance to the lovely, blooming Phillis, she shares her capacity for love and loyalty and that sensitivity and reticence which cause her deep humiliation in a predicament much resembling that of Phillis. As she tells the narrator in confidence:

"My shame and my reproach is this: I have loved a man who has not loved me . . . and I can't make out whether he ever did, or whether he did once and is changed now; if only he did once love me, I could forgive myself."[49]

Yet, when the beloved childhood friend returns to woo her for interested motives (he is penniless) and alienates her by his boorishness, she now almost feels obliged to marry him out of a mistaken but admirable sense of loyalty, until the narrator convinces her of the moral flaw in such a self-sacrificing negation of her own feelings. Thekla cannot even bring herself to accept the widowed innkeeper's proposal of marriage although she cares for him, for would she not be thought a fickle woman, "having loved one man ever since I was a little child until a fortnight ago, and now just as ready to love another?" Eventually however, these two good people are brought together by caring for the innkeeper's sick child. Thekla succeeds in vanquishing her scruples and in her well-deserved happiness can declare "half-laughing": "I am a foolish woman, for I have promised to marry him. But he is still a more foolish man, for he wishes to marry me."[50] Their wedding provides a perfect ending to the narrator's stay in the idyllic village of Heppenheim.

That no such facile conclusion can be found to erase the anguish of unrequited love in "Cousin Phillis" marks the qualitative difference in depth and subtlety between the two stories. For Phillis' disappointment in love is not merely the emotional upheaval of a vulnerable young girl; the subjection of her hopeful innocence to the hardships of experience evokes that larger romantic disillusionment with existing realities characteristic of the entrance into maturity. The author has judiciously avoided a hectic atmosphere, melodramatic actions, and fierce passions in this story. It owes its subtle appeal to its simple plot, its graceful and lyrical descriptions, its understated characterizations, its restrained emotions; indeed the harmonious blending of all these elements and their skillful subjugation to the central theme give "Cousin Phillis" an artistic coherence none of her other stories could achieve.

Through the narrator, Phillis' cousin, who is both participant and witness of the romantic interlude which deeply affects an ardent but very sheltered girl, Mrs. Gaskell maintains a certain esthetic distance. Moreover, events and reactions are rarely analyzed for us by the unintrospective Paul Manning; it is the sheer accretion of subtle descriptive touches which produces the quiet pathos and eventual drama of disappointed love.

That an inexperienced girl should be charmed by a lively and sophisticated man, should come to believe he loves her, and then be heartbroken to discover that he has married abroad and forgotten her is hardly an arresting situation; it is, of course, the attributes investing both characters and situations which give richness to the story.

For Phillis' innocence obviously exemplifies that beauty of unspoiled human nature (also reflected in her parents' virtuous and dedicated lives) which harmonizes with the unmarred loveliness of pastoral nature and of her rustic home—appropriately named "Hope Farm." Paul's comparing her to "a rose that had come to full bloom on the sunny side of a lonely house, sheltered from storms" is thus particularly relevant. And descriptions of the peaceful atmosphere of the farm and of the unmarred prettiness of its surroundings subtly enhance our sense of the inner quietude of lives spent away from the hectic pace of city life and as yet untouched by the inroads which the building of the railroad (the occasion of Paul's presence in the vicinity) may effect. The picture which greets Paul on the September afternoon of his second visit reflects the beauty and harmony of a wholesome and uncomplicated mode of life:

> The vine-leaves over the window had a tinge more yellow, their edges were here and there scorched and brown; there was no ironing about, and cousin Holman sate just outside the house, mending a shirt. Phillis was at her knitting indoors: it seemed as if she had been at it all the week. The many-speckled fowls were pecking about in the farmyard beyond, and the milk-cans glittered with brightness,

hung out to sweeten. The court was so full of flowers that they crept out upon the low-covered wall and horse-mount, and were even to be found self-sown upon the turf that bordered the path to the back of the house. I fancied that my Sunday coat was scented for days afterwards by the bushes of sweetbriar and the fraxinella that perfumed the air. From time to time, cousin Holman put her hand into a covered basket at her feet, and threw handfuls of corn down for the pigeons that cooed and fluttered in the air around, in expectation of this treat.[51]

It is easy to feel that in such a world Phillis has indeed been protected from dismaying experiences, yet even when we first meet her, a small but significant descriptive detail hints at her state of innocence. That "pinafore," which she wears "over her gown" and which Paul on first meeting her finds "odd" in someone "so old, so full grown as she was," is later seen as an emblem of the loving reluctance in Phillis' parents to think of her as anything but a child to be sheltered from the problems of maturity as long as possible.[52]

Yet, even as Phillis' harmonious interaction with her circumscribed world is conveyed in charming vignettes of farm activities that show her "kneeling down with her pinafore full of corn and meal, and tempting the little timid downy chickens upon it, much to the anxiety of the fussy ruffled hen, their mother," "sitting on the horse-mount, with her basket of peas, and a basin in which she was shelling them," "leading the row of farm-servants, turning the swathes of fragrant hay with measured movement," "standing by the dresser, cutting up a great household loaf into hunches of bread for the hungry labourers who might come in any minute,"[53] the precariousness of her state is also hinted at. For other interests and yearnings show that she is hardly the archetypal rustic heroine whose greatest asset is her simple grace in performing household tasks. Her Latin studies with her father already suggest rather unusual interests, but the sophistication which Paul glimpses on his very first visit as he walks home from the field with the Reverend Holman and his daughter reveals their uncommon sensitivity and intellect:

At a certain point, there was a sudden burst of the tawny, ruddy evening landscape. The minister turned round and quoted a line or two of Latin.

"It's wonderful," said he, "how exactly Virgil has hit the enduring epithets, nearly two thousand years ago, and in Italy; and yet it describes to a T what is now lying before us in the parish of Heathbridge, county ——, England."

"I daresay it does," said I, all aglow with shame; for I had forgotten the little Latin I ever knew.

The minister shifted his eyes to Phillis' face; it mutely gave him back the sympathetic appreciation that I, in my ignorance, could not bestow.[54]

Paul's discovery soon after on "a small shelf of books" of "Virgil, Caesar, a Greek grammar—oh, dear! ah, me! and Phillis Holman's name in each of them!" helps to convince him that his rustic young cousin would make too formidable a wife for someone as self-satisfied as he. Accordingly, he tells us, "I gave my Cousin Phillis a wide berth, although she was sitting at her work quietly enough, and her hair was looking more golden, her eyelashes longer, her round pillar of a throat whiter, than ever."[55]

The later tableau of Phillis "peeling apples with quick dexterity of finger, but with repeated turnings of her head towards some book lying on the dresser by her," suggests her versatility even as the next scene prepares us for the fascination which Paul's superior, Mr. Holdsworth, will exercise on an ardently inquisitive young woman. As Phillis who, like Margaret Hale in *North and South*, is wrestling with the difficulties of Dante's *Inferno*, proclaims her need for help with the language, the stage is set for her tragic experience. For Paul with naïve enthusiasm points out that Holdsworth, "a regular first-rate fellow!" who "can do anything," and who acquired Italian when "he had to make a railway through Piedmont, which is in Italy I believe" would be an appropriate mentor. The suggestion is met by Phillis with only four words: "Oh, dear! I wish" before "she stopped."[56]

When Mr. Holdsworth is introduced to Paul's relatives (he comes to the farm to recuperate from an illness), Phillis and her father respond enthusiastically to his experience of the world and his scientific proficiency. For not only Phillis, but the remarkable Reverend Holman, who combines with admirable versatility the duties of minister and farmer (even his prayers are interrupted by injunctions concerning the care of a sick cow for "asking a blessing and neglecting the means" to him "is a mockery"), yearn for the wider experience which knowledge can give and which the universe outside their rural world to a certain extent exemplifies. Not only great literature, but the achievements of science fascinate them both, though even the Reverend is unaware that the marvels of engineering can keep a young girl spellbound. When Paul's father, the great inventor, demonstrates the features of a "turnip-cutting machine" he has perfected, Paul depicts for us "the minister sitting with his massive head resting on his hands, his elbows on the table, almost unconscious of Phillis, leaning over and listening greedily, with her hand on his shoulder, sucking in information, like her father's own daughter."[57]

The connection between Phillis' romantic involvement with Holdsworth and her emotional and intellectual susceptibility to his sophistication (her imperviousness to Paul has shown that she does not admire just any young man who crosses her path) is hinted at with that skillful indirectness characteristic of much of the story, as Paul, on revisiting the farm, hears the Reverend's appraisal of his visitor. The minister's inability to resist the attractions of Holdsworth's versatile mind—despite his conscientious scruples about indulging worldly interests—suggests that Phillis, "her father's own daughter," may well be even more susceptible to the charms of this purveyor of experience:

> "Yes! I like him!" said the minister, weighing his words a little as he spoke. "I like him. I hope I am justified in doing it; but he takes hold of me, as it were, and I have almost been afraid lest he carries me away, in spite of my judgment."
>
> "Yes" (once more hesitating), "I like him, and I think he is an upright man; there is a want of seriousness in his talk at times, but, at the same time, it is wonderful to listen to him! He makes Horace and Virgil living, instead of dead, by the stories he tells me of his sojourn in the very countries where they lived, and where to this day, he says—But it is like dram-drinking. I listen to him till I forget my duties and am carried off my feet."[58]

The pathos of Phillis' vulnerability arises from that very innocence of the world which leads her to idealize the sophisticated Holdsworth while it makes her impervious to his insensitivity. Intermittent suggestions of Holdsworth's limitations (such as are implied, for instance, in the Reverend's appraisal of him) subtly prepare us for Holdsworth's easy forgetfulness of a girl who once charmed him enough to make him contemplate marriage to her (he tells Paul of such a plan before his departure to Canada). That Holdsworth for a while actually indulges in "badinage" with a girl like Phillis, whose innocent seriousness is one of her most appealing attributes, hints at the incompatibility of their natures and the consequent precariousness of their relationship.

The author's descriptive approach to her subject effectively suggests the delicate progression of Phillis' secret romantic preoccupation. As the well-regulated, peaceful home life runs its daily course at Hope Farm, nothing seems overtly changed despite the repeated visits of Holdsworth (whose work at the railroad has led to a long stay in the vicinity); we are told that "to Phillis his relation continued that of an elder brother; he directed her studies into new paths; he patiently drew out the expression of many of her thoughts, and perplexities, and unformed theories."[59] Yet telling glimpses into certain reactions of Phillis indicate an involvement: silence and blushing; an abrupt departure from a room; an unusual awareness of Holdsworth's preferences.

The delicacy of nature thus suggested enhances her desolation after Holdsworth's departure, especially since self-consciousness and scrupulosity prevent her from confiding in the protective parents who still think her immune to passion. When on a chill day in December, Paul discovers her huddled under "a great stack of wood in the orchard. . . . making a low moan, like an animal in pain, or perhaps more like the sobbing of the wind," he compassionately discloses Holdsworth's parting confession of caring for Phillis. The resulting joy and relief are a touching prelude to an emotional rebirth which finds its most appropriate expression in the springtime of nature:

> I never saw her so lovely, or so happy. I think she hardly knew why she was so happy all the time. I can see her now, standing under the budding branches of the grey trees, over which a tinge of green seemed to be deepening day after day, her sun-bonnet fallen back on her neck, her hands full of delicate wood-flowers, quite uncon-

scious of my gaze, but intent on sweet mockery of some bird in neighbouring bush or tree. She had the art of warbling, and replying to the notes of different birds, and knew their song, their habits and ways, more accurately than any one else I ever knew. She had often done it at my request the spring before; but this year she really gurgled, and whistled, and warbled, just as they did, out of the very fullness and joy of her heart.[60]

The progression of her agony at Holdsworth's marriage is also etched out with descriptive subtlety, for only Paul witnesses Phillis' brave efforts at resignation, from her first stoical reaction to Holdsworth's letter which the guilty Paul secretly shows her ("There is nothing to be sorry for. I think not, at least. You have not done wrong, at any rate. . . . And he—there's no wrong in his marrying, is there? I'm sure I hope he'll be happy. Oh! how I hope it!") to her assumed matter-of-factness after Holdsworth has tactlessly sent "visiting tickets" to announce his marriage.[61] The full extent of her distraction is dramatically suggested in a later scene when, ignoring her father's depression over the dismissal of a servant, she converses about insignificant matters with seeming composure; though it is hidden from the others by the dining table, Paul notes "the passionate, convulsive manner in which she laced and interlaced her fingers perpetually, wringing them together from time to time, wringing till the compressed flesh became perfectly white."[62]

When Phillis' emotional breakdown comes, it is not a mere melodramatic climax but the appropriate culmination of a series of anguishing experiences. The initial sense of betrayal, the continual self-restraint, the humiliation of having to confess her love to protect Paul when the Reverend chastises him for "raising hopes, exciting feelings" in one "so young, so pure from the world!" are compounded by the guilt of filial disloyalty. The Reverend's failure to understand that her needs are no longer those of a dependent child ("Phillis! did we not make you happy here? Have we not loved you enough? . . . And yet you would have left us, left your home, left your father and your mother, and gone away with this stranger, wandering over the world!")[63] is the final challenge to her much-tried sensibility which destroys all self-control.

If the author avoids the oversimplification of a tragic ending by having Phillis recover from her nearly fatal brain fever, she does not exploit the potential of her delicately modulated story in her conclusion. Endurance should have been taught to Phillis or been apprehended by her more subtly than through the good-natured scolding of an old servant woman. The shrewd common sense, earthy wisdom, and healthy sense of proportion which Mrs. Gaskell so very much appreciated do not unfortunately—either here or in *Ruth* (Betty closely resembles Sally in the novel)—harmonize with the needs of extremely sensitive, finely attuned natures. The injunction to Phillis to practice self-help and to avoid paining her family by her persistent depression surely is not, for all its common sense and realism, a viable solution for Phillis' searing disillusionment with life. Perhaps that is why, despite Phillis' last assertion that "we will go back to the peace of the old days. I know we shall; I can, and I will!"[64] we are left feeling that she may not achieve that capacity to endure which marks a final acceptance of the tragic realities of experience.

If, as we have seen, many of Mrs. Gaskell's stories assert the significance of certain concerns more fully explored in her social novels, other short works like "Mr. Harrison's Confessions" and "My Lady Ludlow" denote the full scope of her achievement as a humorist. Yet of all her stories, "Cousin Phillis" provides perhaps the most instructive insight into her artistic development, for it suggests that the greater psychological insight and technical restraint exhibited in *Sylvia's Lovers* and *Wives and Daughters* could also be exercised within the more exacting limits of the short story.[65]

Her tales of terror, crime, and the supernatural remain intriguing testimonies to a versatility of feelings and interests which few general readers of her novels might suspect. A just assessment of the quality of her mind and imagination must encompass that susceptibility to the irrational of which her social novels and her humorous works afford only intermittent glimpses. Those tales which so clearly reveal that "all through her life, she loved to linger on the borderland"[66] remain the most appropriate corrective to any portrait of her as a simple, serene, well-meaning but utterly conventional novelist whose mental horizons were strictly confined within the boundaries of Victorian propriety and sweet reasonableness.

CHAPTER 6

The Sense of Tragedy: *Sylvia's Lovers*

OF ALL Mrs. Gaskell's novels, *Sylvia's Lovers* (1863) is the least typical in setting, mood, and characterization. She did not use a familiar background or a relatively contemporary period, but chose to depict a critical time in the life of a Yorkshire whaling town at the end of the eighteenth century—when arbitrary impressment by the Admiralty during the war with France produced many private tragedies. For once personal experience could not (as it had in *Mary Barton* or *Cranford*) guarantee the authenticity of her novel: she not only traveled to Whitby to gather impressions but consulted Admiralty records, read in the British Museum, and corresponded with authorities on the subject of the press gangs.[1]

It is hard to know the precise attraction of such a subject for her beyond her personal involvement with seafaring life.[2] Certainly a re-creation of this tumultuous period gave scope to her narrative and descriptive talents and the flair for dialect already demonstrated in her social novels. Buttressed by research and illumined by imagination, her personal observation of life at Whitby ("Monkshaven" in the novel) yielded a work whose historical and indeed general accuracy critics have praised[3] and whose dramatic power is almost immediately evident.

Mrs. Gaskell's reference to *Sylvia's Lovers* as "the saddest story I ever wrote,"[4] confirms one's sense that it is her single large-scale attempt at the tragic mode. Her originality in that mode has been questioned; a Brontë influence has been noted and indeed a specific resemblance to *Wuthering Heights* in its "bleak, northern atmosphere" and in its characters having "some of those elemental qualities that make one feel that tragedy is inherent in the plot."[5] Only the temperamental Sylvia, however, is faintly Brontëan in conception and even she does not possess that "elemental" power, that unearthly passion and rebelliousness, which endows the tragic conflicts of Catherine Earnshaw and Heathcliff with a larger symbolic significance. The relationships in *Sylvia's Lovers* are all far more conventional, while its setting hardly harmonizes with temperament as Emily Brontë's moorland world complements the inner tumults of its inhabitants.

What may account for the suggestion that the work was derivative is a modification in Mrs. Gaskell's approach to the emotions of her characters which can easily be ascribed to increasing artistic maturity, since it is evident in other of her works that are hardly Brontëan in spirit. Many critics agree in classing *Sylvia's Lovers* with "Cousin Phillis" and *Wives and Daughters* as Mrs. Gaskell's outstanding achievements, for all of them share, as Arthur Pollard puts it, "a new technical control, a deeper investigation of individual behaviour, a fresh awareness of the intensity of human passions."[6]

Yet, despite the growth in "technical control" and psychological maturity which the novel exhibits, its basic theme still reflects those characteristic attitudes to general moral questions and specific dilemmas of the conscience which had so deeply affected the handling of *Mary Barton*, *Ruth*, and—to a lesser extent—*North and South*. Moreover, both characters and situations in *Sylvia's Lovers* have elements in common with those in her earlier works, especially *Mary Barton*.

As in the case of *Mary Barton*, Mrs. Gaskell initially considered a title for *Sylvia's Lovers* far more pertinent to her central theme and to the status of the only character in her works who, along with John Barton, deserves to be considered a tragic hero: Philip Hepburn, whose single-minded passion for the beautiful but frivolous Sylvia destroys him. Though the following comment to her publisher George Smith is jocular in tone (and shows that carelessness about details which some of her critics deplore), it sufficiently suggests the emphasis she had in mind:

> What do you think of "Philip's Idol;" then again you may say people will call it "Philip's Idle,"—I don't think I care about the title much. "Philip's darling" does not quite express the same thing as *idol*, but perhaps sounds better. Only I would rather have it "idol" if you don't mind. "Monkshaven" might do, might it not? Very stupid though "Sylvia's Lovers," but then there is a "Nanette & her lovers," is there not? and published by you too.[7]

It is surprising that Ward calls her suggestion "a title of deep meaning, but a meaning only made clear in the last scene of the story"[8] when, from the very beginning, she suggests the enslavement of the serious, solemn, rather prosaic young shopman by his frivolous young cousin Sylvia and then delineates the progressive moral damage wrought by a romantic *idée fixe* in a seemingly most unromantic nature. Equally inappropriate is Elizabeth Haldane's comment that "the mean actions of Philip, with all his high professions, make one feel he was 'no gentleman' any more than was George Eliot's Stephen."[9] Such critical judgments—in the twentieth century—of a character whose tragedy is obviously that passion impels him to "mean actions" despite his genuine "high professions" indirectly suggests the lack of sophistication Mrs. Gaskell had to contend against in her own century. The title eventually chosen probably won out because of the immediacy of its romantic appeal.

Significantly enough, John Barton and Philip Hepburn not only share a prominence unacknowledged by the author's title and the claim to a tragic stature, but both are destroyed because an obsessive commitment to a particular objective leads them to deny the claims of a higher morality. Mrs. Gaskell's basic standards have not really altered since she destined not only John Barton but Ruth to inexorable retribution for their uncontrolled passions. The qualitative change in her art lies in a more sophisticated apprehension of the complex motivations often responsible for the betrayal of those values which ought most to be cherished.

True, she had depicted Barton's anguish with a measure of

psychological insight. Yet his tragic stature was almost guaranteed by the social context of the novel; Barton was, after all, largely a victim of social evils, his downfall being caused as much by a failure of social duty in others as by a blind irrational rebelliousness of his own. As for Ruth, her initial ignorance and innocence almost inevitably implied a tragic sense of waste in her fall. But in Philip Hepburn, she faced the difficult task of sympathetically charting the fate of a human being essentially responsible for his choices. By making his reprehensible actions not only psychologically plausible but in some sense morally defensible, she was transcending the restrictive conception of morality which had extended some leniency only to transgression prompted by social suffering (Barton), betrayal (Ruth), or selfless loyalty (the Bensons' lie in *Ruth* and that of Margaret Hale in *North and South*). Yet her final judgment of Philip demonstrates that commitment to absolute spiritual values which had deeply affected her view of human error from the very beginning and inhibited a more complex psychological evaluation of character.

Conventional moral standards likewise underlie the portrait of Sylvia, despite its greater psychological subtlety. Only through the qualitative change in exercising moral judgment which humor provided did Mrs. Gaskell produce in *Wives and Daughters* two sophisticated portraits of frivolity. Yet her treatment of Sylvia does show a sense of the tragic potential in vain and superficial impulses absent in the portrayal of Mary Barton. That Sylvia has certain attributes of Mary is unmistakable. Indeed Sylvia's possible choice between a serious, reliable, devoted if rather commonplace lover (Philip) and one who is thoughtless, erratic, but personally attractive (the adventurous "specksioneer" —harpooner—Charley Kinraid) does not have to have been inspired by Hetty Sorrel's predicament in *Adam Bede*[10]: Mary Barton faced precisely such a decision between the plain Jem Wilson and the dashing Harry Carson. Also like Mary, Sylvia somewhat redeems her frivolity by her attachment to her father, whose passionate temper she shares. And just as Mary's spiritedness and impatience are contrasted with the restraint and resignation of Margaret Legh, so Sylvia's flightiness is opposed to the self-discipline of Hester Rose who, unlike Sylvia, knows how to appreciate Philip's basic virtues. Even such a minor character as the coarse and insensitive Molly Corney has a predecessor in Mary's co-worker, Sally Leadbitter.

Enough has been said to suggest that *Sylvia's Lovers*, despite the originality of its historical setting, reflects earlier inspirations in its theme and characterization, and, if it brings a far greater psychological sophistication to its probing of ethical questions, abides by the same moral considerations which guided the portrayal of the erring John Barton and Ruth.

Perhaps the novel's most impressive achievement is a technical one, the triumph over the difficulties of welding setting, story, character, and theme into a coherent structure.[11] With the exception of a few chapters near the conclusion (Philip's aimless wanderings before his final return to Monkshaven), the progression of external events concurs with the development of character to provoke the dramatic, psychologically authentic actions that produce tragedy for at least two of the three central characters. The whole subject of press gangs, which the author had gone to some pains to document and which, like Melville in *Billy Budd*, she handles with a deep awareness both of the destructiveness of arbitrary power and of the tragic impossibility of defying its demands during a national emergency, never monopolizes the reader's attention at the expense of characterization. Almost from the very first, in the exciting scene in which, as the whaling fleet returns from its long voyage, some of the young sailors are set upon by the press gang, she is not merely re-creating a historic phenomenon, but laying the groundwork for her story of ill-fated passion. For Sylvia Robson's first shocked encounter with the arbitrary, cruel treatment of those who "shut up in terrible, dreary, Arctic seas from the hungry sight of sweethearts and friends, wives and mothers" have been yearning for the peace and comfort of home, must predispose her to admire someone who revolts against such treatment. When, a few days after this first incident, Sylvia overhears the story of the heroic resistance to a second impressment attempt by Charley Kinraid, she will, like Desdemona, love a man for the dangers he has passed. As her father will say much later: "I belie' me she first began to think on him time o 'th' fight aboard th' *Good Fortune*, when Darley were killed; and he would seem tame-like to her, if he couldn't conquer press-gangs and men-o'-war." When she first meets him, significantly enough at the dramatic burial of Darley—a victim of the harsh impressment tactics—Sylvia looks upon Kinraid, still weak from his wounds, with "her tear-stained face full of shy admiration of the nearest approach to a hero she had ever seen."[12]

Sylvia's romantic infatuation with the young whaling fisherman is thus largely a tribute to the heroic stature which his rebellion against a hated authority gives him not only in her eyes but in those of the whole town. Thus, that fierce insularity and reckless spirit of resistance of the "wild north-eastern people" (aptly illustrated in an initial descriptive chapter) influences Sylvia's personal involvement. Nor is she immune to the town's pride in its dangerous and exciting way of life. Charley's exploits on whaling voyages (appropriately embellished in tall tales which Sylvia's father, now a farmer but once himself a harpooner, matches with spectacular adventures of his own) might have sufficed to exercise on the susceptible girl a fascination which a sober shopman like Philip Hepburn could hardly hope to counteract. After all even her sedate mother had in her courting days succumbed to the spell of Mr. Robson's seafaring tales.

As the novel proceeds, the author consistently adapts her historical material to the dramatic and psychological needs of her story. Thus, the serious repercussions of the press-gang activities in this Yorkshire port function as turning points in the fate of her three protagonists. For Charley's sudden impressment on a deserted stretch of coast will tempt his rival Philip—the only witness—to keep silent about Charley's fate, thereby earning the punishment of "those who act a lie" when Charley returns years later to claim a betrothed who believes him dead. The culmination of the hostility between the naval authorities and the town in the reckless assault of the Monkshaven residents against the "Randyvowse," as the press-gang rendezvous was popularly called (an actual riot described in Admiralty records),[13] has a decisive effect on Sylvia's relations to Philip. As her personal life is laid waste by the arrest and execution of her father (who has been instrumental in provoking the rebellion), her desire to provide security for her bereaved mother and her despair at the supposed death of her lover and the hanging of her father effect a dispassionate assent to marry Philip, a man whom she cannot love and with whom she does not even share a temperamental affinity. Thus, external circumstances tragically conspire to further Philip's misguided aims, and a most unpromising marriage grows out of the interaction of climactic general events with personal destinies, out of the repercussions of a hardly defensible national morality on the ethical conduct of private citizens.

Such a tragic conjunction of events and character is effective because of the author's discrimination and insight in portraying the conflict and in analyzing the temperament of her protagonists. By acquainting us very early with the devious techniques of the press gang, she has authenticated the sudden, ruthless seizure of the defenseless Charley; by charting the conflicting emotions of Philip toward Sylvia and his rival before this event, she has prepared us for the temptation which it will incite. Accordingly, there is no sense here of an artificial manipulation of plot (such as we have much later in the novel when Philip coincidentally meets Charley on the battlefield of St. Jean d'Acre and saves his life) or of an arbitrary handling of character. Again, the obsessive hatred of the press gang which Sylvia's father consistently demonstrates, combined with his childish impulsiveness and self-importance, make him a most likely leader of the reckless assault on the "Randyvowse." Sylvia's tenderness toward her father and regard for her mother prepare us for the terrible despondency about the death of one parent and anxiety for the welfare of the other which will lead her unwittingly to repay in kind Philip's failure of honesty and loyalty, to accept a marriage blighted from its beginning by her emotional indifference.

Throughout, the author has sought to authenticate the psychological sources of her tragedy by the careful analysis of temperament and motivations. Even general comments on the mores and attitudes of the time illumine the specific problems of her protagonists. She indirectly suggests that their lack of self-knowledge is not just an individual trait but a social characteristic with attractive as well as unfortunate aspects. For the "analysis of motive or comparison of characters and actions," so limited in an unsophisticated rural region and social class "even at this present day of enlightenment," and much more so "sixty or seventy years ago," can also, the author suggests, be viewed as an appealing freedom from "self-consciousness":

. . . taken as a general rule, it may be said that few knew what manner of men they were, compared to the numbers now who are fully conscious of their virtues, qualities, failings, and weaknesses, and who go about comparing others with themselves–not in a spirit of Pharisaism and arrogance, but with a vivid self-consciousness that more than anything else deprives characters of freshness and originality.[14]

Again she implies, through a general comment on Sylvia's instinctive understanding of the servant Kester, that the supremacy of feeling over reason which so tragically governs the behavior of Philip, Sylvia, and Mr. Robson is more than a personal expression of temperament:

It is astonishing to look back and find how differently constituted were the minds of most people, fifty or sixty years ago; they felt, they understood, without going through reasoning or analytic processes; and, if this was the case among the more educated people, of course it was still more so in the class to which Sylvia belonged.[15]

But it is her analysis of character which demonstrates most clearly her conscientious acknowledgement of man's complex nature and motivations. All three actors in the tragedy–even the least subtly conceived, Charley Kinraid–have some conflicting attributes that transcend predictability, and because she avoids stereotypes she succeeds as never before in creating psychological as well as dramatic suspense.

Her understanding of human paradoxes is evident in her basic conception of Philip's temperament and inclinations. She betters Emily Brontë's insights in realizing that a deeply romantic emotion is as, if not more than, likely to find root in a seemingly prosaic and restrained nature as in an overtly imaginative and passionate one. For Philip encompasses feelings akin to Heathcliff's in a temperament like that of Edgar Linton, while he has none of the personal attractions which make them appropriate heroes of fiction. Everything about him indeed tends to negate the reality of his emotional life; his seriousness, his sobriety (he advises Sylvia to purchase grey duffle for her cloak rather than the red which she frivolously desires), his commitment to the unimaginative life of a shopkeeper, his prudent acceptance of the necessity for impressment, his bookishness. His very ungainliness, his stooping shoulders, his somewhat irregular features seem to preclude romantic tendencies in him and romantic appeal to others: Bell Robson's sad realization that this nephew of hers is too "old-fashioned" for Sylvia appears well-founded.

And yet from the very beginning his uncommon, unreasonable devotion is deftly suggested by the eagerness with which he greets any occasion to be with Sylvia (when Sylvia rushes out of the shop at the sound of some excitement in the street, "Philip followed, because she went"). The very attributes in Sylvia that fascinate him show his susceptibility to a temperament opposed to his own. We soon find out that he is immune to the loving regard of the thoughtful, quiet, hard-working Hester Rose who in so many ways resembles him, because his fancy has been caught by the little cousin "Sylvie" (as he tenderly calls her despite her objections) whom the author shows us as:

> . . . ready to smile or to pout, or to show her feelings in any way, with a character as undeveloped as a child's: affectionate, wilful, naughty, tiresome, charming, anything, in fact, at present that the chances of an hour called out.[16]

That Philip is not really interested in reforming the undisciplined Sylvia is evident when he abandons all attempts to teach his unwilling pupil the rudiments of writing and spelling because his efforts to form her mind impede his attempts to win her heart. Much of the pathos of his involvement indeed derives from his lack of self-righteousness and personal vanity: the thoughtless, mercurial nature of his beloved is precious to him despite his own commitment to gravity, self-restraint, and perseverance. He even attempts to assume a guise which will appeal to her immature fancy. Philip's preparations for the New Year's party which proves so ill-fated to his hopes reflect (as the author herself suggests) a desire to project the correct image for Sylvia, which is moving from one vantage point if absurd from another:

> At this hour, all the actors in this story having played out their parts and gone to their rest, there is something touching in recording the futile efforts made by Philip to win from Sylvia the love he yearned for. But, at the time, any one who had watched him might have been amused to see the grave, awkward, plain young man

studying patterns and colours for a new waistcoat, with his head a little to one side, after the meditative manner common to those who are choosing a new article of dress.[17]

The same pathos informs his reckless decision to enlist after Sylvia has driven him from home with her savage vow never to forgive him. He yearns to resemble that very Charley Kinraid whose attributes had earlier seemed to him reprehensibly frivolous, thinking that he might perhaps win Sylvia again by being "gay, and brisk, well-dressed like him, returning with martial glory to Monkshaven."[18]

Not only does the basic conception of Philip show the author's understanding of contradictory impulses but, interestingly enough, the very tendency to oversimplify human nature which she avoids functions as a tragic weakness in the novel. For Philip's rash generalization about Charley's character plays a significant part in his unfortunate decision to keep silent about the latter's impressment. His assumption that Charley merely dallies with Sylvia, based on previous evidence of his flighty behavior, seems to him a moral justification for keeping from Sylvia Charley's sudden abduction and his message promising faithfulness to his betrothed. Philip's belated recognition of his failure to judge Charley correctly is conveyed in a pathetic self-exoneration after his life has been ravaged by Charley's unexpected return and Sylvia's implacable hatred. Preparing to save his rival from death on the battlefield of St. Jean d'Acre, he blurts out only one statement: "I niver thought you'd ha' kept true to her!"[19]

While the author has appropriately provided us as well as Philip with good reasons to doubt Charley's faithfulness (Philip learns that the sister of Coulson, his co-worker, has died of grief at being abandoned by him and later overhears other stories of his conquests), she has yet endowed him with traits sufficiently appealing to make his eventual loyalty to Sylvia believable. She shows us at one point that Sylvia's "innocence" "inspired him with respect, and kept him in check"; she suggests his honest intentions through the frank avowal of his feelings to Sylvia's father and his own solemn engagement; she reveals his capacity for sentiment in such a romantic gesture as the tying of Sylvia's ribbon round his hat. Yet she also presents sufficient evidence of a lack of depth and sensitivity that will later explain his rapid recovery from the shock of finding Sylvia married to Philip. While wooing Sylvia, he has given his cousin Bessy Corney enough proof of his affection to make her believe in an engagement. And if he is capable of feeling "respect" for Sylvia, he also demonstrates in courting her a confidence in his manly attractiveness and a pleasure in exercising his will which are not characteristic of a very choice and delicate nature. Thus he succeeds in extorting from Sylvia that kiss which she had refused him in the game of forfeits because, as Molly Corney shrewdly surmises, "Charley is not t' chap to lose his forfeit."[20]

By sustaining the portrait of a superficial and willful but not coarse and ruthless character, Mrs. Gaskell has avoided a stereotyped contrast between the reckless indifference of a Don Juan on the one hand and the devotion of a true lover on the other. She has made possible the far more subtle opposition of two different kinds of love between whose quality and essence Sylvia will learn too late to discriminate. Molly's reference to Charley exhibiting high spirits at the New Year's party long after Sylvia has gone home by dancing a hornpipe over the now empty plates of the feast shows how skillfully the author can strike the right balance in her assessment of his frivolous but well-meaning nature (he is not after all flirting with other girls in his display of merry unconcern). Even as she demonstrates the lightness of Charley's nature, she suggests the qualitative difference in Philip's passion through his reaction to the other's behavior. His own vulnerability is evident in his mistaken assumption that Charley has now proved his indifference to Sylvia:

> Philip hardly knew what he said in reply, the mention of that *pas seul* lifted such a weight off his heart. He could smile now, after his grave fashion, and would have shaken hands again with Kinraid had it been required; for it seemed to him that no one, caring ever so little in the way that he did for Sylvia, could have borne four mortal hours of a company where she had been, and was not; least of all could have danced a hornpipe, either from gaiety of heart, or even out of complaisance. He felt as if the yearning after the absent one would have been a weight to his legs, as well as to his spirit; and he imagined that all men were like himself.[21]

This explanation of Philip's feelings shows the complex ramifications of that wider misjudgment of Charley we have already mentioned. Philip's mistrust of his intentions regarding Sylvia rests to some degree on the psychological basis of wish-fulfillment, since the conformity of external evidence to Philip's wishes increases its validity for him. Yet that misjudgment also reveals him as the victim of his own intense capacity to love: for if that love makes him eager to shield Sylvia from a possible seduction, it also makes him incapable of conceiving the reality of an emotion not as deep and faithful as his own. Such a forceful tragic conception is, of course, not fully sustained by Mrs. Gaskell, for the same conflict between religious commitments and instinctive sympathies which so strongly affected her handling of the social novels is still present in this far more sophisticated work. Accordingly, she cannot sustain the tragic vision of a hero largely victimized by the very attributes which grant him nobility even as they preclude self-restraint, a vision which Hardy will so beautifully project in *Jude the Obscure*. Indeed that novel is pertinent in another way, since Sue Brideshead's final abnegation is based on values very similar to those which inform Mrs. Gaskell's assessment of earthly love. She cannot help suggesting in *Sylvia's Lovers* that a deep involvement in such love implies a sinful neglect of spiritual devotion to divine authority. In that light, Philip's moral evaluation of Charley marks the reckless assumption of a power to judge others which is outside the province of mere human beings: "Philip took upon himself to decide that, with such a man as the specksioneer, absence was equivalent to faithless forgetfulness."[22]

It is, however, the very earnestness and depth of Philip's passion, the overwhelming force of his yearning for its fulfillment which (though in many ways seemingly admirable) the author views as the most serious transgression from virtue, more to be condemned than a misplaced emphasis on human love or a failure to withhold judgment from another human being, though it is clearly related to both. For she shows us that in ardently seeking to effect the realization of his hopes, Philip, like John Barton, forfeits completely the selfless resignation to a higher will and judgment which she believes alone can rightly rule man's destinies. Thus, before his departure on that trip to London (and that fateful meeting with Charley on the sands), Philip's sinful blindness is suggested, as he expresses thankfulness for what appear to be fortuitous circumstances to win Sylvia—he now has a responsible position and Kinraid is about to leave Monkshaven for a long time:

So this night his prayers were more than the mere form that they had been the night before; they were a vehement expression of gratitude to God for having, as it were, interfered on his behalf, to grant him the desire of his eyes and the lust of his heart. He was like too many of us: he did not place his future life in the hands of God, and only ask for grace to do His will in whatever circumstances might arise; but he yearned in that terrible way after a blessing which, when granted under such circumstances, too often turns out to be equivalent to a curse. And that spirit brings with it the natural and earthly idea that all events that favour our wishes are answers to our prayers; and so they are in one sense; but they need prayer in a deeper and higher spirit to keep us from the temptation to evil which such events invariably bring with them.[23]

The concluding statement in the above paragraph prepares us for that appraisal of Philip's feelings and actions when Charley is impressed, which again reflects Mrs. Gaskell's tendency to evaluate weaknesses of character in spiritual terms. She shows some psychological insight into a nature obsessed with one desire by revealing the potential for hostility and sophistry in a desire for wish-fulfillment. But the distinct form that sophistry assumes reveals Philip's failure of generosity to others and honesty with himself to be not a moral weakness but a religious transgression:

. . . it took him some time before he could reason himself into the belief that his mad, feverish wishes, not an hour before—his wild prayer to be rid of his rival, as he himself had scrambled onward over the rocks alongside of Kinraid's path on the sands—had not compelled the event.

"Anyhow," thought he, as he rose up, "my prayer is granted. God be thanked."[24]

In charting the emotions leading Philip to hide what he has seen, she is again influenced by her conception of his weakness as a spiritual sin. His feeling that he is not bound by any promise to deliver Kinraid's message, since he has not clearly expressed any reply to Kinraid's injunction ("he knew he had spoken hoarsely and low . . . . he doubted if Kinraid had caught his words") is termed a prompting of "the dread Inner Creature, who lurks in each of our hearts" and which now speaks to him the sophistical words: "It is as well: a promise given is a fetter to the giver. But a promise is not given when it has not been received." As Philip hesitates whether to write the truth to his uncle, "he sate, pen in hand, thinking himself wiser than conscience." Yet the rigor of her judgment is softened by the suggestion that there are attenuating circumstances in his fall from righteousness, for it is while thus toying with his decision that he overhears the sailors' "jesting mention of his [Kinraid's] power amongst women, and one or two girls' names were spoken of in connection with him":

> Hepburn silently added Annie Coulson and Sylvia Robson to this list; and his cheeks turned paler as he did so. Long after they had done speaking about Kinraid, after they had paid their shot, and gone away, he sate in the same attitude, thinking bitter thoughts.[25]

The author implies that not only jealous vindictiveness tempts Philip to choose silence but also a genuine concern to protect Sylvia; the mention of Annie Coulson, a tragic victim of Kinraid's indifference particularly suggests this intention. So later on, she may condemn Philip's adherence to his indirect lie; his feeling that Kinraid "was not capable of an enduring, constant attachment" is called a "poor opiate to his conscience." She may also point to the sophistry of his rationalizations as he argues himself and Sylvia into believing that Kinraid is in truth "dead": if not in reality, he tells himself, "as good as dead to her; so that the word dead might be used in all honest certainty, as in one of its meanings Kinraid was dead for sure." Yet she also suggests the devotion to another's welfare which has made him persevere in his tacit lie. Though, upon his return from London, Philip has sympathized with Sylvia's suffering in her mistaken belief that Charley is dead (as the discovery of his hat washed on the shore seems to indicate), his protective impulse prevails:

. . . for all his pity, he had now resolved never to soothe her with the knowledge of what he knew, nor to deliver the message sent by her false lover. He felt like a mother withholding something injurious from the foolish wish of her plaining child.[26]

The author may denounce the distortion of values induced by passion in showing Philip's unholy satisfaction at Sylvia's utter dependence on him during her father's imprisonment (when Sylvia and her mother stay with him overnight to see Robson off to prison in the morning: "he had a warm sympathy with the miserable distress of the wife and daughter; but still, at the back of his mind, his spirits danced, as if this was to them a festal occasion.")[27] But she also emphasizes the generosity and devotion which he exhibits in his efforts to save the misguided Mr. Robson.

Thus, though her strict judgment of Philip as essentially a spiritual transgressor often casts doubt on the value of his love, her partial commitment to that value and to the tragic implications of Philip's ignorance of more pedestrian emotions testifies to her recognition of complexities and paradoxes in her hero's predicament. Though Philip's exclusive concern with another human being is adjudged sinful, she cannot help paying tribute to such devotion and suggesting the tragedy of its failure to be appreciated. From the first (as in this early passage), her condemnation of the spiritual deficiencies in Philip's love is counteracted by her affirmation that the failure of such unusual fidelity to find its reward is inherently tragic:

To Philip she was the only woman in the world; it was the one subject on which he dared not consider, for fear that both conscience and judgment should decide against him, and that he should be convinced against his will that she was an unfit mate for him, that she never could be his, and that it was waste of time and life to keep her shrined in the dearest sanctuary of his being, to the exclusion of all the serious and religious aims which, in any other case, he would have been the first to acknowledge as the object he ought to pursue. For he had been brought up among the Quakers, and shared in their austere distrust of a self-seeking spirit; yet what else but self-seeking was his passionate prayer, "Give me Sylvia, or else I die"? No other vision had ever crossed his masculine fancy for a moment; his was a rare and constant love that deserved a better fate than it met with.[28]

And much as she has stressed the moral weakness of his behavior, she endows his self-justification at Charley's return with the pathos only a selfless and generous love could command. That Philip's arguments may have been sinfully sophistical, he himself hints at, but even that weakness seems insignificant in the light of his admirable devotion:

"He didn't love yo' as I did. He had loved other women. I, yo'—yo' alone. . . . I—I wish God would free my heart from the pang; but it will go on till I die, whether yo' love me or not. . . . How was I to know he would keep true to thee? It might be a sin in me, I cannot say; my heart and my sense are gone dead within me. I know this: I've loved yo', as no man but me ever loved before. Have some pity and forgiveness on me, if it's only because I've been so tormented with my love!"[29]

Thus, despite the inexorable moral demands she makes upon her characters, she often does justice to the contradictory impulses in man's nature and aspirations which make it so very hard for him to meet the standards of righteous conduct. She seems at times even prepared to admit that in the light of human exigencies those standards themselves are rather difficult to determine.

This scrupulosity in taking into account the complex human motivations which make many moral decisions extremely perplexing and moral responsibility itself almost indefinable is also evident in her portrayal of Sylvia. For she convinces us that the interaction of two incompatible beings like Philip and Sylvia as tragically victimizes the one as the other. Though Sylvia's early frivolity and impulsiveness, and her eventual lack of mercy and charity, would seem to make her the significant agent of Philip's destruction, the author avoids the oversimplified standard portrayal of woman as the heartless destroyer of man's peace of mind. She projects convincingly the seeming paradox of two very dissimilar natures basically destroyed by the very same flaw: the inability to control their passions.

From the very beginning Sylvia is shown to be more than a frivolous coquette. For if she is impatient of any general injunctions to be reasonable ("dunnot lecture me; I'm none for a sermon hung on every peg o' words. I'm going to have a new cloak, lass, and I cannot heed thee if thou dost lecture"), she nevertheless shows respect for opinions contrary to her own and an admiration for qualities she does not possess as she acknowledges the significance of her mother's injunctions regarding the purchase. Her perception of the qualitative difference between her parents' temperaments, indeed her awareness of her own flightiness, are also suggested in her recognition that:

". . . mother's words are scarce, and weigh heavy. Feyther's liker me, and we talk a deal o' rubble; but mother's words are like to hewn stone. She puts a deal o' meaning in 'em."[30]

Her thoughtlessness and superficiality are demonstrated at the time of Darley's funeral when she attends the church service "for the ends of vanity"—(to see fashionable attire so as to determine the cut of her cloak) and the funeral "for curiosity and the pleasure of the excitement." Yet she is not immune to feeling, for at the spectacle of the burial, "Sylvia's tears rained down her face"; nor, as has been suggested, is she incapable of appreciating virtue in others. Hester's selfless action in taking care of Darley's invalid sister during the ceremony inspires in her "the simple, purifying pleasure of admiration of another."[31]

The very fact that she can commend Hester's action, yet "without having a pang of self-depreciation" marks her as basically a creature of instinct, as wild as that "briar rose" which Philip so appropriately chooses as a pattern in the ribbon he gives her. But her instincts, as in the very example just given, often serve her constructively in default of reason and learning in assessing character. She can uncannily detect the discrepancy between Philip's "practice and preaching," as he opposes resistance to what he considers lawful impressment while he consistently defies the law by selling smuggled goods. She knows precisely how to keep her restless father in good temper when rheumatism forces him to stay home (she secretly arranges the arrival of the tailor to keep him company) and how to charm the rough but devoted servant, Kester, into assisting her with her plan. Though she is governed by impulses, they can as often be manifestations of kindness as of willfulness: she offers Kester part of the precious material for her own cloak and, after she has stubbornly refused to bid farewell to Philip before his London voyage, she surprises him by shouting "Good-bye, Philip" from the window.

We have seen that the particular temper of the times and of her own community assists Sylvia's romantic feeling for Kinraid; her instinctive appreciation of a way of life that is untamed and excitingly unpredictable also plays its part. If the rejection of such—to her—pedestrian pursuits as reading, writing, and geography ("Greenland is all t' geography I want to know. Except, perhaps, York. I'd like to learn about York, because of t' races, and London, because King George lives there")[32] shows her immaturity, it also suggests a not unattractive impulse to escape the discipline of civilization. Though the distinction between town and country (in part exemplified by Philip's life in Foster's shop and Sylvia's at Haytersbank Farm on the wild moorland heights) is not a focal element in the tragedy, it nevertheless plays a role in charting the incompatibility of these two people. Much as Sylvia may be to blame in her behavior as Philip's wife, there is pathos in her predicament—suggested in part by the painful contrast between the stultifying demands of civilized life and the freedom and satisfying interaction with nature formerly made possible by life on the farm:

> Sitting in the dark parlour at the back of the shop, and doing "white work," was much more wearying to her than running out into the fields to bring up the cows, or spinning wool, or making up butter. She sometimes thought to herself that it was a strange kind of life, where there were no outdoor animals to look after; "the ox and the ass" had hitherto come into all her ideas of humanity; and her care and gentleness had made the dumb creatures round her father's home into mute friends, with loving eyes looking at her as if wistful to speak in words the grateful regard that she could read without the poor expression of language.
>
> She missed the free open air, the great dome of sky above the fields. . . .[33]

Because Sylvia's failure to appreciate Philip and her romantic infatuation with Charley spring partly from her peculiar temperament (which resembles Catherine Earnshaw's in its longing for the freedom and wildness of nature), her moral culpability is markedly attenuated. Though the reality of her passion for Kinraid is not as skillfully conveyed as Philip's single-minded devotion to her, enough emotion is suggested to make her seem almost as poignantly victimized as the man to whom she is indifferent. Her passionate assertion of loyalty to Charley when the latter on his return accuses her of faithlessness conveys an emotion as selfless and fervent in its own way as Philip's defense of his own action:

"Oh, Charley! . . . dunnot cut me to the quick; have pity on me, though he had none. I did so love thee; it was my very heart-strings as gave way, when they told me thou was drowned—feyther, and th' Corneys, and all, iverybody. . . . I went mourning for thee all the day long—dunnot turn away from me; only hearken this once, and then kill me dead, and I'll bless yo'—and have niver been mysel' since; niver ceased to feel t' sun grow dark and th' air chill and dreary, when I thought on t' time when thou was alive. I did, my Charley, my own love! And I thought thou was dead for iver, and I wished I were lying beside thee. Oh, Charley! . . .[34]

And if her commitment to a loveless marriage is a failure of honesty, it is shown to have been her only alternative if she was to provide security for her ailing mother:

"And feyther was taken up, and all for setting some free as t' press-gang had gotten by a foul trick; and he were put i' York prison, and tried, and hung!—hung, Charley!—good, kind feyther was hung on a gallows; and mother lost her sense and grew silly in grief; and we were like to be turned out on t' wide world, and poor mother dateless—and I thought yo' were dead—oh! I thought yo' were dead, I did—oh, Charley, Charley!"[35]

Even the hatred and vengefulness shown in her oath never to forgive Philip are an outgrowth of the outraged sense of injustice provoked by her father's execution. Not only had the riot followed the "foul trick" of luring Monkshaven citizens into the square by ringing the fire bell, but a servant at the Randyvowse to whom Robson had shown kindness that night had given the fatal testimony against him. The fact that she has, as she herself says, "turned savage" and cannot conceive of bringing herself to grant the dying informer's request for forgiveness ("my flesh and blood wasn't made for forgiving and forgetting")[36] shows both a reprehensible failure of mercy and charity but also a commendable instinctive loyalty to those she has loved. And though her rage at Philip is partly the result of bitterness at her father's fate, it is also provoked by his treachery, which she justifiably feels has "spoilt my life." Moreover, while she takes a destructive oath against him, she also, for her child's sake, takes a destructive one against herself, since she swears at the same time never to see Charley again.

Thus the author succeeds in giving Sylvia's feelings and actions a complexity which makes her weaknesses part of a tragic pattern of interacting emotions and circumstances. But, as in her treatment of Philip, her assessment of Sylvia's guilt is also qualified by religious considerations. Sylvia has sinned by generally setting too much store on earthly vanities and pleasures, by specifically placing (like Philip) earthly love above higher duties, and in her fatal oath, by taking the judgment of another human creature upon herself. Sylvia has in fact been shown throughout as sadly lacking spiritual devotion; she had, after all, gone to Darley's funeral only "for the ends of vanity"; even her contrite mood after the ceremony had not restrained her instinctive rebelliousness, "a hatred and desire of revenge on the press-gang, so vehement that it sadly militated against her intention of trying to be good." Both she and her mother are usually remiss in their religious duties, and when they do attend services on the Sunday preceding Robson's judgment, it is "with a strange, half-superstitious feeling, as if they could propitiate the Most High to order the events in their favour, by paying Him the compliment of attending to duties in their time of sorrow which they had too often neglected in their prosperous days."[37] Because she can barely read, Sylvia is ignorant of the Bible, and part of the softening of her feelings toward Philip comes through the influence of Hester Rose's mother who introduces her to it. So the wildness which denotes her to be a true child of nature also marks her failure to subvert her emotions to higher spiritual aims, a failure best exemplified by that almost sacrilegious vindictiveness which lays waste her husband's life and eventually causes him to starve in a wretched hovel while she lives in comparative peace and comfort. The inexorable result of such a sin must be the untimely loss of a love whose value she has only slowly and painfully learned to appreciate.

Despite her concern with the attenuating circumstances for Philip and Sylvia's behavior, the scope of Mrs. Gaskell's tragic vision is confined, as it was in *Mary Barton* and *Ruth*, by her commitment to the affirmation of divine justice. If she sometimes shows her two characters victimized by unfavorable circumstances and defensible weaknesses, nevertheless her final judgment rests on the premise that their tragic fate is the outcome of a spiritual sin which, like that of Ruth, can only find ultimate forgiveness beyond earthly boundaries. So, as Philip lies dying (mortally wounded after saving his child), he reveals to Sylvia his recognition that his moral failure has been a religious transgression: "I ha' made thee my idol; and, if I could live my life o'er again, I would love my God more, and thee less; and then I shouldn't ha' sinned this sin against thee." As he senses the "numbness" of death "stealing up him," he recognizes the absoluteness of his responsibility for straying from the path of virtue:

> All the temptations that had beset him rose clearly before him; the scenes themselves stood up in their solid materialism—he could have touched the places, the people; the thoughts, the arguments that Satan had urged in behalf of sin, were reproduced with the vividness of a present time. And he knew that the thoughts were illusions, the arguments false and hollow; for in that hour came the perfect vision of the perfect truth; he saw the "way to escape" which had come along with the temptation; now, the strong resolve of an ardent boyhood, with all a life before it to show the world "what a Christian might be;" and then, the swift, terrible Now, when his naked, guilty soul shrank into the shadow of God's mercy-seat, out of the blaze of His anger against all those who act a lie.[38]

So Sylvia too measures the full sinfulness of her failure of love and pathetically asks Hester: "If I live very long, and try hard to be very good all that time, do yo' think, Hester, as God will let me to him where he is?"[39]

The forgiveness which they mutually extend to each other is but an imperfect symbol of that higher forgiveness which Philip is convinced God's "pity" will allow them to gain; their brief reunion is but a prelude to that final reunion which will only take place when Philip is purged from his sin:

"I think and do believe as we shall meet together before His face; but then I shall ha' learnt to love thee second to Him; not first, as I have done here upon the earth."[40]

The conclusion of *Sylvia's Lovers* is surely intended to leave us with the sense that the tragic fates of Philip and Sylvia are the inexorable outcomes of a culpable failure to follow the dictates of righteousness. The work as a whole, however, reflects, as we have shown, a much more tentative appraisal of the nature and limits of human responsibility. The author's tragic vision is informed throughout by her religious conviction that man is totally liable for his sins and that his transgressions must inevitably invoke the exercise of retributive justice. Yet that vision is also qualified by her instinctive apprehension of the attenuating factors governing man's decisions: the imponderable effect of external circumstances on his emotions and his actions, the paradoxical nature not only of his feelings and behavior but of the moral dilemmas which confront him.

In many works which preceded *Sylvia's Lovers*, Mrs. Gaskell had demonstrated that concern for the ambiguities of moral decisions which had led Emile Montégut to characterize her as "le romancier des cas de conscience."[41] But she had never before so painstakingly attempted to chart those conflicting and contradictory elements which make questions of conscience at times dilemmas which even the best intentions can hardly hope to resolve without tragic repercussions. The intricacy of ethical problems was so personally real and meaningful to her that even the need to make a relatively insignificant decision (whether she should allow herself to purchase a handsome house) would impel her to "long for the old times when right and wrong did not seem such complicated matters," to yearn for some soothing influence which would "shame the demon (I beg its pardon) Conscience away," to conceive of "Heaven" as "a place where we shan't have any conscience."[42] When incorporated in her treatment of ill-fated love in *Sylvia's Lovers*, that recognition of moral complexities succeeded in endowing the novel with tragic dimensions that far transcended her earlier appraisals of man's nature and destiny.

Notes and References

The number in brackets following a letter quoted from manuscript is that given to it in the collected letters, not available when this study was being written (See Bibliography, Diary and Correspondence). The numbers have been inserted to facilitate reference.

CHAPTER ONE

1. For details on her attitude and on her daughters' adherence to her wishes see Gerald De Witt Sanders, "Preface," *Elizabeth Gaskell* (New Haven, 1929), pp. v–vi.

2. Margaret Lane, "Books in General," [review of A.B. Hopkins' *Mrs. Gaskell: Her Life and Work*] *New Statesman and Nation,* XLIII (March 15, 1952), 324. Cf. Marjory A. Bald, *Women-writers of the Nineteenth Century* (Cambridge, 1923), p. 100: "Some people are so apt to consider literary women as psychological curiosities, that they never pause before any cases which present no enigmas. . . . Mrs. Gaskell will never have much standing among those who hanker for sensations or problems."

3. Charles Dickens, Letter to Mrs. Gaskell, December 5 [really 4], 1851, *The Letters of Charles Dickens,* ed. Walter Dexter (Bloomsbury: Nonesuch, 1938), II, 361. The reference is to *Cranford,* then being published in *Household Words.* In a letter of July 1, 1851 to Mrs. Smith, Charlotte Brontë says of Mrs. Gaskell: "She is a woman of many fine qualities and deserves the epithet which I find is generally applied to her—charming." *The Brontës: Their Lives, Friendship and Correspondence, The Shakespeare*

Head Brontë, ed. Thomas James Wise and John Alexander Symington (Oxford, 1932), III, 254.

4. George Eliot, Letter to Mrs. Peter Alfred Taylor, London, February 1, 1853, *The George Eliot Letters,* ed. Gordon S. Haight (New Haven, 1954), II, 86.

5. Henry James, "Wives and Daughters," *The Nation,* II (January–June 1866), 247. Swinburne was also not immune to Mrs. Gaskell's characteristic attribute. Having spent a "week or ten days" with her at the home of Monckton Milnes (Lord Houghton), he maintained that "no one I think, in so short a time, ever impressed or charmed me more." Fragment of a letter in the Berg Collection, New York Public Library.

6. David Cecil, *Early Victorian Novelists* (Harmondsworth, 1948), p. 152.

7. A. W. Ward, "Biographical Introduction," *Mary Barton and Other Tales, The Works of Mrs. Gaskell* (London, 1906), I, xlvii. Unless otherwise indicated, all subsequent references to Mrs. Gaskell's works are to this edition, The Knutsford Edition, published in 1906 in eight volumes, with extensive introductions by Professor Ward.

8. G. B. Smith, "Mrs. Gaskell and Her Novels," *Cornhill Magazine,* XXIX (January–June 1874), 202.

9. David Masson, "Mrs. Gaskell," *Macmillan's Magazine,* XIII (November 1865–April 1866), 154.

10. The marked incidence of deathbed scenes in *Mary Barton,* often noted by critics, is perhaps a case in point. Maria Edgeworth in a letter to Mary Holland (Mrs. Gaskell's cousin) of December 27, 1848, found the flaw in the novel to be "that it leaves such a melancholy I almost feel hopeless impression," and complained of "too many deaths in the book." "Letters Addressed to Mrs. Gaskell by Celebrated Contemporaries," ed. R. D. Waller, *Bulletin of the John Rylands Library,* XIX (January 1935), 109–10. But Mrs. Gaskell's capacity for morbid anxiety is best exemplified in *My Diary: The Early Years of My Daughter Marianne,* at those moments when she broods not only on the possibility of the child's untimely death but on the danger of lavishing too much affection on an earthly being: "Oh! may I not make her into an idol, but strive to prepare both her and myself for the change that may come any day." Entry of August 4, Tuesday Evening, 1835, p. 11. The book was privately printed in London in 1923 by Clement Shorter.

11. K. L. Montgomery, "Elizabeth Cleghorn Gaskell," *Fortnightly Review,* N.S. XXXVIII (July–December 1910), 461.

12. Elizabeth Haldane, *Mrs. Gaskell and Her Friends* (London, 1931), p. 3.

13. Ward, "Biographical Introduction," p. xliii.

14. "Belles Lettres" (anon. rev. of "A Dark Night's Work"), *Westminster and Foreign Quarterly Review,* N.S., XXIV (July–October 1863), 305.

15. Letter to Eliza [Tottie] Fox, 1853. Quoted by Haldane, p. 244.

16. Smith, p. 212. In 1867 one critic had already noted: "Under her guidance we are always taken into cleanly company, and need never feel ashamed to say where we have been—a comfortable consciousness that does

not remain with us after the perusal of certain younger authors, who yet set up for moralists." "The Works of Mrs. Gaskell," *British Quarterly Review,* XLV (January–April 1867), 400.

17. Letter to Charles Eliot Norton, Manchester, June 3, 1857, *Letters of Mrs. Gaskell and Charles Eliot Norton, 1855–1865,* ed. Jane Whitehill (London, 1932), 3.

18. Letter to Norton, Manchester [1857], *Letters of Mrs. G. and CEN,* pp. 10, 11, 16.

19. Letter to Norton, Manchester, March 9 [1859], *Letters of Mrs. G. and CEN,* p. 34.

20. Letter to Marianne [Polly], The Brotherton Collection, University of Leeds. [93]

21. Letter to Eliza Gaskell, postmarked July 18, 1838, Brotherton Collection. [9]

22. Letter to Catherine [Katie] Winkworth, Lea Hurst, Matlock, Brotherton Collection. [211]

23. Letter to Marianne and Meta, Brotherton Collection. [273]

24. Letter to Mrs. Anne Robson [Nancy] Brotherton Collection. [570]

25. Letter to George Eliot [addressed as "Mr. Gilbert Elliot"], London, June 3 [1859], Yale University Library. Printed in *The George Eliot Letters,* III, 74.

26. Letter to Norton, Silverdale, July 25 [1858], *Letters of Mrs. G. and CEN,* p. 28.

27. Letter to Norton, Manchester, October 25 [1859], *Letters of Mrs. G. and CEN,* p. 38.

28. Letter to Norton, Manchester [1857], *Letters of Mrs. G. and CEN,* p. 16.

29. Though she expresses to Norton (Letter of May 10 [1858]) not only a reluctance to cater to readers but an inability to do so—"I *can* not (it is not *will* not) write at all if I ever think of my readers, & what impression I am making on them," she certainly could not sustain the attitude so colorfully conveyed in the next sentence: " 'If they don't like me, they must *lump* me' to use a Lancashire proverb." *Letters of Mrs. G. and CEN,* p. 20.

30. W. R. Greg, "False Morality of Lady Novelists," *Literary and Social Judgments* (Boston, 1873), pp. 113–14. The article first appeared in the *National Review,* VIII (1859).

31. V. S. Pritchett, "Current Literature: Books in General," *New Statesman and Nation,* N.S., XXI (January–June 1941), 630.

32. Smith, "Mrs. Gaskell and Her Novels" p. 210.

33. Edna Lyall quotes the testimony of Mrs. Gaskell's eldest daughter Marianne (then Mrs. Thurstan Holland) on the author's method of characterization: "I do not think my mother ever *consciously* took her characters from special individuals, but we who knew often thought we recognised people, and would tell her, 'Oh, so and so is just like Mr. Blank,' or something of that kind; and she would say, 'So it is, but I never meant it for him.' And really many of the characters are from originals, or rather are like originals, but they were not conscientiously meant to be like." "Mrs. Gaskell"

in *Women Novelists of Queen Victoria's Reign. A Book of Appreciations by Mrs. Oliphant et al.* (London, 1897), p. 144.

34. Ward, "Introduction to 'Cranford,' Etc.," *Cranford and Other Tales,* II, xvii.

35. William E. A. Axon, "The Homes and Haunts of Mrs. Gaskell," *Bookman* (October 1910), p. 44. One of the best examples of the source-hunting inspired by *Cranford* is the Reverend George Payne's *Mrs. Gaskell and Knutsford* (London, 1906).

36. Margaret Howitt quotes from a letter of Mrs. Gaskell a passage which recalls that difficult time: "Long ago I lived in Chelsea occasionally with my father and stepmother, and *very, very* unhappy I used to be; and if it had not been for the beautiful, grand river, which was an inexplicable comfort to me, and a family by the name of Kennett, I think my child's heart would have been broken." "Stray Notes from Mrs. Gaskell," *Good Words,* XXXVI (1895), 606.

37. Anne Thackeray Ritchie, "Preface," *Cranford* (London, 1892), p. x.

38. Though the author's middle name has usually been associated with James Cleghorn himself, Elizabeth Haldane suggests that Stevenson was paying a debt of gratitude either to James's wife or his mother who "was kind to the young couple" when they lived in Edinburgh. P. 15.

39. Ward, "Biographical Introduction," I, xviii.

40. Mary Ann Lumb's letter is printed in full (from a typescript in the Brotherton Collection) in A. B. Hopkins, *Elizabeth Gaskell: Her Life and Work* (London, 1952), pp. 22–24.

41. The author has left a moving description of the last weeks of Aunt Lumb's life in *My Diary: The Early Years of My Daughter Marianne.* The references to her as "my more than mother," "my most-dearly loved Aunt," clearly reveal Mrs. Gaskell's deep attachment. In referring to her death, she simply says: ". . . on May 1st I lost my best friend." Pp. 28, 29, 28.

42. Two letters to the Howitts (May and August 1838) pay tribute to her childhood. In the first (addressed to both) she recaptures the charm of childhood excursions to a mansion near Knutsford. In the second (written to Mary Howitt), which suggests country homes that William Howitt might wish to visit, she concludes an enumeration with the significant statement: "I am giving but vague directions, but I am unwilling to leave even in thought the haunts of such happy days as my schooldays were." She goes on to describe for their benefit many country customs of Knutsford, and of Cheshire and Lancashire generally, obviously rehearsing them with fondness. "Stray Notes from Mrs. Gaskell," pp. 605–06, 607.

43. Letter to the Howitts of May 1838. "Stray Notes from Mrs. Gaskell," p. 604.

44. Ward, "Introduction to 'Cranford,' Etc.," II, xix; "Biographical Introduction," I, xviii.

45. Letter to Mary Howitt of August 18, 1838. "Stray Notes from Mrs. Gaskell," p. 607.

46. Though studies of Mrs. Gaskell generally assume that she went to this school near Stratford only from 1825 to 1827, Annette Hopkins con-

vincingly argues for a longer stay, adducing as evidence Mrs. Gaskell's own reference in a letter to Walter Savage Landor to five years of schooling. See Hopkins, footnote 1 to Chapter 1, p. 343.

47. Noting the "strong vein of romanticism in Elizabeth Stevenson's nature" which the sketch exemplifies, Annette Hopkins appropriately points out that "this lure of antiquity, this fascination of the gruesome and mysterious to which she responded instinctively speak of a susceptibility that got suppressed by circumstances in the course of her development as a novelist. But it was to crop out with singular power in one or two short tales. And sometimes it would appear in a letter." P. 39.

48. Mrs. Ellis H. Chadwick, *Mrs. Gaskell: Haunts, Homes, and Stories* (New York, 1911), pp. 138, 140.

49. Hopkins, p. 42.

50. A collection of her tales (1859) for which she supplied an introduction that would bind the stories together in *Decameron* fashion. The narrator and her companion become part of a circle of people who gather "round the sofa" of the invalid Margaret Dawson and respectively tell stories after the hostess herself has contributed "My Lady Ludlow."

51. Hopkins, p. 42.

52. Letter to Miss Eliza Gaskell. Quoted by Hopkins, p. 49.

53. Mrs. Gaskell herself characterizes him in a letter to her sister-in-law, Anne Robson as "most reserved in *expressions* of either affection or sympathy." In another letter to the same correspondent (May 10, 1865), after describing her pleasure at her married daughter's visit, she goes on to comment: "But W^{m} trots off to his study, whoever is here all the same." Both letters in the Brotherton Collection. [16 ; 570] To Charles Eliot Norton she also conveys her husband's exclusive preference for his study. *Letters of Mrs. G. and CEN*, pp. 7, 33.

54. Ward, "Biographical Introduction," I, xxi. John Mortimer speaks of him as "a familiar figure in our city streets, a man of dignified and stately presence, one to be singled out in a crowd." "Lancashire Novelists.—Mrs. Gaskell," *The Manchester Quarterly*, XXI (July 1902), 204.

55. A more severe appraisal can be found in Johanna Jacoba Van Dullemen, *Mrs. Gaskell: Novelist and Biographer* (Amsterdam, 1924), and especially in Aina Rubenius, *The Woman Question in Mrs. Gaskell's Life and Works* (Upsala, 1950). The Reverend's attitude toward traveling with his family is clarified by his wife in the same letter to Nancy Robson in which his tendency to retreat to his study is mentioned: "He does not like any of us to go with him when he goes from home, saying it does not give him so much change; and with us he does not make so many acquaintances certainly, as he did at Rome for instance. . . I had got money (from my writing) both to pay for *his* going, & for Meta's, *or* mine, *or* both of us, *with him* but he quite declined it, giving the reason as above: 'being more independent, & getting more complete change.' A letter of Meta Gaskell to her sister Marianne suggests the painfulness of Mrs. Gaskell's disappointment at not hearing from her husband while she had a bad bronchitis. Brotherton Collection.

56. An early letter to Norton (June 3, 1857) broaches a plan with regard to her husband in which her friend is to participate: "*I wish you could persuade him to go to America with you*. . . . I'd soon earn the passage and travelling money. He wants change, and yet hates leaving home. His flesh wants it, but his spirit abhors it, do you understand?" *Letters of Mrs. G. and CEN,* p. 4. In June of 1861, she writes in haste to the William Wetmore Storys to "ask you (if you are at Siena or Spezzia this summer,) to give my dear husband the welcome *there* you have so often and so kindly offered him in Rome." The explanation which follows again throws light on the Reverend's reluctance to travel with "the women of his family" and also demonstrates his wife's sweetly tolerant attitude toward her husband and obvious fondness for him: ". . . he says he feels so much the entire want of *change,* and the desirableness of having no res*ponsib*ility that he would rather not feel that he had any one dependent on him. And yet he would like society, if only to cheer him up a bit,—he is *so* over-worked and I am so sure you would like him—he is such a punster, & so merry when well, & so fond of children——" Berg Collection. [489]

57. Cecil, p. 153.

58. Letter to Mary Howitt of August 18, 1838. "Stray Notes from Mrs. Gaskell," p. 611.

59. Yvonne ffrench, *Mrs. Gaskell* (London, 1949), p. 14.

60. Susanna and Catherine Winkworth, *Memorials of Two Sisters,* ed. Margaret J. Shaen (London, 1908), p. 23. Susanna also suggests the nature of that "charm" which was to win her so many admirers later on: "All her great intellectual gifts—her quick keen observation, her marvellous memory, her wealth of imaginative power, her rare felicity of instinct, her graceful and racy humour,—were so warmed and brightened by sympathy and feeling, that while actually with her, you were less conscious of her power than of her charm." P. 24.

61. Chadwick, p. 239.

62. *Ibid.,* pp. 224–25.

63. That she was herself aware of the artistic gain to be derived from a long accumulation of experience is evident in the advice she gives to an unidentified female correspondent who had sent her a manuscript and obviously sought her opinion regarding a literary career: ". . . viewing the object from a solely artistic point of view a good writer of fiction must have *lived* an active & sympathetic life if she wishes her books to have strength & vitality in them. When you are forty, and if you have a gift for being an authoress, you will write ten times as good a novel as you could do now, just because you will have gone through so much more of the interests of a wife and a mother." Letter of September 25, Eastbourne, Sussex [1862]. Morris L. Parrish Collection. Princeton University Library. [515]

64. Quoted in Ward, "Introduction to 'Mary Barton,' Etc.," *Mary Barton and Other Tales,* I, lxiii.

65. ffrench, p. 27.

66. We get glimpses of the social whirl through the correspondence of the Winkworth sisters. A letter from Emily to Catherine (London, May 8,

1849) mentions Mrs. Gaskell's presence at one of the poet Samuel Rogers' well-known breakfasts along with Mrs. Dickens, Mr. and Mrs. Macready, and Dickens' great friend, John Forster; it also announces an invitation for dinner at Forster's home. Another letter to the same correspondent ten days later enjoins: "Ask Lily [Mrs. Gaskell's nickname] about the breakfast at Monckton Milnes's and Professor Whewell, and Guizot, and Archdeacon Hare, and Maurice and Ludlow." *Memorials of Two Sisters,* pp. 39, 42.

67. His first letter (January 31, 1850) pays a very flattering tribute to her talents: ". . . as I do honestly know that there is no living English writer whose aid I would desire to enlist in preference to the authoress of Mary Barton (a book that most profoundly affected and impressed me), I venture to ask whether you can give me any hope that you will write a short tale, or any number of tales, for the projected pages." *The Letters of Charles Dickens,* II, 202. The ensuing relationship between Mrs. Gaskell and Dickens appears from the latter's correspondence to have been a rather complex combination of distance and intimacy, of affinity and antipathy; admiration, respect, whimsical teasing, polite irritation, lack of candor at one time or another characterize Dickens' approach to his contributor. He did bestow generous praise on her talents as a story-teller, addressing her in his letter of November 25, 1851 as "MY DEAR SHEHEREZADE,—For I am sure your powers of narrative can never be exhausted in a single night, but must be good for at least a thousand nights and one." II, 359. Not only *Cranford, Mary Barton,* and *Ruth,* but even *North and South,* which became such a bone of contention because of its unconscionable length, earned his praises. See Letter of April 13, 1853 (II, 457) and Letter of June 16 [really 15], 1854 (II, 561). Annette Hopkins has devoted one whole chapter of her work on the conflicts concerning the publication of *North and South*; see Hopkins, Chapter VIII, pp. 135–57, a reworking of material in an earlier article.

68. Letter to Eliza Fox [1850]. Quoted by Hopkins, pp. 298–99.

69. Her talents as a hostess won the high approval of Monckton Milnes "whom I very well remember," Ward informs us, "telling me that their house made that city a quite possible place of residence for persons of literary tastes." "Biographical Introduction," I, xxxvi. Her own sketch "Company Manners" suggests a freedom from pomposity and pretensions and a genuine flair for achieving a gracious and diverting informality. *Ruth and Other Tales,* Etc., III, 493–512.

70. *Memorials of Two Sisters,* p. 24.

71. In the first of two letters to Tottie Fox on this subject she herself speaks of "home duties and individual life" as "just my puzzle; and I don't think I can get nearer to a solution than you have done." She goes on to express her conviction that, as far as women are concerned, "it is healthy for them to have the refuge of the hidden world of Art to shelter themselves in when too much pressed upon by daily small Lilliputian arrows of peddling cares; it keeps them from being morbid as you say; and takes them into the land where King Arthur lies hidden, and soothes them with its peace." Yet the problem is not resolved, for "the difficulty is where and when to

make one set of duties subserve and give place to the other." Quoted by Haldane, p. 249. Her ambiguous attitude is also evident in a statement to the female correspondent who had sent her a manuscript (see footnote 63 above): "I do not think I ever cared for fame: nor do I think it *is* a thing that ought to be cared for. It comes and it goes. The exercise of a talent or power *is* always a great pleasure; but one should weigh well whether this pleasure may not be attained by the sacrifice of some duty."

72. Letter to Norton, Manchester [1857], *Letters of Mrs. G. and CEN*, pp. 12–13. In another letter to him (December 10, 1860), the conflicting claims are more sharply suggested in a statement regarding her daughters: ". . . I like to keep myself in readiness to give them sympathy or advice at any moment; and consequently I do not do as I am often tempted to do, shut myself up secure from any interruption in any room." P. 74.

73. Letter to Catherine Winkworth, Lea Hurst, Matlock. Brotherton Collection. [211]

74. Perhaps the most winning evidence of her insatiable curiosity is the whimsical letter she sent to the father of her good friend Eliza (W. J. Fox, Unitarian Minister and M.P.) on discovering that his daughter had become engaged:

> My dear Mr. Fox
>
> Our Times of to-day—well of yesterday—well, tomorrow it will be of some day in dream-land, for I am past power of counting—
>
> Our Times of to-day has taken away my breath—Who—What, Where, Wherefore, Why—oh! do be a woman, and give me all possible details—Never mind the House of Commons: it can keep—but my, our, curiosity CAN'T.
>
> Oh! please telegraph back anything about him—how long known what is he—what *has* he (I live in Manchester city sacred to Mammon,) when did she *first* see him—Where are they going to live—Whole love story, &c., &c., &c.
>
> Write for 26 hours consecutively, and you can't write enough.
>
> WELL TO BE SURE
I THINK I AM
VERY
GLAD
Yours most truly,
E. C. Gaskell

Quoted by Haldane, p. 256.

75. In a letter to her future hosts discussing the impending trip, she reveals her worries about the reception of the biography, dreading the "double power to wound" of adverse criticism, "for if they say anything disparaging of *her* I know I shall not have done her and the circumstances in which she was placed justice." Quoted by Henry James in *William Wetmore Story and His Friends* (Boston, 1903), I, 354. James, who characterizes the happy visit as "a season the perfect felicity of which was to feed all her later time with fond memories, with renewed regrets and dreams," provides dramatic evidence of this reaction in Mrs. Gaskell's letters to her

former hosts. The most moving tribute to her Italian experience is undoubtedly the oft-quoted assertion in one of the letters: "It was in those charming Roman days that my life, at any rate, culminated. I shall never be so happy again. I don't think I was ever so happy before. My eyes fill with tears when I think of those days, and it is the same with all of us. They were the tip-top point of our lives. The girls may see happier ones—I never shall." Pp. 354, 355–56.

76. The details of the actual encounter between Mrs. Gaskell and Norton were rehearsed by her daughter Meta in a letter to Norton; see "Introduction," *Letters of Mrs. G. and CEN*, p. xix. In her letter (April 22 [1862]) acknowledging the announcement of Norton's engagement, Mrs. Gaskell paid tribute to the qualities which had endeared Norton to her: "I am so particularly glad to think of your being married; almost as if you were my own son; for I have often thought that of all the men I ever knew you were not only the one to best appreciate woman; but also the one to require along with your masculine friendships, the sympathetic companionship of a good gracious woman." *Letters of Mrs. G. and CEN*, p. 98.

77. Annette Hopkins has made a detailed study of the correspondence between Mrs. Gaskell and George Smith; see Chapter XI, pp. 200–24. One cannot resist presenting here two assessments of George Eliot quoted by Hopkins which reflect the characteristic conflict of values in Mrs. Gaskell, the gravitation between a standard conception of morality and a far more sophisticated appraisal of human behavior. Having in a previous communication expressed her disapproval of George Eliot's unorthodox relationship with George Henry Lewes by "hoping against hope" that she had not written *Adam Bede* since "Miss Evans' life—taken at the best construction, does so jar against the beautiful book," she demonstrates in a subsequent letter the breadth of imagination and spirit which so often obviated against her more conventional tendencies, despite an instinctive timidity even here still clearly perceptible: "Do you know I can't help liking her—*because* she wrote those books. Yes I do! I *have* tried to be moral, & dislike her & dislike her books—but it won't do. There is not a wrong word, or a wrong thought in them. I do believe—and though I should have been more 'comfortable,' for some indefinable reason, if a *man* had written them instead of a *woman*, yet I think the author must be a noble creature: and I shut my eyes to the awkward blot in her life." Pp. 207, 208.

78. *The George Eliot Letters*, III, 198–99. The extent of Mrs. Gaskell's enthusiasm for George Eliot's work—whose power she immediately recognized—is particularly evident in an admission to Norton regarding a projected work of her own: "Not a line of the book is written yet,—I think I have a feeling that it is not worth trying to write; while there are such books as Adam Bede & Scenes from Clerical Life—I set 'Janet's Repentance' above all, still.—" Letter of October 25 [1859], *Letters of Mrs. G. and CEN*, p. 39.

79. Even two out of the three poems published in *Household Words*, "Bran" and "The Scholar's Story," are based on Breton ballads. Both in her correspondence and in her works, Mrs. Gaskell demonstrates a great facility in the French language, particularly in what foreigners find most

difficult, the correct use of idiomatic expressions (she even employs one—*au pied de la lettre*—for humorous purposes in a speech of Cynthia's in *Wives and Daughters*). Though she claims in one letter (introducing W. R. Greg to Emile Souvestre) that she "cannot write good and grammatical French," the French that she finally lapses into is easy and fluent and perfectly carries out the vivacity and whimsicality of her particular mood. Letter of March 18th. Parrish Collection. Printed in full in M. L. Parrish, *Victorian Lady Novelists* (London, 1933).

80. Madame Mohl's youth has been interestingly described by Kathleen O'Meara in the first (the January number) of a series of four articles entitled "Madame Mohl, Her Salon and Her Friends," *Atlantic Monthly*, LV (January–June 1885), 74–79. Both before and after her marriage, she attracted in her salon men like Thiers, Mérimée, De Tocqueville, Guizot, Cousin, Benjamin Constant, "in fact, the cleverest men of the day," as Kathleen O'Meara puts it (February 1885, p. 170). That Madame Mohl greatly prized certain emotional qualities in Mrs. Gaskell is movingly suggested in a letter to Madam Sherer in which she laments the author's death: "I am sure you will feel for me when I tell you that I have lost my dear Mrs. Gaskell, the best friend I had in England, perhaps anywhere. . . . To say what I have lost would be impossible. . . . Oh, dear! My heart feels like a lump of lead in me. If you had known what a heart *she* had! But no one did." (Quoted by Kathleen O'Meara, March 1885, p. 327.) Mrs. Gaskell has given a lively description of life in the Mohl household during one of her visits in a letter to Emily (Winkworth) Shaen. Printed in full by Haldane, pp. 296–300.

81. In a letter to Norton of July 13, 1863, she recalls those trying times: "Last autumn and winter was *such* hard work—we were often off at nine,—not to come home till 7, or ½ past, too worn out to eat or do anything but go to bed. The one thought ran thro' all our talk almost like a disease." *Letters of Mrs. G. and CEN*, p. 107.

82. The very letter (September 8, 1865) announcing to Norton the "terribly grand thing! and a secret thing too!"—the purchase of a house "for Mr. Gaskell to retire to and for a home for my unmarried daughters"—has an intensely pathetic reference to the unrecapturable past; speaking of some American visitors, she says: "We hope they were the forerunners of you all in your times. But life never flows back,—we shall never again have the old happy days in Rome, shall we?" Her subconscious fears had already been touchingly suggested in an earlier letter (February 5, 1865) in which she conveyed to Norton her desire to visit him in America: "Sometimes I dream I go over to Boston and see you and Susan and the little ones. But I always pass into such a cold thick damp fog, on leaving the river at Liverpool that I never get over to you." *Letters of Mrs. G. and CEN*, pp. 125, 121. Her fatigue is very evident in a letter of [August 31st?] 1865 to her prospective son-in-law Thurstan Holland in which she almost immediately tells him: "I am so tired & worn out I must refer you to Minnie [Marianne] for all particulars" and concludes a discussion of her daughter's health with "I am so tired I hardly know what I say." One senses that shopping for the new house cannot fully account for the lassitude; sig-

nificantly enough she is also discussing provisions for a will. Yale University Library. [581]

83. Letter to Anne Robson. Brotherton Collection. [16]

CHAPTER TWO

Mary Barton

1. For details on the favorable reception, see Ward, "Introduction to 'Mary Barton,' Etc.," pp. lvii–lix. How much Carlyle's sympathetic praise meant to her is evident in Mrs. Gaskell's reference to it in her letter to Miss Lamont (January 5 [1849]): ". . .when I am over-filled with thoughts arising from this book, I put it all aside, (or *try* to put it aside,) and think of his last sentence. "May you live long to write good books, or *do silently good actions which in my sight is far more indispensable.*" Parrish Collection. [39]

2. The unfortunate social conditions prevailing in Lancashire in the years immediately preceding the publication of *Mary Barton* are clearly indicated by the following statement from Donald Read's study, "Chartism in Manchester" (in Asa Briggs, *Chartist Studies,* London, 1959): "During the latter part of 1846 and throughout 1847 the trade depression which had returned in the summer of 1845 became increasingly severe. In May 1847 the *Manchester Examiner* calculated that 84,000 operatives were working short-time and that 24,000 were unemployed. Only 77,000 were working full-time. . . . Cholera too was spreading. Altogether, the year 1847 was a terrible one." Pp. 61–62.

3. Harriet Martineau, "Preface," *Illustrations of Political Economy* (London, 1843), I, xii.

4. Mrs. Trollope's consistent liveliness and shrewdness of observation compensate for her weaknesses, and she manages to sustain suspense with an ingenuity worthy of Dickens; indeed she creates a heroine far more clever and sophisticated than most Dickensian ladies. In comparison with Charlotte Elizabeth (Mrs. Tonna) and even Mrs. Trollope, Mrs. Gaskell seems quite liberal in her attitude to social agitation. Whereas she could write sympathetically of John Barton who "became a Chartist, a Communist," the author of *Helen Fleetwood* inveighed against Socialism as "the moral Gorgon upon which whomsoever can be compelled to look must wither away . . . the last effort of Satanic venom wrought to the madness of rage by the consciousness of his shortened time" (*The Works of Charlotte Elizabeth* [Tonna], New York, 1849, I, 628) and Mrs. Trollope decided not to continue the career of her workman hero beyond his youth at a time "when those in whose behalf she hoped to move the sympathy of their country are found busy in scenes of outrage and lawless violence, and uniting themselves with individuals whose doctrines are subversive of every species of social order" ("Preface," *The Life and Adventures of Michael Armstrong, the Factory Boy,* London, 1840, p. iv).

5. Mrs. Gaskell was to use almost the very same terms in *Mary Barton* in her reference to "two worlds." As Kathleen Tillotson points out, the dire sense of separateness between classes had already been suggested much earlier by Carlyle's reference in *Sartor Resartus* to "two Sects" who "will one day part England between them," to "two contradictory, uncommunicating masses." *Novels of the Eighteen-Forties* (London, 1961), p. 82.

6. Tillotson, p. [202].

7. Arnold Kettle, "The Early Victorian Social-Problem Novel," *From Dickens to Hardy,* ed. Boris Ford (London, 1958), p. 179.

8. Louis Cazamain, *Le Roman Social en Angleterre (1830–1850)* (Paris, 1904), pp. 388, 385. I have supplied English versions of Cazamain's text since the work has never been translated.

9. Thus, although doubtful of the appropriateness of using "Fiction" as "the vehicle for a plain and matter-of-fact exposition of social evils," the critic of the *Athenaeum* (writing on October 21, 1848) could not deny the accuracy of the portrayal: "But we have met with few pictures of life among the working classes at once so forcible and fair as 'Mary Barton.' The truth of it is terrible." P. 1050. On the appearance of a third edition, the reviewer of *Fraser's Magazine* dramatically announced that if readers wished to be enlightened on such burning questions of the day as "why poor men, kind and sympathising as women to each other, learn to hate law and order, Queen, Lords and Commons, country-party, and corn-law leaguer, all alike," "what can madden brave, honest, industrious North-country hearts, into self-imposed suicidal strikes, into conspiracy, vitriol-throwing, and midnight murder," "what drives men to gin and opium," his advice (repeated with rhetorical fervor at the mention of each significant issue) was "let them read *Mary Barton.*" XXXIX (April 1849), 430.

10. W. R. Greg, "Mary Barton," *Mistaken Aims and Attainable Ideals of the Artizan Class* (London, 1876), p. 113. The article originally appeared in *The Edinburgh Review,* April 1849.

11. *Ibid.,* pp. 135–37, 139.

12. Cazamian, p. 382.

13. Cecil, p. 181.

14. Ward, "Introduction to 'Mary Barton,' Etc.," p. lii.

15. Letter to Miss Ewart. Quoted by Haldane, pp. 46–47.

16. Arthur Pollard, "The Novels of Mrs. Gaskell," *Bulletin of The John Rylands Library,* XLIII (March 1961), 410.

17. Elizabeth Barrett Browning, Letter to Miss Mitford, December 13, 1850, *The Letters of Elizabeth Barrett Browning,* ed. Frederic G. Kenyon (New York, 1897), I, 472.

18. Indeed the initial impulse, as expressed in her Preface, does not even suggest any didactic intention: she tells us that, despite a previous intention of expressing her "deep relish and fond admiration of the country" in a story, "I bethought me how deep might be the romance in the lives of some of those who elbowed me daily in the busy streets of the town in which I resided." "Preface to the Original Edition of 1848," I, lxxiii.

19. *Ibid.*

20. *Ibid.*, p. lxxiv; *Mary Barton. A Tale of Manchester Life*, p. 95.

21. Mrs. Gaskell has herself testified to the meaningfulness of the character of John Barton. In the unfinished draft of a letter to the sister-in-law of W. R. Greg, she thus attests to his focal position in the novel: "Round the character of John Barton all the others formed themselves; he was my hero; *the* person with whom all my sympathies went, with whom I tried to identify myself at the time, because I believed from personal observation that such men were not uncommon, and would well reward such sympathy and love as should throw light down upon their groping search after the causes of suffering, and the reason why suffering is sent, and what they can do to lighten it." Quoted in Ward, "Introduction to 'Mary Barton,' Etc.," I, lxiii. She is even more explicit regarding the importance of the character in her letter to Miss Lamont, January 5 [1849]: "'John Barton' was the original name, as being the central figure to my mind; indeed I had so long felt that the bewildered life of an ignorant thoughtful man of strong power of sympathy, dwelling in a town so full of striking contrasts as this is, was [*sic*] a tragic power, that in writing he was [one word illegible] hero; and it was a London thought coming through the publishers that it must be called *Mary* B. So many people overlook John B or see him merely to misunderstand him, that if you were a stranger and had only said that one thing (that the book sh[d] have been called *John B.*) I should have had pleasure in feeling that my own idea was recognized." Parrish Collection. [39]

22. *Mary Barton*, pp. 4, 8.

23. *Ibid.*, pp. 22, 20–21, 20, 22.

24. For, Margaret Legh (Mary's friend) who is here speaking goes on to say, "Every sorrow in her mind is sent for good." *Ibid.*, p. 50. Such a providential view of suffering is of course essentially alien to Barton's temperament.

25. *Ibid.*, pp. 68, 71, 72.

26. *Ibid.*, p. 73.

27. *Ibid.*, pp. 96, 114. For details on the rise of the movement which incorporated in a "People's Charter" (May 8, 1838) its six demands for social reform (manhood suffrage, voting by ballot, salaried Members of Parliament, abrogation of property requirements for Members, electoral districts of equal population, and yearly elections) and its first great defeat by the Parliamentary rejection of the Charter (July 12, 1839), see Elie Halevy, *A History of the English People, 1830–1841,* trans. E. I. Watkin (London, 1927), pp. 295–335. Donald Read's specific study of Chartist agitation in Lancashire indirectly vindicates the accuracy of Mrs. Gaskell's portrayal of the conflict between masters and men in the difficult years 1839–42. The following characterization of the operatives' mood could serve as an appropriate footnote to John Barton's tragedy: "The mood of despair prevailed throughout. Despair spurred the operatives to take up Chartism in the hope of improving their conditions, but despair with Chartism itself quickly undermined whatever prospects of success the movement might have had." "Chartism in Manchester," in Briggs, *Chartist Studies,* p. 42.

28. *Mary Barton*, pp. 219, 194–95.
29. *Ibid.*, pp. 195, 195–96.
30. *Ibid.*, pp. 217, 219.
31. *Ibid.*, pp. 430, 431.
32. Tillotson, p. 211.
33. Kettle, p. 181.
34. *Mary Barton*, p. 196.
35. *Ibid.*, pp. 23–24.
36. *Ibid.*, p. 24.
37. Her tendency to relate the phenomenon of social discontent with the impulse to question and negate divine injunction is partly conveyed in that letter to Mrs. Greg in which she also stresses the importance of John Barton. Having indicated as part of her conception the effect of "the seeming injustice of the inequalities of fortune," which "must bewilder an ignorant man full of rude, illogical thought, and full also of sympathy for suffering which appealed to him through his senses," she goes on to point out: "I fancied I saw how all this might lead to a course of action which might appear right for a time to the bewildered mind of such a one, but that this course of action, violating the eternal laws of God, would bring with it its own punishment of an avenging conscience far more difficult to bear than any worldly privation." Quoted in Ward, "Introduction to 'Mary Barton,' Etc.," p. lxiii.
38. See Chapter 5 for a discussion of this motif in the short stories.
39. George Orwell, *A Collection of Essays* (New York, 1954), p. 182.
40. Margaret Legh endures her blindness without repining and cautions Mary of the need for "being patient," pointing out that "waiting is far more difficult than doing. . . . but it's one of God's lessons we all must learn, one way or another." *Mary Barton*, p. 164.
41. Tillotson, p. 221.
42. "Preface," *Mary Barton*, p. lxxiv.
43. Letter to Mrs. Greg. Quoted in Ward, "Introduction to 'Mary Barton,' Etc.," p. lxiii.
44. The difference between Mary and the standard heroines of fiction was acclaimed by one critic: "Compare Mary Barton with the Evelinas, Cecilias and Belindas which superseded the Romances of the Forest, the Children of the Abbey, and the Haunted Towers of the age which preceded theirs! Mary Barton is no heiress, nursed in the lap of luxury, living upon the produce of other people's labour . . . refined, generous, capricious, indolent, dying first of ennui, then of love, and lastly falling a prey to a fortune-hunter, or a military swindler. No; Mary Barton is one of Labor's daughters—heiress of all the struggles, vicissitudes and sufferings consequent upon the ignorance and prejudices of the society into which she was born." *Westminster and Foreign Quarterly Review*, LI (April–July 1849), 48. The difficulty of moving the focus away from John Barton in accordance with the publisher's preference for a novel entitled *Mary Barton* may partly account for the limitations of the portrayal of Mary and even for structural weaknesses. Annette Hopkins, who feels that once "pushed in the foreground,"

the character "becomes alive," notes that nevertheless "the scar left by this major operation remains." P. 77.

45. *Mary Barton,* pp. 90, 131, 90.
46. *Ibid.,* p. 89.
47. *Ibid.,* pp. 148, 149, 150.
48. *Ibid.,* pp. 340–41.
49. *Ibid.,* p. 380.
50. *Ibid.,* pp. 98–99.
51. *Ibid.,* pp. 113–14.
52. *Ibid.,* pp. 137–38.
53. *Ibid.,* pp. 247, 425.
54. *Ibid.,* p. 429. As a manuscript entitled "Conclusion yet to be written" indicates, the author had originally conceived of a far more obdurate Carson who "gave him [Barton] in charge to the police" and was only "softened by the agony which ended in death" as Barton was being taken to prison. Only "as the breath fled" after Barton's "last penitent cry" for divine forgiveness did Carson become capable of forgiving. The Forster Collection, Victoria and Albert Museum. The final version enabled her to convey far more appropriately her conviction of the essential brotherhood of man.
55. *Ibid.,* p. 448.
56. *Ibid.,* p. 451.

North and South

57. Ward, "Introduction to 'North and South,'" *North and South,* IV, xix.
58. Cazamian, p. 408.
59. *Ibid.*
60. Her artistic consciousness was soon to be evident in her annoyance at the curtailment of the novel enforced upon her by Dickens and indeed at the whole method of writing for serial publication. In a letter to Mrs. Jameson, whose advice she requests on possible revisions before republication, she complains of having been forced "to write pretty hard without waiting for the happy leisure hours," and that "at last the story is huddled and hurried up" because she was limited to 20 numbers. In her next letter she again regrets the adverse circumstances of the novel's production: "If the story had been poured just warm out of the mind, it would have taken a much larger mould. It was the cruel necessity of compressing it that hampered me." *Anna Jameson. Letters and Friendships* (*1812–1860*), ed. Mrs. Steuart Erskine (London, 1915), pp. 296, 297–98. For the actual changes made see A. Stanton Whitfield, *Mrs. Gaskell. Her Life and Work* (London, 1929), Appendix II, p. 219. Almost the only available comments from the author on work actually in progress relate, interestingly enough, to *North and South.* In a letter to John Forster of April 1854 she ponders the possibility of adding to the novel a young girl "to be in love with Mr Thornton in a kind of passionate despairing way,—but both jealous of Margaret, & yet angry that she gives Mr Thornton pain—I know the kind of wild wayward character that grows up in lonesome places, which has a sort

of Southern capacity of hating & loving." The British Museum. [191] Her letter to Catherine Winkworth from Lea Hurst (October 1854) is both whimsical and lively on the subject of her work. She has renounced the temptation of outings: "So *ought* not M. Hale to stand a good chance. I do think she is going on well. I am satisfied. Not that I have written so much, but so *well.* There's modesty for you." She requests her opinion on whether "a fire burning down Mr Thornton's mills *and house* as a *help* to failure" would be appropriate and announces: "M H has just told the lie, & is gathering herself up after her dead faint; very meek & stunned & humble." Brotherton Collection. [211] For other comments in a letter to Emily Winkworth see Haldane, p. 97.

61. "Modern Novelists—Great and Small," *Blackwood's Edinburgh Magazine,* LXXVII (January–June 1855), 559.

62. *Ibid.,* p. 560.

63. Thus, like Thornton, the mill-owner Robert Gérard Moore's view of his workmen is at first narrow since he believes that "in treating them justly, I fulfil my whole duty towards them"; Caroline Helstone, like Margaret Hale, sees the limitations of Moore's behaving "as if your living cloth-dressers were all machines like your frames and shears," and regrets that he does not "expect them to love [him]." Moore's eyes are eventually opened to the sufferings of the deprived and he is converted to social sympathy, to "something . . . beyond a man's personal interest." *Shirley* (London, 1960), pp. 70, 538.

64. Cazamian sees the basic contrast Mrs. Gaskell herself originally experienced between the worlds of country and city as the product of her sensibility: initially her senses and imagination sharply separated "the sunny green country side" from "the black cities of noise and smoke." P. 409.

65. Kettle, p. 183.

66. "He [Barton] felt the contrast between the well-filled, well-lighted shops and the dim gloomy cellar, and it made him moody that such contrasts should exist. They are the mysterious problem of life to more than him." *Mary Barton,* p. 69.

67. *Ibid.,* p. 432.

68. Perhaps this limitation accounts for the rather ambiguous praise bestowed upon the work by her formerly severe critic, W. R. Greg: "I do not think it as thorough a work of genius as 'Mary Barton'—nor the subject as interesting as 'Ruth'—but I like it better than either, and you know how, in spite of my indignation, I admired the first." Quoted in Ward, "Introduction to 'North and South,' " p. xix.

69. Cazamian, p. 419.

70. Charlotte had asked: "Do you, who have so many friends,—so large a circle of acquaintance,—find it easy, when you sit down to write, to isolate yourself from all those ties, and their sweet associations, so as to be your *own woman,* uninfluenced or swayed by the consciousness of how your work may affect other minds, what blame or what sympathy it may call forth? . . . . are you never tempted to make your characters more amiable than the Life, by the inclination to assimilate your thoughts to the thoughts

of those who always *feel* kindly, but sometimes fail to *see* justly?" Letter of July 9, 1853, quoted by Mrs. Gaskell in *The Life of Charlotte Brontë* (New York, n.d.), pp. 450–51.

71. See the discussion of William Stevenson in Chapter I. In delineating Mr. Hale, Mrs. Gaskell was probably influenced by the experiences of J. A. Froude (see Whitfield, p. 25 and Rubenius, pp. 246–47) and of Travers Madge (Chadwick, p. 224). The resemblance between Mr. Hale and Mr. Pomfret in Henry F. Chorley's *Pomfret* (1845) was first noted in the *Athenaeum* review of *Wives and Daughters* (March 3, 1866, p. 295); see also Rubenius, pp. 247–48. It is intriguing to find the Reverend Brontë (seemingly of a temperament so different from Hale's) claiming in a letter to Mrs. Gaskell that, despite the general opinion of him as "a somewhat extraordinary and eccentrick personage," he is "in some respects a kindred likeness to the father of Margaret . . . peacable, feeling, sometimes thoughtful—and generally well-meaning." Letter of November 3, 1856, "The Reverend Patrick Brontë and Mrs. E. C. Gaskell," *Transactions and Other Publications of the Brontë Society*, VIII (1936), 99.

72. *North and South*, pp. 9, 42.

73. *Ibid.*, pp. 78–79.

74. *Ibid.*, p. 79.

75. *Ibid.*, p. 70.

76. *Ibid.*, p. 18.

77. *Ibid.*, p. 71.

78. *Ibid.*, p. 73.

79. *Ibid.*, pp. 83, 73.

80. *Ibid.*, pp. 92–93.

81. *Ibid.*, p. 93.

82. *Ibid.*, pp. 93, 93–94.

83. *Ibid.*, pp. 94, 96.

84. *Ibid.*, pp. 97, 97–98, 98.

85. *Ibid.*, pp. 99–100, 101, 99.

86. *Ibid.*, pp. 137, 138.

87. *Ibid.*, pp. 140, 141.

88. *Ibid.*, p. 142.

89. *Ibid.*, pp. 142, 143.

90. Kettle, pp. 182–83.

91. Pritchett, p. 91.

92. *North and South*, pp. 103, 118, 178.

93. *Ibid.*, pp. 104, 156, 159, 156.

94. *Ibid.*, pp. 172, 185, 193–94.

95. *Ibid.*, pp. 181, 197.

96. *Ibid.*, p. 209.

97. *Ibid.*

98. *Ibid.*, pp. 211–12.

99. *Ibid.*, p. 226.

100. *Ibid.*, p. 214.

101. *Ibid.*, pp. 222–23.

102. "Modern Novelists—Great and Small," *Blackwood's*, p. 560.

103. See footnote 60 in this chapter. The reason Mrs. Gaskell gives in her letter is not fully illuminating; once "mills and *house*" were destroyed, "then Margaret would rebuild them larger & better & need not go & live there when she's married." But it certainly suggests Margaret's role as Thornton's rescuer at a time of great crisis.

104. *North and South*, p. 387.

105. *Ibid.*, pp. 389, 515.

Ruth

106. ffrench, p. 37.

107. Copy of a letter to Anne Robson, Brotherton Collection. [148] That her mood while preparing to write *Ruth* was rather uneasy is evident in a letter to her daughter Marianne [1852]: "When Ruth will be published whether this year, next, or 10 years hence I don't know. It is not *written* yet—although Agnes Sanders was told at a Leamington Library that it was coming down next day. I have never asked for any copies for myself. But, as I say again, *when* or *if ever* I shall finish it I don't know. I hate publishing because of the talk people make, which I always feel as a great impertinence, *if they address their remarks to me* in any way." She goes on to announce the arrival of visitors "(to go off from Ruth, the very thought of which makes me X. & the dress & order subjects)." Berg Collection. [140]

108. Letter to Eliza Fox, quoted by Haldane, pp. 244–45. The pervasiveness of conservative attitudes toward this subject is aptly illustrated by Josephine Butler's description (in *An Autobiographical Memoir*) of the attitudes of Oxford University students to *Ruth* when it was first published: "A moral lapse in a woman was spoken of as an immensely worse thing than in a man. . . . A pure woman, it was reiterated, should be absolutely ignorant of a certain class of evils in the world, albeit those evils bore with a murderous cruelty on other women. One young man seriously declared that he would not allow his own mother to read such a book. . . . Silence was thought to be the great duty of all on such subjects." Quoted by Rubenius, p. 190. The incongruous persistence of such views into the twentieth century is demonstrated by K. L. Montgomery in 1910: "Only recently, in one of the spasms of prudery which periodically attacks censors, a certain Middlesex County Circuit refused to admit *Ruth* in its public library as unfit for the young person, who reads Zola in sixpenny translations or gloats over the latest murder details in the evening issues." "Elizabeth Cleghorn Gaskell," *Fortnightly*, p. 459.

109. Copy of a letter to Anne Robson, Brotherton Collection. [148]

110. Emile Montégut, "Mary Barton—Ruth," *Ecrivains Modernes de l'Angleterre* (Paris, 1889), p. 47.

111. Those are the terms used by Mrs. Gaskell in a letter to Mrs. Jameson of March 7 [1853] to characterize the failing of which readers have accused her: ". . . I am surprised to find how very many people—good kind people—and *women* infinitely more than men, really and earnestly disapprove of what I have said and express that disapproval at considerable pains to

themselves, rather than allow a 'demoralising laxity' to go unchecked." *Anna Jameson. Letters and Friendships*, pp. 294–95.

112. For details on the favorable reception by Mrs. Jameson, Archdeacon Hare, Richard Cobden, Frederick Denison Maurice, Florence Nightingale, and Mrs. Stanley, see Ward, "Introduction to 'Ruth,' Etc.," III, xiii–xvi. The many compensations for the pain of public disapproval are evident in a letter of Catherine Winkworth to Emma Shaen of March 23, 1853 which mentions that aside from "all the evil that is said" there is also "the very highest praise from Mr. Scott and Bunsen, and from Mr. Maurice and Archdeacon Hare, from Hallam and Monckton Milnes, besides many other less celebrated names, each testifying moreover to its meeting with appreciation among the best of their friends." *Memorials of Two Sisters*, p. 103. Elizabeth Barrett Browning's commendatory letter must have been particularly gratifying since her admiration for *Ruth* in part impelled her to address Mrs. Gaskell for the first time (she was also aware of those positive feelings toward her which had led Mrs. Gaskell to apply to Kenyon for an autograph letter): ". . . I write—and thank you from my heart for your sympathy and appreciation—I love and honour your books—especially 'Ruth' which is noble as well as beautiful, which contains truths purifying and purely put, yet treats of a subject scarcely ever boldly treated of except when taken up by unclean hands—" She not only goes on to express hopes for a future visit, but graciously announces: "I write for my husband as well as for myself—He is not a thick and thin novel-reader like me, but he was absorbed in your Ruth and feels all my feelings on it." "Letters Addressed to Mrs. Gaskell by Celebrated Contemporaries," *Bulletin of the John Rylands Library*, pp. 141, 142. Mrs. Gaskell's great dependence on critical approval is well demonstrated by the ecstatic delight she felt at being praised by one magazine; the satisfaction of approbation vents itself in an appealing informality of expression as she informs Catherine Winkworth: "The *North British Review* had a *delicious* review of 'Ruth' in it. Who the deuce could have written it? It is so truly religious, it makes me swear with delight. I think it is one of the Christian Socialists, but I can't make out which. I must make Will find out!" Quoted by Haldane, p. 68. Not only that review, which is indeed full of praise for many aspects of the work, but other favorable judgments, such as those in the *Westminster* and the *Gentleman's Magazine* must have proved very consoling.

113. Charlotte Brontë's reaction is quoted by Mrs. Gaskell in *The Life of Charlotte Brontë*, p. 422. Interestingly enough the question Charlotte raised before the work was even finished (she had only read Mrs. Gaskell's outline) was almost echoed though in a more sentimental vein by Elizabeth Barrett Browning in her first letter to Mrs. Gaskell (see footnote 112): "Was it quite impossible but that your Ruth should *die*? I had that thought of regret in closing the book—Oh, I must confess to it—Pardon me for the tears' sake!—" P. 141. For the other opinions quoted in the text see George Eliot's letter to Mrs. Peter Alfred Taylor, *The George Eliot Letters*, p. 86, and Hopkins, p. 127.

114. Cecil, p. 182.

115. "Ruth and Villette" [the review is unsigned but attributed to George Henry Lewes by George Eliot herself in one of her letters], *Westminster Review,* III (January and April 1953), 476.

116. Such an approach to rehabilitation shows a remarkable resemblance to Hawthorne's handling of the question of Hester Prynne's redemption in *The Scarlet Letter* (1850). There may be a reminiscence of Hawthorne in Lewes' reference to the ostracized fallen woman in fiction, "a scarlet letter flaming upon her breast, attracting every eye." Though Mrs. Gaskell was later to praise highly Hawthorne's *The Marble Faun* and was familiar with *The Scarlet Letter,* it is impossible to know whether she had read it before writing *Ruth.* Surprisingly enough, the resemblance between the two works seems hardly to have been noticed. John Mortimer, in discussing *Ruth,* briefly comments: "In some of the features of this story, one is irresistibly reminded of Hawthorne's 'Scarlet Letter'." "Lancashire Novelists.–Mrs. Gaskell," *Manchester Quarterly,* p. 217.

117. Lewes, pp. 476, 477.

118. *Ibid.,* p. 480.

119. Greg, "False Morality of Lady Novelists," p. 114.

120. "The Lady Novelists of Great Britain," *Gentleman's Magazine,* XL (July–December 1853), p. 22.

121. Cecil, p. 182. A comment by David Masson is particularly pertinent: "Passion . . . lay out of her domain; and both 'Ruth' and 'Sylvia's Lovers' rested on a delineation of passions with which the writer was either unable or, as I rather believe, unwilling to grapple firmly. The literature of passion can only be treated worthily by persons who, whether for good or bad, are indifferent to the thought how their work may be judged by the standard rules of the society in which they move; and this was not the case with one of the most sensitive and delicate-minded women who ever wrote in England." "Mrs. Gaskell," *Macmillan's Magazine,* p. 155.

122. Letter to Mrs. Schwabe, Manchester [1853], The Manchester Central Library. [162]

123. The German words are from a brief reference to the opinion of Chevalier Bunsen (the Prussian ambassador) given in a letter of Catherine Winkworth to Emma Shaen (March 23, 1853), the rest from the translated letter of Bunsen to Susanna Winkworth (February 3, 1853). *Memorials of Two Sisters,* pp. 103, 99.

124. *The Life of Charlotte Brontë,* p. 422.

125. Greg, "False Morality of Lady Novelists," p. 114.

126. *Ruth,* pp. 43–44.

127. Indeed, Johanna Van Dullemen argues, even her ignorance of such facts would be hard to believe since "a girl of 16 who is constantly with girls her own age and those girls her fellow-dressmakers, must have had some idea of irregular attachments." P. 124.

128. *Ruth,* p. 14.

129. *Ibid.,* p. 18.

130. *Ibid.,* p. 22.

131. *Ibid.,* pp. 32–33.

132. *Ibid.*, p. 40.
133. *Ibid.*, pp. 54, 54–55.
134. *Ibid.*, p. 64.
135. *Ibid.*, pp. 128–29. From the beginning, the full significance of this approach was not recognized. The critic of the *North British Review* who in 1853 had singled out this passage for praise as an example of the novel's "perfect simplicity, truthfulness . . . together with its exquisite purity of feeling" skirted the issue of Ruth's physical experience as he commended the author's handling of the heroine: "Ruth is still the simple girl, country-bred, delighted with the new sight of mountain-scenery, with all her sympathies not deadened, but heightened, by the new power which has been developed in her, the entire devotion of a most humble, most trustful love." XIX (May–August 1853), 151.
136. *Ruth*, p. 93.
137. *Ibid.*, p. 71.
138. *Ibid.*, p. 118. Cf. Pastor Dimmesdale's speech interceding for Hester Prynne's right to keep Pearl in *The Scarlet Letter:* ". . . it is good for this poor, sinful woman that she hath an infant immortality, a being capable of eternal joy or sorrow, confided to her care,–to be trained up by her to righteousness,–to remind her, at every moment, of her fall,–but yet to teach her, as it were by the Creator's sacred pledge, that, if she bring the child to heaven, the child will also bring its parent thither!" (Boston, 1960). P. 114.
139. *Ibid.*, pp. 118–19.
140. *Ibid.*, p. 119.
141. The first point of view is well represented by the critic of the *Athenaeum* in his review of *Ruth*, January 15, 1853, p. 77; for the opposing view see Montégut, "Mary Barton–Ruth," pp. 53–54. Charlotte Brontë, who shrewdly guessed that the Reverend Benson's action would arouse much criticism, missed the ambiguities involved in that action when she expressed her conviction that "it is explicitly shown that this step was regarded by the author as an error, and that she unflinchingly follows it up to its natural and fatal consequences. . . ." Letter to Mrs. Gaskell, February 1853, *Shakespeare Head Brontë*, IV, 49.
142. *Ruth*, p. 120.
143. *Ibid.*, p. 121.
144. *Ibid.*, p. 358.
145. *Ibid.*, p. 153.
146. For the intriguing resemblance between such misgivings and Mrs. Gaskell's own anxious feelings with regard to her child Marianne, see Chapter 1, footnote 10.
147. *Ruth*, p. 296.
148. *Ibid.*, p. 283.
149. *Ibid.*, pp. 238, 334, 347, 348.
150. As far as W. R. Greg was concerned, Bradshaw displayed in his reaction to Ruth "a brutal, savage violence and a coarse, unfeeling cruelty, which we need not scruple to affirm constituted a far greater sin than poor

Ruth had committed, or would have committed had her lapse from chastity been wilful and persistent instead of unconscious, transient, and bitterly and nobly atoned for." He goes on to comment appropriately: "Something of this very conviction was evidently in Mrs. Gaskell's mind; and we can scarcely doubt that she placed Mr. Bradshaw's hard and aggressive Pharisaism in such strong relief and contrast by way of insinuating the comparative moral we have boldly stated. In any case such is the resulting impression which must be left in the reader's mind." "False Morality of Lady Novelists," p. 113. If the character of Mr. Bounderby in Dickens' *Hard Times* owes something to that of Mr. Bradshaw, as Ward suggests ("Introduction to 'Ruth,' Etc.," p. xxiii) so does that of Mr. Gradgrind in the same work (see Sanders, p. 51) particularly in the relationships of both fathers to their daughter and son. Indeed, as Cazamian notes, "many incidents and characters from *Hard Times* (1854) have been inspired by *Ruth* (1853)." *Le Roman Social en Angleterre*, p. 385 (note).

151. *Ruth*, pp. 321, 320, 323, 324.

152. Though Greg's criticism of Mrs. Gaskell—that she "scarcely seems at one with herself" in the handling of Ruth—applies to his discussion of the character of Bradshaw and the "impression" it is intended to create, the same comment could be made with regard to Jemima.

153. *Ruth*, pp. 351, 353.

154. Pollard, p. 414.

CHAPTER THREE

"Mr. Harrison's Confessions"

1. "Company Manners," III, 508.

2. See the discussion of the inception of *Mary Barton* in Chapter 2.

3. Letter to the Howitts, May 1838, "Stray Notes from Mrs. Gaskell," pp. 604–5.

4. *Cranford and Other Tales*, II, p. 1.

5. She herself told Ruskin that she "never meant to write more" than the first paper, "so killed Captain Brown very much against my will." Quoted in Ward, "Introduction to 'Cranford,' Etc.," p. xii. Dickens' enthusiasm probably was responsible for the continuation of the sketches. See for example his comment on the next installment: "If you were not the most suspicious of women, always looking for soft sawder in the purest metal of praise, I should call your paper delightful, and touched in the tenderest and most delicate manner. Being what you are, I confine myself to the observation that I have called it A Love Affair at Cranford, and sent it off to the printer." Letter of December 21, 1851, *The Letters of Charles Dickens*, II, 364.

6. Hopkins, p. 97; Ward, "Introduction to 'My Lady Ludlow,' Etc.," *My Lady Ludlow and Other Tales*, V, xxii.

7. "Mr. Harrison's Confessions," *My Lady Ludlow and Other Tales*, pp. 414, 447.

8. *Ibid.*, p. 487.

9. *Cranford*, p. 137.
10. "Mr. Harrison's Confessions," pp. 470–71.
11. *Ibid.*, p. 481.
12. See footnote 5 above.

Cranford

13. *Cranford*, pp. 4–5.
14. *Ibid.*, p. 5.
15. *Ibid.*, p. 9.
16. *Ibid.*, p. 10.
17. *Ibid.*
18. *Ibid.*, pp. 11–12.
19. Dickens, who felt that all Mrs. Gaskell's references to his work should be excised, since, as he explained in his letter of December 5 [really 4], 1851, "with my name on every page of Household Words, there would be —or at least I should feel—an impropriety in so mentioning myself," makes a particular reference to this section of the *Cranford* paper although he had already made several changes (*e.g.*, the substitution of a rather silly punning joke for a mention of the Bath swarry in *Pickwick Papers*). He tells her: "I was particular, in changing the author, to make it 'Hood's *Poems*,' in the most important place—I mean where the Captain is killed—and I hope and trust that the substitution will not be any serious drawback to the paper in any eyes but yours." *The Letters of Charles Dickens*, II, 361. One wonders whether Dickens was so particularly eager to remove the mention of his work from this one incident because he was loath to have such sad connotations attached to it.
20. *Cranford*, p. 22. She speaks of "one of those whimsical thoughts which come unbidden into our heads, in times of deepest grief. . . ."
21. *Ibid.*, pp. 3–4.
22. *Ibid.*, pp. 2, 6, 17.
23. *Ibid.*, p. 50.
24. *Ibid.*, p. 89.
25. *Ibid.*, pp. 108–9.
26. *Ibid.*, p. 76.
27. Arthur Pollard makes a somewhat similar point in stating that Miss Matty "represents human values over against social conventions." "The Novels of Mrs. Gaskell," p. 407.
28. *Cranford*, pp. 40–41.
29. *Ibid.*, pp. 42–43.
30. *Ibid.*, p. 48.
31. *Ibid.*, p. 152.
32. *Ibid.*, p. 101.
33. *Ibid.*, p. 118.
34. *Ibid.*
35. *Ibid.*, p. 192.
36. Cecil, p. 169.
37. *Cranford*, p. 168.

38. *Ibid.*, p. 96. Commenting on Miss Matty's limited skills, the narrator says: "No! there was nothing she could teach to the rising generation of Cranford, unless they had been quick learners and ready imitators of her patience, her humility, her sweetness, her quiet contentment with all that she could not do." P. 158.

39. *Ibid.*, pp. 120–21.

40. *Ibid.*, p. 15.

41. *Ibid.*, p. 140.

42. Letter to Ruskin, quoted by Ward, p. xii.

43. Anne Thackeray Ritchie suggests that the genial, eccentric, and understanding spirit of Cranford was hardly limited to the small town: "I am sure Cranford existed in the quarter of Paris where my own youth was passed. I can remember it in Kensington also, though we did not quite go to the length of putting our cows into gray flannel dressing-gowns. . . . Perhaps Cranford did not even stop at Kensington, but may have reached farther afield, taking Chiswick on its way." "Preface," *Cranford*, p. viii. Ward quaintly tells us that "an American young person told a friend of mine that it had taken her long to realise that Cranford was not a New England village." "Introduction to 'Cranford,' Etc.," p. xvii.

44. She apparently had a "Cranford Abroad" in mind. See Ward, "Introduction to 'Cranford,' Etc.," p. xvii. Her attempt ten years later to revive the characters of *Cranford* in a small story, "The Cage at Cranford" (published in *All the Year Round*, November 28, 1863), was not successful, however. One cannot agree with Annette Hopkins that the work is "the most striking instance of the author's genius for recapturing the original tones of her story." P. 108. On the contrary, the true spirit of humor and whimsy seems to have evaporated. There is real gaucherie in the attempt to connect all of the characters of the original work with such a slight and silly incident as the mistaking of a crinoline cage for a bird cage. The rehearsal of the characteristic idiosyncrasies seems mechanical and uninspired: compare, for instance, the description of Cranford ways quoted earlier in this chapter with the following passage from "The Cage at Cranford": "We called on Miss Matty, of course, and then on Mrs. Hoggins. It seems as if ill-luck would have it that we went to the only two households of Cranford where there was the encumbrance of a man, and in both places the man was where he ought not to have been—namely in his own house, and in the way." *The Cage at Cranford and Other Stories*, ed. Paul Beard (London, 1937), p. 34.

45. Ruskin wrote to Mrs. Gaskell that once he had recovered from his "passion at Captain Brown's being killed," he "enjoyed mightily" the reading of *Cranford*, adding "I do not know when I have read a more finished little piece of study of human nature. . . . nor was I ever more sorry to come to a book's end." Letter of February 21, 1865, quoted in Ward, "Introduction to 'Cranford,' Etc.," p. xxiv. There are several references to the reading aloud of *Cranford* by George Eliot in George Henry Lewes' Journal. *The George Eliot Letters*, II, 310–11. Mrs. Gaskell spoke of preferring it in the letter to Ruskin quoted by Ward, p. xi. In the very first letter which Norton wrote to Mrs. Gaskell (June 5, 1855) he mentioned his father's attachment to the book: "It was indeed, I think, the last book that he cared

to hear." *The Letters of Mrs. G. and CEN*, p. (1). The general popularity of the work is thus suggested by Annette Hopkins: "It has been rendered not only into German but French and Hungarian. It has been frequently dramatized, as frequently illustrated. It has appeared in de luxe editions and in cheap editions. It has fallen into the hands of textbook makers and been forced to stagger under a corpus of notes and study aids for the edification of American school children." P. 103.

"My Lady Ludlow"

46. Paul Elmer More, "Mrs. Gaskell," *The Nation*, LXXIV (April 11, 1907), 333.
47. Ward, "Introduction to 'My Lady Ludlow,' Etc.," p. xiv.
48. "My Lady Ludlow," p. 141.
49. *Ibid.*, p. 29.
50. *Ibid.*, p. 19. The tale exhibits that flair for suspense and melodrama so evident in many of her short stories.
51. *Ibid.*, p. 24.
52. *Ibid.*, pp. 215–16.
53. *Ibid.*, pp. 143–44.
54. *Ibid.*, pp. 137–38.
55. *Ibid.*, p. 179.
56. *Ibid.*, p. 207.

Wives and Daughters

57. Quoted by Chadwick, p. 66.
58. Henry James refers specifically to that subtitle to suggest the nature of his appreciation of the work: "If an author can be powerful, delicate, humorous, pathetic, dramatic, within the strict limits of homely prose, we see no need of his 'dropping into poetry,' as Mr. Dickens says. It is Mrs. Gaskell's highest praise to have been all of this, and yet to have written 'an everyday story' (as, if we mistake not, the original title of 'Wives and Daughters' ran) in an everyday style." "Wives and Daughters," p. 247. There is no evidence that the subtitle was ever intended as the title of the work.
59. See "Concluding Remarks" by Frederick Greenwood (editor, the *Cornhill Magazine*) appended to *Wives and Daughters. An Every-day Story*, VIII, 756–61.
60. Previous planning no doubt accounts for the latter. Annette Hopkins points out that an outline of the story in the letter to Smith "shows that barring a few trifling changes, the novel adheres strictly to the original plan. Thus . . . she was able to preserve unity and continuity in a way that she might not have been able to do had she composed it as she went along." P. 293. A more careful organization did not, however, preclude certain blunders: Sanders notes that Miss Browning is first called Sally, then Clarinda in chapter XIII and finally becomes Dorothy in chapter XXVI. Pp. 136–37.
61. Although W. E. A. Axon in his review of Mrs. Chadwick's book (see Chapter 1, footnote 35) denies her contention that Charles Darwin suggested Roger Hamley, Darwin's career must have been on Mrs. Gaskell's

mind since, according to Ward, she drew in one letter a comparison between Roger's expedition and that of Darwin. "Introduction to 'Wives and Daughters,'" p. xxvi.

62. That certain more minor elements in Mrs. Gaskell's plot bear a great similarity to aspects of *A Diary,* by the Swedish novelist Fredrika Bremer (some of whose novels she knew and with whom she became personally acquainted), was first suggested by the critic of the *Athenaeum* in his initial review of the work (March 3, 1866, p. 295) and subsequently demonstrated in great detail by Aina Rubenius. See her comparison of *Wives and Daughters* with *A Diary* (in which there is an incident extremely similar to that involving Cynthia, Mr. Preston, and Molly with regard to Cynthia's letters) and with *The Home* (in which two brothers resemble Osborne and Roger Hamley, and a Judge and his foster daughter have a relationship rather like that of Dr. Gibson and Cynthia). Pp. 264–72. Though Miss Rubenius tactfully concludes her painstaking examination by suggesting that since the two Bremer novels had been read by Mrs. Gaskell before her own career as a writer began, there is "at least a possibility that the events and characters from *A Diary* and *The Home* which she made use of, were not realized by her to be anything but her own large stock of material" (p. 277), all the evidence of comparable passages points to a somewhat more conscious process of imitation—the result perhaps of sheer fatigue and flagging powers of invention.

63. David Cecil calls Mrs. Jamieson (of *Cranford*) and Mrs. Gibson "figures in Jane Austen's manner; sisters of Mrs. Bennet and Lady Bertram." P. 169. Henry James indirectly suggests another predecessor when he notes that "the very nicest art was yet required to keep her [Mrs. Gibson] from merging, in the reader's sight, into an amusing caricature—a sort of commixture of a very mild solution of Becky Sharp with an equally feeble decoction of Mrs. Nickleby." "Wives and Daughters," p. 247. The conjunction of these two characters in James's mind appropriately reflects Mrs. Gaskell's characterization of Mrs. Gibson as a compound of studied hypocrisy (Becky) and deluded vanity (Mrs. Nickleby).

64. *Wives and Daughters*, pp. 133, 186.
65. *Ibid.*, pp. 108, 355.
66. *Ibid.*, p. 413.
67. *Ibid.*, p. 412.
68. *Ibid.*, pp. 416–17.
69. *Ibid.*, pp. 208, 198.
70. *Ibid.*, pp. 742–43.
71. James, p. 247.
72. Cecil, p. 168.
73. James, p. 247.
74. *Wives and Daughters*, pp. 249–50.
75. *Ibid.*, pp. 540, 256–57.
76. *Ibid.*, pp. 695, 254, 257.
77. *Ibid.*, pp. 254, 437–38, 254.
78. *Ibid.*, pp. 254, 472.

79. *Ibid.*, p. 509.
80. *Ibid.*, pp. 266, 413, 272.
81. *Ibid.*, p. 308. It is intriguing to note that Cynthia professes here a limitation very reminiscent of Miss Matty's endearing failure to comprehend scientific principles. Such a similarity suggests how positively the author felt toward the fallible Cynthia.
82. *Ibid.*, p. 309.
83. James, p. 247.
84. *Wives and Daughters*, p. 250.
85. *Ibid.*, p. 185.
86. *Ibid.*, pp. 455, 405.
87. *Ibid.*, pp. 576–77.
88. *Ibid.*, p. 485.
89. *Ibid.*, pp. 171, 329.
90. Thomas Seccombe, "Elizabeth Cleghorn Gaskell," *Bookman*, September 1910, p. 243.

CHAPTER FOUR

1. How much Mrs. Gaskell did justice to her subject is suggested by such a study as Margaret Lane's *The Brontë Story*: *A Reconsideration of Mrs. Gaskell's Life of Charlotte Brontë* (London, 1953) which, as its title indicates, examines the first biography of Charlotte Brontë in the light of subsequent knowledge. Probably the only essential failure in Mrs. Gaskell's approach is seen as the neglect of the early writings of Branwell and Charlotte which she had at her disposal but only used very scantily. Restrictive circumstances conspired to prevent her from revealing the content of those four significant letters to Mr. Heger which illumine the depth and hopelessness of Charlotte's attachment to her Belgian teacher. The basic lines of Mrs. Gaskell's study are, however, shown to be permanently sound, there being ample warrant for her general appraisal of the Reverend Brontë (apart from some of the eccentric behavior she attributed to him), of the Reverend Carus Wilson, and even of Mrs. Robinson in her relation to Branwell Brontë. See pp. 64, 161–64, 34, 54–55, 170.

2. Her sensitivity to the criticism which had assailed the biography and with which she had to cope on her return from the lovely visit to Italy is suggested by a cryptic passage in a letter to Norton (June 3, 1857): "I found trouble enough awaiting me from the publication of my Life of C. B. or rather not 'awaiting' me, but settled without me, settled for the best, all things considered, I am sure, Well! we won't speak any more of that." *Letters of Mrs. G. and CEN*, p. 3.

3. For the details of the inception of the work see pp. 10–12 of the "Preliminary" section devoted to Mrs. Gaskell in Clement K. Shorter, *Charlotte Brontë and Her Circle* (New York, 1896) and Chapter XXXV: "Mrs. Gaskell's Biography," *Shakespeare Head Brontë*, IV, 186–246. The letter written by Charlotte's best friend, Ellen Nussey, to the Reverend Brontë (June 6,

1855) is particularly instructive in clarifying not only the immediate circumstances under which the project was initiated ("the misinterpretations and the malignant spirit" of a magazine article on *Jane Eyre*) but the factors determining the choice of Mrs. Gaskell and the kind of responsibility that was to be placed on her: "I wish Mrs. Gaskell, who is every way capable, would undertake a reply, and would give a sound castigation to the writer. Her personal acquaintance with Haworth, the Parsonage, and its inmates, fits her for the task, and if on other subjects she lacked information I would gladly supply her with facts sufficient to set aside much that is asserted, if you yourself are not provided with all the information that is needed on the subjects produced. Will you ask Mrs. Gaskell to undertake this just and honourable defence? I think she would do it gladly. She valued dear Charlotte, and such an act of friendship, performed with her ability and power, could only add to the laurels she has already won." *Shakespeare Head Brontë*, IV, 189.

4. It is not surprising that she would find the work of writing at times trying, both mentally and physically. Thus she complains to Emily (Winkworth) Shaen in a letter of September 8, 1856 about the "dreary work" of "looking over, correcting, interweaving, &c. &c. &c. . . ." connected with receiving the juvenilia ("that mass of minute writing"), the addition of which necessitated the redoing of forty pages; she mentions having produced "120 *new* pages while we were absent on one holiday, which was no holiday to me"; she describes a working day at Dumbleton and Boughton from nine to one thirty and then "till 5—or past: having just a run of a walk before 7 o'clock dinner," adding: "I got through an immense deal: but I found head & health suffering—I could not sleep for thinking of it." Brotherton Collection. [308] To Mrs. Jameson she likewise revealed the arduousness of her task: "It is a most difficult undertaking. I have constantly to rewrite parts in consequence of gaining some fresh intelligence, which intelligence ought to have found place at some earlier place than the time I am then writing about." *Anna Jameson. Letters and Friendships,* p. 298. The mechanics of the work were surely only one of the problems she was then contending with.

5. Quoted by Hopkins, p. 160.

6. Her description of her awed reaction to Mr. Brontë while visiting Haworth is a case in point. She explains that the Reverend "was very polite and agreeable to me; paying rather elaborate old-fashioned compliments, but I was sadly afraid of him in my inmost soul; for I caught a glare of his stern eyes over his spectacles at Miss Brontë once or twice which made me know my man." She whimsically goes on to explore further the reason for her feelings: "Moreover to account for my fear—rather an admiring fear after all—of Mr. Brontë, please take into account that though I like the beautiful glittering of bright flashing steel I don't fancy firearms at all, at all—and Miss Brontë never remembers her father dressing himself in the morning without putting a loaded pistol in his pocket, just as regularly as he puts on his watch. There was this little deadly pistol sitting down to breakfast with us, kneeling down to prayers at night to say nothing of a loaded gun hang-

ing up on high, ready to pop off on the slightest emergency." Letter of September 1853, *Shakespeare Head Brontë*, IV, 91.

7. It is interesting to compare Mrs. Gaskell's formal description of the meeting between Charlotte Brontë and Harriet Martineau, to whom Currer Bell was as yet not known, with the lively and whimsical description of the event she had given in a letter to her friend Ann [Annie] Shaen: ". . . Mr. & Mrs. R. Martineau and Harriet M. sat with early tea before them, awaiting six o'clock, & their mysterious visitor, when lo! and behold, as the clock struck, in walked a little, very little, bright haired sprite, looking not above 15, very unsophisticated, neat & tidy. She sat down & had tea with them; her name being still unknown; she said to HM. 'What did you really think of "Jane Eyre"?' HM. I thought it a first rate book, whereupon the little sprite went red all over with pleasure. After tea Mr. & Mrs. RM. withdrew, and left sprite to a 2 hours tête-a-tête with H. M. to whom she revealed her name & the history of her life." Brotherton Collection. [60] Another lively account is to be found in a letter to Mrs. Froude in which she refers to the Reverend Brontë as Charlotte's "wayward eccentric wild father." Incomplete text in Berg Collection. [78] Her elaborate letter to Catherine Winkworth relating to Charlotte Brontë (August 25, 1850) best reveals the kind of censorship she exercised over her own correspondence when she incorporated it in the biography—in order, for instance, to understate the behavior of the Reverend Brontë and to minimize the unattractive details of Charlotte's appearance. Thus the Reverend's reaction to Charlotte's announcement that she had written a book—*Jane Eyre*—is toned down in the biography (though she had said to Catherine of Charlotte's account "I think I can remember the exact words," she claims in the biography where the words are evidently altered to be "pretty sure they are quite accurate.") The two versions seem worth quoting for the different portrait of the Reverend which their subtle variations reveal—and the sense of authenticity which is conveyed in the first version of the Reverend's response to Charlotte's request that he read her work:

Letter	*Biography*
"I can't be troubled to read MS"	"I am afraid it will try my eyes too much."
"I hope you have not been involving yourself in any such silly expense."	"My dear! you've never thought of the expense it will be! It will be almost sure to be a loss, for how can you get a book sold. No one knows you or your name."
Brotherton Collection. Also in *Shakespeare Head Brontë*, III, 140–46.	*The Life of Charlotte Brontë*, p. 276

When in the biography she quoted from this same letter her description of

Charlotte, she omitted the following details: "a reddish face"; "many teeth gone; altogether *plain.*"

8. Relying on Charlotte's statements, Mrs. Gaskell had violently denounced the behavior of Mrs. Robinson with regard to Branwell, quite blatantly accusing her of seducing the young tutor in her household and, by breaking Branwell's heart, behaving destructively not only to him but to his whole family. For they were directly victimized by Branwell's progressively destructive addiction to drink and opium after the experiences of being dismissed by Mr. Robinson and later (after Mr. Robinson's death) learning of his wife's remarriage. See *The Life of Charlotte Brontë*, pp. 227–28, 234–35, 236–38 (Doubleday reprints the first edition). The initial denunciation (pp. 227–28) was, when expurgated, replaced by the cryptic statement: "Of the causes of this deterioration I cannot speak; but the consequences were these" and a brief insertion regarding the reasons for the Brontë family's concern which made no mention of Mrs. Robinson; the other two sections were largely deleted. Mrs. Robinson was dissuaded from suing for libel, settling for a public apology by Mrs. Gaskell (conveyed through her solicitors, and published in *The Times* and the *Athenaeum*), the removal of all unsold copies, and the elimination of all offending passages regarding her from future editions. The changes were made in the third edition.

9. The work provoked objections even from those who had figured in a rather minor capacity in the biography. Mrs. Gaskell's general assessment of the regional temperament aroused the animosity of Yorkshiremen. The Haworth servants who had been called "wasteful" exacted a testimonial to the contrary from Mr. Brontë. See *Shakespeare Head Brontë*, IV, 226. Harriet Martineau had, as Mrs. Gaskell put it in a letter to Ellen Nussey (June 16 [1857]): "written sheet upon sheet regarding the quarrel ? misunderstanding? between her and Miss Brontë." Berg Collection. [352] John Stuart Mill objected to Mrs. Gaskell's publication of a letter from Charlotte criticizing the writer [Harriet Taylor, later Mrs. Mill] of the *Westminster Review* article on "The Emancipation of Women"; see *Shakespeare Head Brontë*, IV, 233–36, for the interesting exchange of letters between Mill and Mrs. Gaskell. George Henry Lewes wrote requesting the addition of a "phrase" regarding his appraisal of *Shirley* in the *Edinburgh Review* "intimating that it is *not* a disrespectful article to women, although maintaining that in the *highest* efforts of intellect women have not equalled men." "Letters Addressed to Mrs. Gaskell by Celebrated Contemporaries," p. 137. One is not surprised to find Mrs. Gaskell in exasperation writing to William Fairbairn: "I have had a preface to my (forthcoming) third edition sent to me, which I dare not insert there; but it is too good to be lost, therefore I shall copy it out for you: 'If anybody is displeased with any statement in this book, they are requested to believe it withdrawn, and my deep regret expressed for its insertion, as truth is too expensive an article to be laid before the British public.' But for the future I intend to confine myself to lies (*i.e.* fiction). It is safer." Quoted by Whitfield (pp. 158–59) who estimated the date of the letter as "probably June, 1857." Mrs. Gaskell appropriately be-

gins her above-mentioned June letter to Ellen Nussey discussing reactions to the biography with the statement: "I am in the Hornet's nest with a vengeance," perhaps a reference to the term "wasp nest" used earlier by Charlotte's other great friend, Mary Taylor, in adumbrating the dangerous situation Mrs. Gaskell would encounter "by speaking the truth of living people." Letter of April 19, 1856, *Shakespeare Head Brontë*, IV, 198.

10. Naomi Lewis, "Books in General" [Review of Margaret Lane's *The Brontë Story*], *New Statesman and Nation*, XLV (March 7, 1953), 266.

11. Thus she begins her discussion of Charlotte's first stint as a governess with the following comment: "I intend carefully to abstain from introducing the names of any living people, respecting whom I may have to tell unpleasant truths, or to quote severe remarks from Miss Brontë's letters; but it is necessary that the difficulties she had to encounter in her various phases of life, should be fairly and frankly made known, before the force 'of what was resisted' can be at all understood." *The Life of Charlotte Brontë*, p. 142.

12. Mary Taylor paid tribute to the biography's general fidelity to truth in expressing to Ellen Nussey her objection to projected revisions of the first edition: "As to the mutilated edition that is to come, I am sorry for it. Libellous or not, the first edition was all true, and except the declamation all, in my opinion, useful to be published. Of course, I don't know how far necessity may make Mrs. Gaskell give them up. You know one dare not always say the world moves." *Shakespeare Head Brontë*, IV, 229.

13. *The Life of Charlotte Brontë*, pp. 59, 67. In the revised version the sharp edges were smoothed away; "the errors which he certainly committed" became "the errors which he was believed to have committed"; the devastating "willing to sacrifice everything but power" was eliminated altogether as well as the whole reference to the specific "disagreeable qualities" of the Reverend Wilson.

14. Not only did the Wilson family for a while consider a libel suit against Mrs. Gaskell but Mr. Wilson's son-in-law, the Reverend H. Shepheard, published a pamphlet impressively entitled "A Vindication of the Clergy Daughters' School and of the Rev. W. Carus-Wilson from the Remarks in 'The Life of Charlotte Brontë.'" The whole question is dealt with in Appendix I: "The Cowan Bridge Controversy," *Shakespeare Head Brontë*, IV, 297–314.

15. The letter is that of June 16 [1857], to Ellen Nussey, Berg Collection.

16. Her letter to Emily (Winkworth) Shaen of September 8, 1856 relates the circumstances in which, with the help of Sir James Kay-Shuttleworth, she received a great deal of material including the manuscript of *The Professor*. Brotherton Collection. [308] She cites the Reverend's encouraging words in a letter to Ellen Nussey of July [1855], in which she also describes how the Reverend Nicholls "yielded to Mr. Brontë's impetuous wish," getting for her "all the materials he could furnish me with"—mainly letters to Emily between the years 1839 and 1843. Stanley Withers Collection, Manchester Central Library. [257] The Reverend Brontë wrote several letters to Mrs. Gaskell specifically intended to give her information about himself, his marriage, and especially his children—their temperament, their

schooling, and occupations (with the emphasis, of course, falling most often on Charlotte). See letters of July 24, 1855 (pp. 91–92), July 30, 1855 (pp. 93–95), August 27, 1855 (pp. 95–97) in "The Reverend Patrick Brontë and Mrs. E. C. Gaskell," *Transactions and Other Publications of the Brontë Society*, VIII (1936). Though in a letter to Mr. Gaskell he denied that he had made his children eat only vegetable food and had performed what he called "The Eccentrick Movements ascribed to me" (Letter of April 7, 1857, p. 128), his general reactions to accusations of oddness in a letter of July 30 to Mrs. Gaskell seem on the whole reasonable and good-natured. Both in this and in an earlier letter he extended generous praise to the biography (pp. 126, 129). He even tried to console Mrs. Gaskell for her tribulations by deeming them "what has been, is, and ever will be the lot of eminent writers." Letter of August 24, 1857, p. 133. Regarding the revised edition, he asserted that "All reasonable persons must be satisfied, since in it there is much to praise and little or nothing to blame." Letter of September 9, 1857, p. 135.

17. See footnotes 6 and 7 of this chapter.

18. *The Life of Charlotte Brontë*, p. 50. The Reverend Brontë's specific reaction to the stories in the letter of July 30 mentioned above was: "I have no objection whatever to you representing me as a little eccentric since you and other friends will have it so; only don't set me on in my fury to burning hearth rugs, sawing the backs of chairs, and tearing my wife's silk gowns." P. 129.

19. *Ibid.*, p. 51.

20. Hopkins, p. 165.

21. *The Life of Charlotte Brontë*, p. 242.

22. *Ibid.*, pp. 118–21.

23. *Ibid.*, p. 140.

24. Letter to Ellen Nussey, July [1855], Stanley Withers Collection, Manchester Central Library.

25. Shorter, p. 3. A letter from Mrs. Gaskell to an unknown correspondent (Silverdale, August 23 [185?]) shows the care she exercised in performing the necessary research for the work. She prefaces her request for information about "the character of the population she [Charlotte Brontë] lived amongst,—the character of the individuals amongst whom she was known," and about places and possible "local publications" illustrative of regional "customs" and "character" with the following statement: "Her father has requested me to write her life; and I want *every particular* I can collect, not necessarily for publication, but to trust to my honour and discretion, and to enable me to form a picture of her character & a drama of her life in my own mind." Berg Collection. [266]

26. *The Life of Charlotte Brontë*, pp. 72, 76, 77.

27. *Ibid.*, p. 81.

28. *Ibid.*, pp. 333, 391, 372, 287.

29. *Ibid.*, p. 71.

30. *Ibid.*, pp. 45, 55, 47.

31. *Ibid.*, p. 78.

32. *Ibid.*, p. 79.

33. *Ibid.*, p. 351.
34. *Ibid.*, pp. 101, 110–11.
35. *Ibid.*, pp. 165–66.
36. *Ibid.*, p. 285. See above Chapter 1, footnote 71. Mrs. Gaskell praised Charlotte Brontë in her letter to Mrs. Froude because "she possesses a charming union of simplicity and power; and a strong feeling of responsibility for the gift which she had given her." Berg Collection. Aina Rubenius suggests that the writing of the biography played some part in Mrs. Gaskell's serious concern in the following years with the problem of household versus artistic duties by having "forced her to consider the problem as it affected that writer, whose situation in that special case was so like her own." P. 62.
37. *The Life of Charlotte Brontë*, p. 302.
38. See Shorter's index for other instances of what he calls the "hiatuses and blunders" of the biography. See also *Shakespeare Head Brontë*, IV, 218, for the two inaccuracies regarding Branwell's love affair.
39. Letter to Ellen Nussey, June 16 [1857], Berg Collection.
40. "Contemporary Literature," *Westminster Review*, LXVIII (July–October 1857), 162. Perhaps of the many tributes earned by the biography (it won high praise from Kingsley and Guizot, for instance) those of such discerning critics as George Eliot and George Henry Lewes are now most meaningful. Writing to Sarah Hennell on April 16 [1857], George Eliot comments in the following way on what she calls "*one* new book we have been enjoying": "Deeply affecting throughout:—in the early part romantic, poetic as one of her own novels; in the later years tragic, especially to those who know what sickness is. Mrs. Gaskell has done her work admirably, both in the industry and care with which she has gathered and selected her material, and in the feeling with which she has presented it." *The George Eliot Letters*, II, 319. To the same correspondent she conveys on May 22 both her reaction and that of Lewes after mentioning the raising of objections by others against the biography: "We thought it admirable—cried over it—and felt the better for it." II, 330. Given Lewes' discrimination, the following statement in his letter to Mrs. Gaskell of April 15, 1857 may well be the most impressive testimony to the biography's excellence: "The book will, I think, create a deep and permanent impression; for it not only represents a vivid picture of a life noble and sad, full of encouragement and healthy teaching, a lesson in duty and self-reliance; it also, thanks to its artistic power, makes us familiar inmates of an interior so strange, so original in its individual elements and so picturesque in its externals—it paints for us at once the psychological drama and the scenic accessories with so much vividness—that fiction has nothing more wild, touching, and heart strengthening to place above it." "Letters to Mrs. Gaskell from Celebrated Contemporaries," p. 137.

CHAPTER FIVE

1. Like many of her stories, most of these appeared in *Household Words*.
2. A letter to Norton of September 3, 1858 reveals her eagerness to

change editors; she declares herself "so out of heart" regarding news from Norton (obviously in relation to the publication of a story in America), adding: "I know it is fated to go to this new Dickensy periodical [*All the Year Round*], and I did so hope to escape it." *Letters of Mrs. G. and CEN*, p. 34.

3. Miriam Allott, *Elizabeth Gaskell* (London, 1960), 39.

4. Chadwick, p. 126. How skillful a teller of such stories she continued to be is suggested by Anne Thackeray Ritchie in a charming evocation: ". . . the remembrance of *her voice* comes back to me, harmoniously flowing on, with spirit and intention, and delightful emphasis, as we all sat indoors one gusty morning listening to her ghost stories . . . . mystery was there, romantic feeling, some holy terror and emotion, all combined to keep us gratefully silent and delighted." "Preface," *Cranford*, p. ix.

5. "Clopton House," *Mary Barton and Other Tales*, I, 506.

6. Haldane, pp. 5–6.

7. The best example of the likely conjunction of a humorist's imagination with a strong impulse to sentimentality and an almost morbid fascination with the sensational and the uncanny is to be found in the very writer for whom Mrs. Gaskell produced so many of her minor works; one need hardly wonder that Dickens would so eagerly court her contributions, for their temperaments were in many ways similar. Mrs. Gaskell shows her flair for conjoining the comic and the bizarre in the little story "Curious if True" in which a traveller who has lost his way finds himself entertained at a strange château near Tours. We soon discover that all of the assembled company are characters from familiar fairy tales (indeed the traveller is himself assumed to be "Jean de Géanquilleur"). In a crowning display of whimsy the hostess is depicted as mourning the death of her husband killed by her brothers to protect her ("a miserable passage in my life, which has been represented in a false light. . . . I was young and curious–he was justly angry with my disobedience") and, when the traveller remarks on the "peculiar tint" of her late husband's beard in a portrait, ruefully commenting: "Yes; the painter did not do it justice. It was most lovely, and gave him such a distinguished air, quite different from the common herd." *Cousin Phillis and Other Tales*, VII, 273, 275, 276.

8. "Libbie Marsh's Three Eras," *Mary Barton and Other Tales*, p. 484. This story was first published in 1847 with "The Sexton's Hero" in *Howitt's Journal* in which in 1848 "Christmas Storms and Sunshine" also appeared. The three were published together in 1848 as *Life in Manchester* by Cotton Mather Mills.

9. "The Sexton's Hero," *Mary Barton and Other Tales*, II, 493, 497, 500.

10. "The Heart of John Middleton," *Cranford and Other Tales*, II, 408, 409.

11. Swinburne apparently first called attention to the resemblance (see Haldane, p. 79). In all likelihood it was "The Moorland Cottage" which incited the young Matthew Arnold to a display of emotion whose comic self-consciousness his sister cleverly describes in a letter to Doctor Arnold: "Matt is stretched full length on a sofa reading a Christmas tale of Mrs. Gaskell's which moves him to tears, and the tears to complacent admiration

of his own sensibility." Quoted by Haldane, p. 79.

12. "The Moorland Cottage," *Cranford and Other Tales*, pp. 294, 302, 282, 283, 290.

13. *Ibid.*, pp. 287, 303.

14. Ward, "Introduction to 'Cranford,' Etc.," p. xxvii.

15. In this story she also anticipates Tennyson's "Enoch Arden" in her tale of a second marriage threatened by the return of a first husband shipwrecked at sea and believed dead. It is interesting to see how much more richly Mrs. Gaskell later developed this theme of an untimely reappearance in *Sylvia's Lovers*. In the short story, despite a few complications, the problems raised are soon resolved by the accidental death of the first husband; in the novel, the return of the man to whom Sylvia was solemnly engaged marks the tragic permanent destruction of her life with her husband.

16. There are in this tale (based on an actual story related in Green's *History of Knutsford*) intriguing resemblances between Mr. Wilkins and another attorney, Mr. Wickfield of *David Copperfield*. Each is weakened in spirit by the untimely loss of a beloved wife, is devoted to his daughter, and is made uneasy by the clerk whom he is forced to take into partnership. Mr. Dunster and Uriah Heep are also conceived in a somewhat similar way: both are ugly, ungainly, poorly dressed, and both lack openness and generosity. Ellinor and Agnes share intelligence, courage, and that altruism and great loyalty to their fathers which makes self-sacrifice possible. (Another minor Dickens influence is perceptible in the reference to the child Ellinor as "old fashioned," an echo of the epithet applied to Paul Dombey in *Dombey and Son.*)

17. The principle is also exemplified in the small story "Right at Last" in which a young doctor finds that his attempts to hide his family's disgrace (his father was a convict) are vain when a servant threatens to reveal it (he has uncovered evidence in the bureau from which he stole money) if he is prosecuted for theft. With the help of his courageous wife who enjoins him not to hide any longer, the doctor faces up to the truth, achieving peace of mind and an eventual triumph over ostracism. *Cousin Phillis and Other Tales*, VII, 278–99. Truth also inevitably comes to the fore in "The Grey Woman," when the heroine is forced to tell her tragic story to her daughter because she has discovered that the beloved prospective husband of her child is the son of the man whom her husband had murdered. *Cousin Phillis and Other Tales*, pp. 304, 361.

18. "A Dark Night's Work," *Cousin Phillis and Other Tales*, pp. 435, 428, 424.

19. *Ibid.*, pp. 475–76, 476, 477, 557.

20. "The Well of Pen-Morfa," *Cranford and Other Tales*, p. 263.

21. "Half a Lifetime Ago," *Round the Sofa, My Lady Ludlow and Other Tales*, pp. 315–16.

22. "The Crooked Branch," *Cousin Phillis and Other Tales*, p. 258.

23. *Cranford*, p. 110.

24. "The Squire's Story," *Cranford and Other Tales*, p. 533.

25. "The Grey Woman," pp. 309–10.

26. "The Squire's Story," pp. 545–46.

27. "The Grey Woman," pp. 359–60. For the authentic background which probably influenced Mrs. Gaskell's treatment of the band of robbers, see Ward, "Introduction to 'Cousin Phillis,' Etc.," pp. xxviii–xxxi. There are interesting similarities in the plight of this heroine and that of the defenseless Marquise de Gange in "French Life," whose hopeless attempts to escape murder at the hands of her husband and her brothers-in-law are depicted in all their morbid and grotesque details even to her efforts at "pushing her long black hair down her throat" in order to throw up the poison which she has been forced to swallow, her only other alternatives having been death by pistol or by sword. It is not difficult to see why the author would have been impelled to retell this story which, she informs us, she read during her stay in Avignon, for it has all the sensational attributes which so strongly moved her imagination. *Cousin Phillis and Other Tales,* pp. 664–78. Though in "The Grey Woman" she reverses the tradition of the wicked French maid, she follows it in "Crowley Castle," where the faithful maid of the young Theresa Crowley poisons the wife of Theresa's cousin to enable her mistress to marry him; when she later feels rejected by the innocent Theresa, she accuses her of complicity in the crime, thereby destroying all chances of happiness for the young couple. Pp. 681–720.

28. "The Grey Woman," pp. 325, 331.

29. "The Old Nurse's Story," *Cranford and Other Tales,* pp. 425, 427, 426, 429, 430.

30. *Ibid.,* pp. 435, 437, 438. Aina Rubenius sees in this motif the influence of *Wuthering Heights.* P. 255.

31. *Ibid.,* pp. 443, 444, 445.

32. "The Poor Clare," *Round the Sofa,* p. 341.

33. "The Doom of the Griffiths," *Round the Sofa,* p. 238.

34. "The Poor Clare," p. 361.

35. "The Doom of the Griffiths," p. 243.

36. "The Poor Clare," pp. 370, 380–81.

37. *Ibid.,* p. 390.

38. "The Doom of the Griffiths," pp. 244, 247, 249.

39. *Ibid.,* p. 276.

40. *Ibid.,* pp. 260–61, 258, 277. According to Mrs. Chadwick, the author may have heard this story "when visiting the lonely valleys of North Wales, a district noted for its ghost stories, curses, and charms." P. 353. To Norton, Mrs. Gaskell claimed as "the only merit" of her story "that it is founded on fact." *Letters of Mrs. G. and CEN,* p. 10.

41. For the author's possible sources, see Ward, "Introduction to 'Cousin Phillis,' Etc.," pp. xxi–xxiii.

42. "Lois the Witch," *Cousin Phillis and Other Tales,* pp. 147–48.

43. *Ibid.,* p. 135.

44. *Ibid.,* pp. 157, 168.

45. This vivid study of the "Cagots," a proscribed people long resident in Brittany, the Pyrenees, and the Landes, while it exemplifies the appeal to her imagination of such elements as mysterious origins, strange fears,

grotesque customs, and savage passions, also shows the rejection by her reason, her intellect, and that spirit of tolerance so evident in *Ruth* of any glaring instances of prejudice and superstition. See especially the conclusion, *Round the Sofa,* p. 235. Her strong objections to any form of tyranny and social corruption are also evident in her fascinating study of the operation of a secret society in Naples (whose activities much resemble those of the present-day Mafia) in "An Italian Institution," *Sylvia's Lovers, Etc.,* VI, 531–[540].

46. Sanders, p. 109.
47. "Lois the Witch," p. 122.
48. "Cumberland Sheep-Shearers," *Ruth and Other Tales,* III, 460, 462.
49. "Six Weeks at Heppenheim," *Cousin Phillis and Other Tales,* p. 374.
50. *Ibid.,* pp. 394, 403.
51. "Cousin Phillis," pp. 78, 12.
52. *Ibid.,* pp. 9, 98.
53. *Ibid.,* pp. 26, 46, 81, 83.
54. *Ibid.,* p. 17.
55. *Ibid.,* p. 19.
56. *Ibid.,* pp. 27–28.
57. *Ibid.,* pp. 24, 34.
58. *Ibid.,* pp. 52–53.
59. *Ibid.,* p. 59.
60. *Ibid.,* pp. 72, 77–78.
61. *Ibid.,* pp. 84, 92.
62. *Ibid.,* p. 95.
63. *Ibid.,* pp. 98, 99–100.
64. *Ibid.,* p. 109.
65. That "Cousin Phillis" denotes to a certain extent a specific response to much more sophisticated requirements is suggested by Sanders' general statement regarding "a change in Mrs. Gaskell's style" when writing for a new magazine: "*The Cornhill* demanded a different type of fiction from that found in Dickens's magazines, and Mrs. Gaskell accommodated herself to this fact." P. 110. But her letters to Norton already clarify her desire to emancipate herself from the standards of *Household Words.* See footnote 2 of this chapter.
66. Chadwick, p. 127.

CHAPTER SIX

1. See Ward, "Introduction to 'Sylvia's Lovers,' Etc.," *Sylvia's Lovers, Etc.,* VI, pp. xvi, xxiii–xxvi.
2. Seccombe maintains that "a visit to the then secluded resort of Ramsay in the Isle of Man and the long (foc'sle) yarns of a brave sailor, who took her and her daughter on rowing expeditions along the coast, caused her mind to revert to the long-cherished project of a story of the sea." "Elizabeth Cleghorn Gaskell," p. 242.

3. Her faithfulness in reproducing the actual details of town and countryside indeed makes it possible, as in *Cranford,* to identify some landmarks and characters. See Chadwick, pp. 376–86. The *Westminster Review* in its initial reception of the novel, paid tribute to its authenticity: "The scene of Mrs. Gaskell's new novel is laid on the chill North country shore, which she knows so well how to depict, and amidst the rough North country folk, whom she draws with such admirable humour and pre-eminent faithfulness." "Belles Lettres," *Westminster and Foreign Quarterly Review,* N.S. XXIII (January–April 1863), 622.

4. Quoted by Ward, "Introduction to 'Sylvia's Lovers,' Etc.," p. xii.

5. Haldane, p. 212.

6. Pollard, p. 423. G. B. Smith in "Mrs. Gaskell and her Novels" speaks of her "greater grasp not only of character but of actual expression" in this work (p. 206), while W. Minto finds that in both *Sylvia's Lovers* and *Wives and Daughters* "she shows greater art in the management of her story." "Mrs. Gaskell's Novels," *Fortnightly Review,* N.S. XXIV (July–December 1878), 369.

7. Hopkins, p. 219. "Too Late" and "The Specksioneer" were also contemplated, according to Ward, p. xiv. In her letter to Norton of August 28, 1861, she is still in large part committed to her initial choice, for she informs him regarding the novel: ". . . it is above half-way done and will I *think* be called 'Philip's Idol.'" *Letters of Mrs. G. and CEN,* p. 94.

8. Ward, "Introduction to 'Sylvia's Lovers,' Etc.," p. xiv.

9. Haldane, p. 219.

10. See Rubenius, p. 258.

11. Indeed only such minor discrepancies as the following one mar a coherence which suggests very careful planning and attention to details: a year after the initial events of the story, which the author has specifically indicated as happening in 1796, Philip crosses the bridge as the bells ring out the new year—1796. Sanders mentions other discrepancies which to him seem to suggest an interval between the writing of the first section and later chapters. P. 114. That she expended great effort on this story is evident in her decision, contrary to usual practice, to rewrite a very significant section—Kinraid's return. Ward, p. xii.

12. *Sylvia's Lovers,* pp. 20, 268, 75.

13. For the original documents consulted by Mrs. Gaskell, see Ward, pp. xxii–xxiii.

14. *Sylvia's Lovers,* pp. 78–79.

15. *Ibid.,* p. 336.

16. *Ibid.,* pp. 28, 26.

17. *Ibid.,* p. 141.

18. *Ibid.,* p. 413.

19. *Ibid.,* p. 456.

20. *Ibid.,* pp. 195, 157.

21. *Ibid.,* p. 175.

22. *Ibid.,* p. 244.

23. *Ibid.,* p. 187.

24. *Ibid.*, p. 235.
25. *Ibid.*, pp. 235, 238.
26. *Ibid.*, pp. 267, 249.
27. *Ibid.*, p. 314.
28. *Ibid.*, p. 136.
29. *Ibid.*, p. 403.
30. *Ibid.*, pp. 14, 13.
31. *Ibid.*, pp. 79, 74, 79.
32. *Ibid.*, p. 114.
33. *Ibid.*, p. 361.
34. *Ibid.*, p. 402.
35. *Ibid.*, pp. 402–03.
36. *Ibid.*, pp. 337, 352.
37. *Ibid.*, pp. 81, 328.
38. *Ibid.*, pp. 523, 526–27.
39. *Ibid.*, p. 529.
40. *Ibid.*, p. 524.
41. Montégut, "Nord et Sud," *Ecrivains Modernes de l'Angleterre,* p. 78.
42. Quoted by Hopkins, pp. 298–99.

Selected Bibliography

PRIMARY SOURCES

Dates of magazine publication for novels, stories, essays are to be found in the text.

Novels

Mary Barton: A Tale of Manchester Life. 2 vols. London, Chapman and Hall, 1848. (Published anonymously)

Cranford. London, Chapman and Hall, 1853.

Ruth. 2 vols. London, Chapman and Hall, 1853.

North and South. 2 vols. London, Chapman and Hall, 1855.

Sylvia's Lovers. 3 vols. London, Smith, Elder and Co., 1863.

Wives and Daughters: An Every-Day Story. 2 vols. London, Smith, Elder and Co., 1866.

Stories and Essays

Life in Manchester by Cotton Mather Mills, Esq. Manchester, 1848. ("Libbie Marsh's Three Eras"; "The Sexton's Hero"; "Christmas Storms and Sunshine")

The Moorland Cottage. London, Chapman and Hall, 1850.

Lizzie Leigh and Other Tales. London, Chapman and Hall, 1855. ("Lizzie Leigh"; "The Well of Pen-Morfa"; "The Heart of John Middleton"; "Disappearances"; "The Old Nurse's Story"; "Traits and Stories of the Huguenots"; "Morton Hall"; "My French Master"; "The Squire's Story"; "Company Manners"; "Mr. Harrison's Confessions"; "Libbie Marsh's Three Eras"; "The Sexton's Hero";

"Christmas Storms and Sunshine"; "Hand and Heart"; "Bessie's Troubles at Home")

Round the Sofa. 2 vols. London, Sampson Low, Son & Co., 1859. ("My Lady Ludlow"; "An Accursed Race"; "The Doom of the Griffiths"; "Half a Lifetime Ago"; "The Poor Clare"; "The Half-Brothers")

Right at Last and Other Tales. London, Sampson Low, Son & Co., 1860.

A Dark Night's Work. London, Smith, Elder & Co., 1863.

The Grey Woman and Other Tales. London, Smith, Elder & Co., 1865. ("The Grey Woman"; "Curious if True"; "Six Weeks at Heppenheim"; "Libbie Marsh's Three Eras"; "Christmas Storms and Sunshine"; "Hand and Heart"; "Bessie's Troubles at Home"; "Disappearances")

BIOGRAPHY

The Life of Charlotte Brontë. London, Smith, Elder & Co., 1857.

PREFACES

CUMMINS, MARIA S. *Mabel Vaughn.* London, Sampson Low, Son and Co., 1857. Mrs. Gaskell affirms the cultural rapprochement leading to greater "understanding" and "sympathy" which an "interchange of novels" between England and America makes possible. She also edits the work, modifying or explaining for English readers such unfamiliar idioms as "a good time."

VECCHJ, COLONEL [C. AUGUSTO]. *Garibaldi at Caprera,* tr. [L. and M. Ellis]. Cambridge, Macmillan and Co., 1862. Praises Garibaldi and describes some of his associates.

DIARY AND CORRESPONDENCE

Reference to the collected letters (indicated by *) published after this study had been written has been included for the reader's convenience.

My Diary: The Early Years of My Daughter Marianne. London, Privately Printed by Clement Shorter, 1923.

Letters of Mrs. Gaskell and Charles Eliot Norton, 1855–1865, ed. Jane Whitehill. London, Oxford University Press, 1932.

* *The Letters of Mrs. Gaskell,* ed. J. A. V. Chapple and Arthur Pollard. Manchester, Manchester University Press, 1966. A comprehensive collection of Mrs. Gaskell's letters arranged mainly in chronological order (undated letters are in a special section). Very useful indexes (family, literary, and general biographical). Introduction discusses significant aspects of the correspondence

(with numerical references to the letters): Mrs. Gaskell's relationship to and evaluation of her children; her social life in Manchester; her friendships with famous people, her travels; her attitudes to her writings and details about the actual "process of composition"; the personal qualities she reveals. A few pages are devoted to the technical aspects of the compilation and arrangement of the letters.

"Letters Addressed to Mrs. Gaskell by Celebrated Contemporaries," ed. Ross D. Waller, *Bulletin of the John Rylands Library,* XIX (January 1935), 102–69. Reprints many of the letters to Mrs. Gaskell in the John Rylands Library, Manchester.

Letters of Mrs. Gaskell in Manuscript: Brotherton Collection, University of Leeds. British Museum. Victoria and Albert Museum. Central Library, Manchester. Berg Collection, New York Public Library. Yale University Library. Morris L. Parrish Collection, Princeton University Library.

COLLECTED WORKS

The Novels and Tales of Mrs. Gaskell. 8 vols. London, Smith, Elder & Co., 1872–73.

The Works of Mrs. Gaskell. 8 vols. Pocket Edition. London, Smith, Elder & Co., 1897.

The Novels and Tales of Mrs. Gaskell, ed. Clement K. Shorter. 11 vols. London, Oxford University Press, 1906–19. [The World's Classics Edition] The most comprehensive edition. Introductions by Shorter.

The Works of Mrs. Gaskell. With Introductions by A. W. Ward. 8 vols. London, Smith, Elder & Co., 1906. [The Knutsford Edition] Extensive biographical and critical material contributed by Ward.

BIBLIOGRAPHIES

GREEN, JOHN ALBERT. *A Bibliographical Guide to the Gaskell Collection in the Moss Side Public Library.* Manchester, Reference Library, 1911.

NORTHUP, CLARK SUTHERLAND, "Bibliography," in Sanders, Gerald De Witt. *Elizabeth Gaskell.* New Haven, Yale University Press, 1929.

PARRISH, M. L. *Victorian Lady Novelists.* George Eliot. Mrs. Gaskell. The Brontë Sisters. First Editions in the Library at Dormy House, Pine Valley, New Jersey, described with Notes by M. L. Parrish. London, Constable and Company Limited, 1938.

SADLEIR, MICHAEL. *Excursions in Victorian Bibliography.* London, Chaundy and Cox, 1922.

SECONDARY SOURCES

The basic approach of many of the writers listed below has been dealt with more fully in the text. Two critical works (indicated by *) published after this study had been written have been included for the reader's convenience.

ALLOTT, MIRIAM. *Elizabeth Gaskell.* London, Longmans, Green & Co., 1960. A lively though somewhat condescending brief study of the major works which terms *Wives and Daughters* "the only novel . . . (*Cranford* is a series of sketches) which a contemporary reader will feel at home with."

ASTALDI, MARIA LUISA. *La Signora Gaskell.* Bocca, 1954. Praises Mrs. Gaskell's humanitarian impulses and her ability to capture the life of her times in the habits, personalities, and modes of expression of her characters as seen "attraverso l'occhio sicuro, tenero e penetrante di una donna."

AXON, WILLIAM E. A. "The Homes and Haunts of Mrs. Gaskell," *Bookman* (October 1910), 43–44. Points to the factual and critical flaws in Mrs. Ellis H. Chadwick's *Mrs. Gaskell: Haunts, Homes and Stories.*

BALD, MARJORY A. *Women-Writers of the Nineteenth Century.* Cambridge, University Press, 1923. Devotes substantial section of the work to Mrs. Gaskell, examining such elements as the evolution of her humor and pathos, her feminine viewpoint, and her moral values. Finds her "peculiar achievement" in "her power of combining the life of genius with a round of common interests."

"Belles Lettres," *Westminster and Foreign Quarterly Review,* N.S. XXIV (July–October 1863), 292–312. Includes a generally favorable review of "A Dark Night's Work."

"Belles Lettres," *Westminster and Foreign Quarterly Review,* N.S. XXIII (January–April 1863), 611–30. A review of *Sylvia's Lovers* in this section praises its authenticity of setting and characterization.

BRIGGS, ASA. *Chartist Studies.* London, Macmillan & Co. Ltd., 1959. A discussion of the progression of the Chartist movement in Manchester ("Chartism in Manchester," by Donald Read) in this collection of essays is very pertinent to an understanding of the social background in *Mary Barton.*

The Brontës: Their Lives, Friendship and Correspondence. The Shakespeare Head Brontë, ed. James Thomas Wise and John Alexander Symington. 4 vols. The Shakespeare Head Press, 1932.

Volumes III (1849–52) and IV (1852–1928) contain many letters which clarify the relationship between Charlotte Brontë and Mrs. Gaskell (both correspondents are represented). Chapters XXXI ("Friendship with Mrs. Gaskell") and XXXV ("Mrs. Gaskell's Biography") of Volume IV are particularly significant.

CAZAMIAN, LOUIS *Le Roman Social en Angleterre (1830–1850)*. Paris, Société nouvelle de librairie et d'édition, 1904. The chapter on Mrs. Gaskell subtitled "L'interventionisme chrétien" suggests the particular influence exerted by the feminine conscience on the movement of "idéalisme interventioniste" by which social novelists (other chapters deal with Dickens, Disraeli, and Kingsley) sought to counteract the evils of materialism in industrial England. Especially meaningful for the intelligence and originality of Cazamian's general thesis on the social novel. Specific discussions of *Mary Barton* and *North and South.*

CECIL, DAVID. *Early Victorian Novelists.* Harmondsworth, Penguin Books, 1948. This extensive, thoughtful consideration of Mrs. Gaskell's artistic merits and deficiencies, though frequently subtle and suggestive, does not do justice to her capacity for transcending the conventions of her femininity and her Victorianism. As in his study of Dickens, Cecil shows his understanding of the nature of English humor.

CHADWICK, MRS. ELLIS H. *Mrs. Gaskell: Haunts, Homes and Stories.* New York, Frederick A. Stokes Company Publishers, 1911. Painstakingly detailed but frequently injudicious exploration of possible correspondences between the author's family relationships, personal experiences, places of residence, and her literary productions. Interesting illustrations of significant "haunts" and "homes."

COLLINS, H. P. "The Naked Sensibility: Elizabeth Gaskell," *Essays in Criticism,* III (January 1953), 60–72. An unduly abstract, rather condescending, highly severe discussion of Mrs. Gaskell's limitations and deficiencies as an artist. She is criticized for conventionality, timidity, the incapacity to transfigure experience which "made an unbroken, unalleviated impact on her mind, her feelings, her nerves," the lack of "dynamic conviction or illusion," the failure "to *think* hard enough." Some praise is bestowed on her humor and irony, her "sympathy with human nature," and especially her "acute feeling for the beauty of the English scene at its best."

"Contemporary Literature: History, Biography, Voyages, and Travels," *Westminster Review,* LXVIII (July–October 1857), 152–62. Contains a review of *The Life of Charlotte Brontë* which, though severely critical of the handling of Branwell Brontë, acclaims the "elevating, assuring, and composing" portrait of Charlotte.

"Contemporary Literature of England," *Westminster and Foreign Quarterly Review,* N.S. IV (July–October 1853), 246–74. *Cranford* (just published in book form) is termed "such a series as no male creature could have written,—only a woman of genius, quick of wit, and not less quick of feeling."

CROSS, WILBUR L. *The Development of the English Novel.* New York, The Macmillan Company, 1911. Sees *Ruth* as an incipient psychological novel and suggests George Eliot's reliance on and emancipation from her predecessor.

ELIZABETH, CHARLOTTE [Mrs. Tonna]. *Helen Fleetwood. The Works of Charlotte Elizabeth.* Volume I. New York, M. W. Dodd, 1849. This denunciation of the evils of child labor in the cotton factories is marred by its unreal characterizations, its sentimentality, and its narrow pietism.

FFRENCH, YVONNE. *Mrs. Gaskell.* London, Home & Van Thal Ltd., 1949. An often perceptive informal combination of biography and criticism, written in a lively if at times eccentric style.

"Mrs. Gaskell." Obit., *Athenaeum,* No. 1986 (November 18, 1865), 689–90. Terms the author ". . . if not the most popular, with small question, the most powerful and finished female novelist of an epoch singularly rich in female novelists."

The George Eliot Letters, ed. Gordon S. Haight. 7 vols. New Haven, Yale University Press, 1954. Many letters in Volumes II and III suggest the mutual regard of George Eliot and Mrs. Gaskell (both correspondents are represented).

GREG, W. R. *Literary and Social Judgments.* Boston, James R. Osgood and Company, 1873. "False Morality of Lady Novelists," an essay reprinted from the *National Review* (1859), contains an extremely perceptive assessment of the weaknesses of *Ruth* as manifestations of a larger conventional bias.

———. *Mistaken Aims and Attainable Ideals of the Artizan Class.* London, Trübner & Co., 1876. Greg's original appraisal of *Mary Barton* in the *Edinburgh Review* is here reprinted. This complex and subtle but one-sided attack on the author for failing to do justice to the masters' viewpoint or to the workers' own responsibility for their plight aptly suggests the values and assumptions of utilitarian capitalism. Invaluable in dealing with Mrs. Gaskell's social novels, especially since Greg may have influenced the modification of her viewpoint in *North and South.*

HALDANE, ELIZABETH. *Mrs. Gaskell and Her Friends.* London, Hodder and Stoughton Limited, 1931. The first work to present extensive correspondence (both from the Brotherton Collection in Leeds and privately owned) that sheds light on Mrs. Gaskell's general opinions and her appraisals of acquaintances and friends (Florence Nightingale, Charlotte Brontë, the Reverend Brontë, Madame Mohl). Many letters are printed in full. Unfortunately the material is poorly organized and is often insufficiently documented.

HALEVY, ELIE. *A History of the English People, 1830–1841,* trans. E. I. Watkin. London, T. Fisher Unwin Limited, 1927. The thoughtful and detailed discussion of Chartist agitation helps to clarify the social and historical setting of *Mary Barton.*

HOPKINS, A. B. *Elizabeth Gaskell. Her Life and Work.* London, John Lehmann, 1952. A work far more distinguished for its biographical than its critical aspects. Indeed what is probably the definitive biography is remarkable for its exhaustive scholarly attention to all the pertinent aspects of Mrs. Gaskell's life and thought. Her correspondence (especially with Dickens, Charles Eliot Norton, and her publisher George Smith) is minutely explored and extensively quoted. Very detailed notes. Attractive illustrations. Some corrections of earlier errors in dating.

———. "Mrs. Gaskell in France 1849–1890," *PMLA,* LIII (June 1938), 545–74. An examination of the extensive popularity of Mrs. Gaskell's work in France. "To have won and held a reading public for forty years in the France of George Sand, Hugo, Dumas *père,* Flaubert, Feydeau, and Zola is no mean achievement."

HOWITT, MARGARET. "Stray Notes from Mrs. Gaskell," *Good Words,* XXXVI (1895), 604–[612]. Extensive quotations from interesting letters written by Mrs. Gaskell to William and Mary Howitt which provide glimpses of her youth in Knutsford and describe quaint customs of the town and region.

JAMES, HENRY. *William Wetmore Story and His Friends.* 2 vols. Boston, Houghton, Mifflin & Co., 1903. The small section in Volume I devoted to Mrs. Gaskell as a friend of the Storys indicates, through her correspondence with them, how pleasurable and meaningful an experience her stay in Rome as their guest proved to be. Significant comments by Mrs. Gaskell on her own *Life of Charlotte Brontë* and Hawthorne's *The Marble Faun.* James's own references to the novelist are invariably more deferential and gracious than illuminating.

———. "Wives and Daughters," *The Nation,* II (January–June 1866), 246–47. In this early review, James's already complex style succeeds in veiling as much as in revealing his critical viewpoint.

Overtly the evaluation is quite favorable, especially with regard to the characterizations of Mrs. Gibson and Cynthia. Enough is said, however, to suggest stronger objections to the intellectual limitations of the writer than James is prepared openly to admit.

Anna Jameson. Letters and Friendships (1812–1860), ed. Mrs. Steuart Erskine. London, T. Fisher Unwin, Ltd., 1915. Several interesting letters of Mrs. Gaskell to Mrs. Jameson discussing the critical reactions to *Ruth* and the problems connected with the writing of *North and South* and *The Life of Charlotte Brontë.*

Kettle, Arnold. "The Early Victorian Social-Problem Novel," in *From Dickens to Hardy,* ed. Boris Ford. Harmondsworth, Penguin Books, 1958. A very thoughtful discussion of the characteristic attributes of the social novel in the forties viewed in the light of earlier manifestations of the genre and of the peculiar social, "ideological," and political circumstances of the period. Meaningful comparisons and contrasts between Disraeli, Mrs. Gaskell, and Kingsley. Kettle's assessment of the strengths and weaknesses of *Mary Barton* and *North and South* is both just and suggestive.

Kingsley, Charles. *His Letters and Memories of his Life.* Edited by his wife. New York, Scribner, Armstrong & Company, 1877. Two letters to Mrs. Gaskell (1853, 1857) warmly praise *Ruth* and *The Life of Charlotte Brontë.*

"The Lady Novelists of Great Britain," *Gentleman's Magazine,* XL (July–December 1853), 18–25. Singling *Ruth* out as "the most striking of our English female novels," the critic praises its denunciation of the double standard, its power of sympathy, its "language" and "wit," but astutely suggests that the heroine should have been "both more alive and less simple."

Lane, Margaret. "Books in General," *New Statesman and Nation,* XLIII, No. 1097 (March 15, 1952), 323–24. A generally favorable review of A. B. Hopkins' *Elizabeth Gaskell. Her Life and Work.*

———. *The Brontë Story: A Reconsideration of Mrs. Gaskell's "Life of Charlotte Brontë."* London, William Heinemann Ltd., 1953. This lively, informal study offers no scholarly documentation but is shrewd, sensible, and balanced in its mainly favorable appraisal of Mrs. Gaskell's work from a much later vantage point. Selections from the *Life* (clearly identified) are combined with Margaret Lane's own contributions (modifications or additions) in one coherent discussion.

The Letters of Elizabeth Barrett Browning, ed. Frederic G. Kenyon. 2 vols. New York, The Macmillan Company, 1897. A discriminating evaluation of *Mary Barton* and praise for the message of *Ruth* are the salient aspects of the few letters referring to Mrs. Gaskell and her works.

The Letters of Charles Dickens, ed. Walter Dexter. 3 vols. Bloomsbury, The Nonesuch Press, 1938. Many letters to Mrs. Gaskell and others in Volume II illumine the intriguingly checkered relationship between two writers whose many temperamental affinities were not always proof against the conflicts arising out of their mutual positions as editor and contributor.

[LEWES, GEORGE HENRY]. "Ruth and Villette," *Westminster Review,* N.S. III (January and April 1853), 474–91. In a sympathetic assessment of Mrs. Gaskell's views on the "fallen woman," Lewes cleverly notes the serious flaw in her conception of a completely innocent and appealing heroine. He sees Charlotte Brontë as far exceeding Mrs. Gaskell in emotional intensity but as lacking the latter's humor, "so strong and so genial."

LEWIS, NAOMI. "Books in General," *New Statesman and Nation,* XLV, No. 1148 (March 7, 1953), 266–67. A lively appraisal of Mrs. Gaskell as a biographer is presented along with the review of Margaret Lane's *The Brontë Story.*

"The Life of Charlotte Brontë. . . ." Anon. rev., *Athenaeum,* No. 1536 (April 4, 1857), 427–29. A very favorable assessment later partially retracted when the threat of a lawsuit cast doubts upon the accuracy and restraint of Mrs. Gaskell as a biographer. (The June 6, 1857 edition of the magazine carried as an advertisement the legal exchange between Mrs. Gaskell's and Mrs. Robinson's solicitors which settled the question of libel.)

MARTINEAU, HARRIET. *Illustrations of Political Economy.* 9 vols. London, Charles Fox, 1834. Such short novels as *The Hill and the Valley* (Volume I) and *A Manchester Strike* (Volume III) are good examples of the presentation in fiction of the principles of political economy as applied to the clash between labor and capital.

"Mary Barton. A Tale of Manchester Life." Anon. rev., *Athenaeum,* No. 1095 (October 21, 1848), 1050–51. Praises the authenticity of the novel and the writer's "power over what is quaint and whimsical."

"Mary Barton. A Tale of Manchester Life." Anon. rev., *British Quarterly Review,* IX (February 1, 1849), 117–36. The "graphic power" and pathos of the book are commended but it is censured for presenting "a one-sided picture" of the conflict between masters and men ("the worst enemy" of the workers is really "their own improvidence").

"Mary Barton. A Tale of Manchester Life." Anon. rev., *Westminster and Foreign Quarterly Review,* LI (April–July 1849), 48–63. Defense of political economy as a valuable means of resolving some of the social conflicts so pertinently depicted in *Mary Barton.*

MASSON, DAVID. "Mrs. Gaskell," *Macmillan's Magazine,* XIII (November 1865–April 1866), 153–56. General assessment of the author at the time of her death. "Other novelists have written books as clever, and many have written books as innocent; but there are few, indeed, who have written books which grown-up men read with delight, and children might read without injury."

MELVILLE, LEWIS. "The Centenary of Mrs. Gaskell," *The Nineteenth Century and After,* No. CCCCIII (September 1910), 467–82. A very severe evaluation of most of the works of Mrs. Gaskell who is termed "an indifferent novelist" and criticized for sensationalism, triteness, sentimentalism, and artificiality in characterization and dialogue—particularly in the social novels. Only *Cranford,* "so pathetic, so tender, so delightful," escapes criticism.

MINTO, W. "Mrs. Gaskell's Novels," *Fortnightly Review,* N.S. XXIV (July to December 1878), 353–69. "There never was a writer so essentially a moralist who had less self-consciousness of a mission to be such, and there have been very few moralists who have combined so much earnestness with so hearty an enjoyment of the sunshine of human existence."

"Modern Novelists—Great and Small," *Blackwood's Edinburgh Magazine,* LXXVII (January–June 1855), 554–68. Suggests in an assessment of *North and South* the influence of Charlotte Brontë on Mrs. Gaskell's conception of the romantic relationship between her two main characters.

MONTÉGUT, EMILE. *Ecrivains Modernes de l'Angleterre.* Paris, Librairie Hachette et Cie, 1889. The section on "Mistress Gaskell" contains discussions of *Mary Barton* and *Ruth* (1853) and of *North and South* (1855). Montégut's subtle apprehension of the power of fiction in an age very vulnerable to "la force du sentiment" is particularized in his praise of the moving simplicity and directness, and the absence of theorizing in *Mary Barton.* His discussion of *Ruth* reveals his psychological insight into the to him characteristically English phenomenon of pharisaism and his essay on *North and South* his understanding of the significance which dilemmas of conscience had for Mrs. Gaskell.

MONTGOMERY, K. L. [Kathleen and Letitia] "Elizabeth Cleghorn Gaskell," *Fortnightly Review,* N.S. XXXVIII (July to December 1910), [450]–463. The social novelist's "fairness of observation" and the story-teller's power of creating suspenseful terror are praised. *Cranford* is classed with *The Vicar of Wakefield* and *The Life of Charlotte Brontë* with Boswell's *Life of Johnson.*

MORE, PAUL ELMER. "Mrs. Gaskell," *The Nation,* LXXXIV (January–June 1907), 331–33. Writing in part to acknowledge the "well-edited" volumes of the recently published Knutsford Edition, More favorably compares the humanizing emotional effect of writers like Mrs. Gaskell and Dickens with that of "our modern fiction of the Zola-Tolstoy school" which "brings only a harsh contraction of spirit." He stresses the significance in Mrs. Gaskell's work of the contrast between town and country.

MORTIMER, JOHN. "Lancashire Novelists.—Mrs. Gaskell," *Manchester Quarterly,* XXI (July 1902), [195]–228. A biographical and critical essay written from the vantage point of familiarity with the Manchester way of life. Some factual inaccuracies.

"New Novels: Wives and Daughters. An Every-Day Story." Anon. rev., *Athenaeum,* No. 2001 (March 3, 1866), 295–96. A very favorable reception with special commendation for the authenticity of the characterizations (e.g., Cynthia). Mention is made of a resemblance between the novel and Fredrika Bremer's *A Diary.*

"North and South." Anon. rev. *Athenaeum,* No. 1432 (April 7, 1855), 403. Greatly praises Mrs. Gaskell's use of dialect but objects to the introduction of so serious an ethical problem as a conflict of conscience into fiction "where only artistic truth is possible."

OLIPHANT, MRS. *et al. Women Novelists of Queen Victoria's Reign.* London, Hurst & Blackett, 1897. Contains a critical evaluation of Mrs. Gaskell by Edna Lyall which praises the "wide human sympathies, . . . tender comprehension of human frailty, . . . bright flashes of humour and . . . infinite pathos" of her works.

O'MEARA, KATHLEEN. "Madame Mohl, Her Salon and Her Friends," *Atlantic Monthly,* LV (January–June 1885), 67–79, 169–84, 318–30, 477–90. Four papers devoted to the fascinating friend of Mrs. Gaskell whom in later years she regularly visited on her trips to France.

PAYNE, REV. GEORGE A. *Mrs. Gaskell and Knutsford.* Manchester, Clarkson & Griffiths, Ltd., 1906. Contains a detailed discussion of the physical similarities between Knutsford and Cranford and of the institutions, anecdotes, customs, and people of the real town which are approximated in *Cranford.* Praises the "good and high moral tone in all her writings."

POLLARD, ARTHUR. "The Novels of Mrs. Gaskell," *Bulletin of The John Rylands Library,* XLIII (March 1961), 404–23. A discriminating assessment of Mrs. Gaskell's achievements which commends her skill in description and narration and her "sure grasp of social reactions especially among the working classes," but also points to the weaknesses of "prolixity, moralizing and occasional tendency to melodrama."

*———. *Mrs. Gaskell: Novelist and Biographer.* Manchester, Manchester University Press, 1965. Provides a brief review of past criticism and some biographical information. It is essentially a series of informal critical discussions of most of the writings, stressing "matters of plot, character, setting, information, and moral purposes as separate entities within each of Mrs. Gaskell's works," and suggesting the evolution of her art toward the greater maturity of insight and craftsmanship exemplified in the last two novels. Pertinent use has been made of the Gaskell correspondence (the author is co-editor of the recently published collected letters). Attractive illustrations.

PRITCHETT, V. S. "Current Literature: Books in General," *New Statesman and Nation,* N.S. XXI (January–June 1941), 630. Taking exception with some of David Cecil's comments regarding the limited scope of Mrs. Gaskell's apprehension, Pritchett, in a subtle appraisal of *North and South,* justly sees it as a characteristically Victorian novel in the extent of its melodrama and moral scrupulosity and suggests the writer's comprehension, if not of economics, of "the men and women of the Industrial Revolution," their mode of life, their characteristic expression.

"Recent Novels," *Fraser's Magazine,* XXXIX (April 1849), 417–32. On the occasion of the third edition of *Mary Barton,* the book is forcefully recommended as a key to the understanding of the social and political problems of the times.

"The Reverend Patrick Brontë and Mrs. E. C. Gaskell," *Transactions and Other Publications of the Brontë Society,* VIII (1936), [83]–100, ([125]–138. Many letters from the Reverend Brontë to Mrs. Gaskell provide not only invaluable insights into the mode of life and temperament of Mr. Brontë as well as of his children but indicate his specific reactions to the initial and revised versions of *The Life of Charlotte Brontë.*

RUBENIUS, AINA. *The Woman Question in Mrs. Gaskell's Life and Works. Essays and Studies on English Language and Literature,* ed. S. B. Liljegren. Volume V. Upsala, A.-B. Lundequistska Bokhandeln, 1950. Conscientious and solid study of Mrs. Gaskell which suggests her gradual emancipation from a conventional concept of the position and duties of woman (partly under the influence of her friends), and the consequent decline of didacticism in her fiction. Specific attitudes toward female factory workers, domestic servants, "fallen" women, and protective legislation are explored in separate chapters. Valuable appendices on "Factory Work for Women," "Literary Influences in Mrs. Gaskell's Works," and "Mrs. Gaskell's Quotations from and References to Other Writers and Works." Extensive bibliography.

"Ruth: A Novel." Anon. rev., *Athenaeum,* No. 1316 (January 15, 1853), 76–78. Though the reviewer praises the subdued handling of events and the characterizations (especially that of Sally) he strongly objects to the Reverend Benson's lie as "a piece of artistic disingenuousness" on the author's part.

"Ruth: A Novel." Anon. Rev., *North British Review,* XIX (May–August 1853), 151–74. A very favorable review of the work which commends" its perfect simplicity, truthfulness . . . its exquisite purity of feeling," the authenticity of its characters, its tolerant approach to illegitimacy, its philanthropic power in furthering social reform.

Sanders, Gerald De Witt. *Elizabeth Gaskell. Cornell Studies in English,* ed. Joseph Quincy Adams, Clark Sutherland Northup, Martin Wright Sampson. New Haven, Yale University Press, 1929. A basically sound and sensible appraisal of Mrs. Gaskell's work which also rectifies some earlier biographical mistakes and contributes some new information. Offers a detailed (though not always accurate) chronology and devotes a special section to the author's handling of dialect. Clark S. Northup's very extensive bibliography of primary and secondary sources (listed by year) is invaluable.

Sargisson, Conrad S. "Mrs. Gaskell's Early Surroundings, and Their Influence on Her Writings," *Bookman,* September 1910, 245–50. A discursive tribute to the spirit of Knutsford and its inhabitants as it was caught by Mrs. Gaskell and translated into her novels. Many photographs by the author; copious illustrations of places in Knutsford relevant to the works.

Seccombe, Thomas. "Elizabeth Cleghorn Gaskell," *Bookman,* September 1910, [237]-244. Sees Mrs. Gaskell as a writer not possessed of "the qualities and the experience of her prodigious rivals [George Eliot, Anthony Trollope, Charlotte Brontë, George Meredith]" but one who "painted with feeling." Emphasizes in special praise of *Mary Barton* her "subordination both of purpose and personality to a virtually new conception of the novel as a harmonious work of art."

Shorter, Clement K. *Charlotte Brontë and Her Circle.* New York, Dodd, Mead and Company, 1896. Contains "Preliminary section" on Mrs. Gaskell which with the help of correspondence clarifies her relationship with Charlotte Brontë and the most significant aspects of the writing and reception of *The Life of Charlotte Brontë*.

Smith, G. B. "Mrs. Gaskell and Her Novels," *Cornhill Magazine*, XXIX (January–June 1874), 191–212. Notes three phases in Mrs. Gaskell's work of which *Mary Barton, Sylvia's Lovers* and *Wives and Daughters* are respectively representative; to the "force . . . truthfulness, and . . . concentrativeness" of her early work are later added "other graces of composition" such as an increased command over characterization and style. The "purity" of the author is especially commended.

Stebbins, Lucy Poate. *A Victorian Album*. New York, Columbia University Press, 1946. Includes section on Mrs. Gaskell. Some inaccuracies in the biographical information as well as wholly undocumented assertions. Suggests the writer's limitations by stating that "Life was too kind to her as a woman to make her a great artist."

Tillotson, Kathleen. *Novels of the Eighteen-Forties*. London, Oxford University Press, 1961. The extensive "Introductory" section is invaluable for its very intelligent and knowledgeable appraisal of the vicissitudes of the novel in the 1840's. The section devoted to *Mary Barton* as both an "outstanding example" of the social novel and as a work which goes beyond it skillfully points up the larger significance of John Barton's character and of the author's "true theme," noting the connection of the work's broadly humanitarian "moral content" with that of Dickens' *Dombey and Son* and Carlyle's *Past and Present*.

Trollope, Frances. *The Life and Adventures of Michael Armstrong, The Factory Boy*. London, Henry Colburn, 1840. In this lively, elaborate, suspenseful novel, Mrs. Trollope brings sentiment and a strong satirical power to bear on her denunciation of child labor in the cotton factories.

Van Dullemen, Johanna Jacoba. *Mrs. Gaskell: Novelist and Biographer*. Amsterdam, H. J. Paris, 1924. The first part of this Dutch doctoral dissertation consists of discussions of nineteenth-century social conditions and earlier social novels (two separate chapters) and of a short biographical chapter. The central critical section lacks a sound organization (indeed there are no paragraphs). The chapter on "Contemporary Criticism and Opinion" is probably the most useful for the general reader.

Ward, A. W. "Introductions" in *The Works of Mrs. Gaskell*. 8 vols. London, Smith, Elder & Co., 1906. [The Knutsford Edition].

Ward provides extensive information on biographical details, on possible sources of inspiration, and on the general social, economic, and historical backgrounds of some of Mrs. Gaskell's works—information on which others have relied heavily. The literary appraisals are rather conventional and indulgent. Unfortunately *The Life of Charlotte Brontë* was omitted (because it had been included in an edition of Charlotte's works).

WHITFIELD, A. STANTON. *Mrs. Gaskell: Her Life and Work.* London, George Routledge & Sons, Ltd., 1929. The few contributions to biographical knowledge were unfortunately only documented as "Private information." Some previously unpublished letters are printed in full. The limitations of *Ruth* and the power of *Sylvia's Lovers* are correctly assessed. Includes a chart of Mrs. Gaskell's family tree.

WINKWORTH, SUSANNA AND CATHERINE. *Memorials of Two Sisters,* ed. Margaret J. Shaen. London, Longmans, Green, and Co., 1908. Invaluable evaluations of the young Mrs. Gaskell, information on the critical reception of *Mary Barton* and *Ruth,* as well as interesting references to the writing of *The Life of Charlotte Brontë* are to be gotten from the correspondence of the three sisters (there are also letters to and from Emily Winkworth) who were close friends of the author in Manchester.

WOLLWEBER, CAROLA. *Der Soziale Roman der Mrs. Gaskell.* Mainz, Georg Aug. Walter's Druckerei, 1928. This rather slight German doctoral dissertation devotes its introduction to political, economic, spiritual and literary approaches to the working class problem in the nineteenth century and its main section to simple discussions of the workmen and masters' types in Mrs. Gaskell's novels (mostly in *Mary Barton* and *North and South*) and to such religious figures as Mr. Hale and the Reverend Benson.

"The Works of Mrs. Gaskell." *British Quarterly Review,* XLV (January and April 1867), 399–429. A very insular and narrowly moralistic evaluation of Mrs. Gaskell which takes issue with her tolerant handling of the question of lying and guilt, but praises her generally elevated "tone" and "matter" and asserts that "in the art of telling a story she has no superior—perhaps no equal."

*WRIGHT, EDGAR. *Mrs. Gaskell: The Basis for Reassessment.* London, Oxford University Press, 1965. A generally thoughtful and thorough critical discussion of Mrs. Gaskell's works which sees as "the basis for reassessment" the steady "development" in maturity and complexity of her social views and writing technique. Emphasis is placed on the writer's growth away from didacticism as this "novelist of the individual and his relationships becomes more aware of her natural bent as a social observer." More sociological than esthetic, the approach stresses the significance of religious tradition and social change in the world of Mrs. Gaskell's novels. Concluding chapters on technique suggest "a controlling art that moulds the structure of Mrs. Gaskell's work, and that develops to accommodate her changing purpose as a novelist."

Index